महाराजकनिष्कलेख

།རྒྱལ་པོ་ཆེན་པོ་ཀ་ནིཥ་ཀ་ལ་སྤྲིངས་པའི་འཕྲིན་ཡིག།

Mahārājakaniṣkalekha

།སློབ་མ་ལ་སྤྲིངས་པའི་སྤྲིང་ཡིག།

Śiṣyalekha

Invitation to Enlightenment

Invitation to Enlightenment

Letter to the Great King Kaniṣka
by Mātṛceṭa

Letter to a Disciple
by Candragomin

Translated with
an Introduction and Notes
by Michael Hahn

Dharma Publishing

TIBETAN TRANSLATION SERIES

Library of Congress Cataloging-in-Publication Data

Mātṛceṭa.
[Mahārājakaniṣkalekha. Polyglot]
Invitation to enlightenment : letter to the great king Kaniṣka / Mātṛceṭa ; letter to a disciple by Candragomin ; translated with an introduction and notes by Michael Hahn.
p. cm. — (Tibetan translation series)
English, Tibetan and Sanskrit.
Includes bibliographical references and index.
ISBN 0-89800-299-0. — ISBN 0-89800-298-2 (pbk.)
1. Religious life—Buddhism—Early works to 1800.
I. Hahn, Michael, 1941– . II. Candragomin. Śiṣyalekha. English and Sanskrit. III. Title. IV. Series.
BQ5385.M3616 1998
294.3′444—dc21 98-14406 CIP

Frontispiece: Sarasvatī, Goddess of Learning and the Literary Arts (dByans can ma), late 17th century, Tibet. Courtesy of the Los Angeles County Museum of Art, from the Nasli and Alice Heeramaneck Collection, Museum Associates Purchase.

Reproduction of the Sanskrit manuscript of Candragomin's Śiṣyalekha, manuscript Add. 1161, by permission of the Syndics of Cambridge University Library.

Produced under the auspices of the Yeshe De Project.

Typeset in Adobe Palatino with Bellevue italic dropcaps.

Printed and bound by Dharma Press, Berkeley, CA.

10 9 8 7 6 5 4 3 2 1

Dedicated to
Western students of the Dharma

Contents

Publisher's Preface

Among the many masters in the Indian Mahāyāna tradition, Matṛceṭa and Candragomin are renowned for their comprehensive knowledge of Sanskrit and their ability to express profound dimensions of meaning through poetic imagery. Although separated by centuries, they shared similar qualities: Both were endowed with great intellectual skills, and both are venerated for the depth of the devotion that infuses their writings with extraordinary insight and compassion.

Tibetan historians equate Matṛceṭa with Aśvaghoṣa, author of the Buddhacarita, an epic poem on the life of the Buddha preserved in the Tanjur, although recent scholars doubt this association. While accounts of Matṛceṭa vary in specific details, they agree that in his early years he was a philosopher devoted to the Hindu god Śiva, who promised him he would never be defeated in debate by any human being, for Śiva would personally come to his aid and use his magic to assist him. Matṛceṭa became so formidable in debate that he was renowned as Durdharṣakāla: He who is difficult to defeat. Driven by pride, he challenged and overcame the Buddhists in both northern and western India.

Since it was the rule in those times for philosophers overcome in debate to become the disciples of the winner, those who lost to Matṛceṭa had to abandon the Buddhadharma and follow the doctrines he propounded, which glorified war and animal sacrifice. When no scholar in his region remained to challenge him, Matṛceṭa, seeking to extend his power, sought his mother's advice on how to proceed.

Tibetan historians record that his mother, inspired by the compassionate protectress Tārā, sought a skillful way to humble her son and introduce him to the Buddha's teachings. She advised him to go east to the province of Magadha, where the great master Nāgārjuna had transmitted the teachings of the Middle Way, and Buddhist scholars had trained in his style of dialectic. "Here the Buddhists are comparable in number to the hairs on a horse's ear, but in Magadha they are as many as the hairs on a horse's body. No one gains fame in debate without defeating the Buddhists of Magadha."

As Matṛceṭa made his way to Magadha, the scholars of that region were filled with dismay, for his reputation was well known, and there were none who had the skills to defeat him. Their thoughts turned to their greatest philosopher, Nāgārjuna, then living in his hermitage on Śrī Parvata, far to the south. They wrote a letter imploring him to come quickly, saying, "If the wind fails to blow from the south, the Dharma will be no more in Magadha." Tying the letter to a raven's neck, they prayed that the bird would speed to Śrī Parvata and that Nāgārjuna would respond to their request.

Nāgārjuna received the message, but his disciple Āryadeva pleaded with the master to be allowed to go in his place. So Nāgārjuna gave Āryadeva his final training by arguing Matṛceṭa's views so convincingly that Āryadeva thought his master had somehow been transformed into his future opponent. Āryadeva applied all his skills to defeating Nāgārjuna, who praised his disciple's accomplishment, but warned that Āryadeva would now suffer the karma of having defeated his teacher. On the way to the north, Āryadeva lost one eye, some say by giving it to a god disguised as a Hindu woman, others by losing it to a branch that sprang back upon him along the way.

When Āryadeva arrived at Nālandā, he found that Matṛceṭa had already vanquished all the Buddhist paṇḍitas and it was no longer permitted to express Buddhist teachings or to challenge Matṛceṭa's system. Entering Nālandā disguised as a grass cutter, Āryadeva tricked Matṛceṭa into challenging him to debate and used his powers to prevent Śiva from assisting Matṛceṭa.

Three times Āryadeva bested Matṛceṭa; when Matṛceṭa, humiliated, sought to escape, Āryadeva locked him inside a temple library. Here Matṛceṭa unwrapped a book, intending to use its cover to hang himself. The book fell open, and Matṛceṭa's eyes glanced at a passage predicting his own service to the Buddhadharma. Reading further, he was filled with appreciation for the Buddha. He marveled at the Enlightened One's great compassion and wisdom, which had no equivalent in the doctrine he was following.

Overwhelmed, he composed the Viśeṣa-stava, verses in praise of the Buddha, extolling the differences between the Enlightened One and all others. (The author of this stotra, which occupies the place of honor as the first text in the Derge Tibetan Tanjur, is recorded in that edition under the name Udbhaṭasiddhasvāmin, "most excellent accomplished master," which Tibetan tradition recognizes as an honorific for Matṛceṭa.) Requesting ordination, Matṛceṭa entered the Sangha. From the depth of his realization and devotion, he composed many stotras, hymns of praise imbued with the qualities of enlightened vision.

Candragomin was born some centuries after Matṛceṭa, when the great Mahāyāna philosophical schools founded on the lineages of Nāgārjuna and Asaṅga were in full flower. Transmitted through such great masters as Āryadeva, Buddhapālita, and Bhavaviveka, Nāgārjuna's teachings on śūnyata had given rise to the Mādhyamika school, and the lineage of Asaṅga, transmitted through Vasubandhu, Dignāga, and other outstanding masters, had nourished the Yogācāra tradition and its related philosophical systems, Cittamātra and Vijñānavāda. Within the Mādhyamika school had arisen two major interpretations of Nāgārjuna's works: Prāsaṅgika and Svātantrika, as clarified in the works of Buddhapālita and Bhāvaviveka. Home to the most brilliant scholars of India, Nālandā had developed from a monastery into a great university that attracted students from all parts of India and beyond. At the head of Nālandā's masters was the monk-scholar Candrakīrti, the foremost proponent of Prāsaṅgika.

Tibetan historians describe Candragomin as an anāgārika, a renowned scholar and Buddhist, but not a fully ordained monk. Devoted to Avalokiteśvara and Tārā, he propitiated both of them early in life as he composed the Candravyākaraṇa, his major grammatical work. He then went to Nālandā, and outside its walls met with Candrakīrti, who was addressing the tīrthikas (non-Buddhists) gathered there.

As Candragomin stood by, Candrakīrti, assuming the newcomer wished to debate him, asked where he was from and what subjects he knew. Candragomin replied that he was from the south, and named as his subjects grammar, the Eight-thousand-line Prajñāpāramitā Sūtra, and the Mañjuśrī-nāmasaṁgīti, texts that represent the whole of the fields of language, Sūtra, and Tantra. By this statement, Candrakīrti recognized the speaker as Candragomin, and arranged for him to be formally welcomed by the Sangha of monks.

When Candragomin said that this was not appropriate, as he was not fully ordained, Candrakīrti advised Candragomin to carry a statue of Mañjuśrī as he entered Nālandā; the monks would welcome Mañjuśrī, and Candragomin would receive the honor his knowledge merited. As he carried the statue, Candragomin composed verses of such eloquent praise and devotion to the great Bodhisattva that the statue turned its face to one side, as if listening and wondering, "Did I really inspire such beauty?" From that day the statue became known as Mañjuśrī with the Head Inclined to the Left.

It is said that Candrakīrti and Candragomin then engaged in a debate that continued for seven years and attracted the interest of everyone in the region. Candrakīrti took the Prāsaṅgika position transmitted through the followers of Nāgārjuna, while Candragomin took the view of the Vijñānavādins, who followed in the lineage of Asaṅga.

While Candrakīrti was a great master of dialectic and the most skilled in expressing the depth of Nāgārjuna's doctrine, Candragomin's words came from the heart, for he was able to embrace and express the vastness of enlightened nature. Day after day, Candrakīrti was at the point of success, only to find that Candragomin returned on the morrow with fresh new arguments that Candrakīrti had to begin anew to refute.

Accounts describe how, considering that someone must be instructing his partner in debate, Candrakīrti followed Candragomin to his place of meditation, where he found him receiving teachings from a stone statue of the Bodhisattva Avalokiteśvara, or, as some say, of the Ārya Tārā. Upon Candrakīrti's entrance, the statue resumed the rigidity of stone, but its finger remained in the pointing position of teaching the Dharma. With this, the debate came to an end. Seeking to know why Avalokiteśvara supported Candragomin and not himself, Candrakīrti prayed to the compassionate Bodhisattva, who in a dream revealed that Candragomin was in greater need of his blessing, since Candrakīrti was already blessed by Mañjuśrī.

Candragomin continued to compose texts on a wide range of subjects, all of which convey a powerful joining of compassion, insight, and great technical expertise. Few can match his mastery of expression, which Western languages, even in the hands of skilled translators, lack the depth of associations to convey. In his Śiṣyalekha, or "Letter to a Disciple," the imagery carries multiple dimensions of meaning, for what appear to be elaborate flights of imagination are actually reflections of symbolic images deeply imprinted on human consciousness. These images are manifestations of karma accumulated through lifetimes; unrecognized and unacknowledged, they are now accessible only in nightmares or as hidden terrors that come upon us unaware.

These images surface in our experience as frustration, aggression, and other destructive qualities such as hatred or anger. They are found in each of the six realms of existence, which represent the range of experience accessible to the human psyche: the attachment to desire of the god realms, the driven striving and wrath of the demigods, the confusion, anger, and willful destruction of the human realm, the dullness and emotional vulnerability of the animals, the endless grasping and revulsion of the hungry ghosts, and the torments and terrors of the hells. When conditions favor, this secret karma finds expression in our thoughts and erupts unpredictably in our actions, in what the Western mind might view as evil, or, in its most extreme, as demonic possession.

To save us from perpetuating such suffering, the Buddha, in his infinite compassion, taught the reality of karma and the folly of ignoring its operations. He showed how to mitigate karma through mindfulness and discipline, and how to penetrate it completely through the Bodhisattva's power of samādhi. In this spirit, Candragomin uses poetic imagery to express the powerful reality of karma, how our actions foster attachments that support our understanding of self, and how focusing on the self enmeshes us in suffering and distracts us from higher priorities. He holds a mirror to our psyche, encouraging us to look fearlessly at the workings of karma. Only by knowing karma can we begin to free ourselves of the negative effects of our actions.

In translating the works of these two great masters, Michael Hahn has given readers access to teachings that are readily grasped on the external level, yet, as is true of all Dharma teachings, carry the potential for awakening the seed of enlightenment. At this critical point of Dharma transmission, the śāstras, the clearly-worded yet penetrating teachings by masters of the enlightened lineage, provide a sound foundation for the path that transforms mind and heart into the highest expression of human nature.

Śāstras focus on specific aspects of the Buddha's teachings, bringing out their depth and scope and presenting them in ways we can readily comprehend. They hold the key to the comprehensive understanding that can continue to develop Western languages into vehicles more capable of transmitting the full meaning of Dharma. We can all hope that this understanding and commitment to improvement will continue to increase, so that the full meanings of the Buddhist teachings grow ever clearer.

While I have not personally reviewed this translation with the original, Dr. Hahn, like other noted European scholars, has a special affinity for Sanskrit and spares no effort to bring out the beauty of the original to the best of his ability. He has done a great service in making these works available, and we hope that these translations will inspire others to follow his example. For the future of the Dharma, and for the benefit of future generations, I urge scholars to continue to translate both Sūtras and śāstras, confident that meaning beyond the apparent awaits discovery, and that newly effective ways can be found to convey it.

Tarthang Tulku
November, 1997

Preface

Twenty-five years have passed since I first began to read the printed text of Candragomin's "Letter to a Disciple" together with the old palmleaf manuscript of its original Sanskrit that is reproduced at the end of this book. About ten years ago, Dharma Publishing invited me to publish this letter in the Tibetan Translation Series along with Mātṛceṭa's "Letter to the Great King Kaniṣka." A first draft of the English translation was written in the summer of 1986 and a little later I had the opportunity for a first revision when a Dharma Publishing representative visited Germany and came to my place for five days.

Due to personal as well as scholarly distractions, this second draft lay dormant for almost ten years until I decided to go to Berkeley in August of 1996 and October of 1997 and work there on the final revision of the translation together with the staff of Dharma Publishing. Thanks to the perseverance and dedication of Zara Wallace, the translation could be greatly improved. Particularly with the "Letter to a Disciple," which is written in a rather ornate and embellished style, it was by no means easy to produce a translation that on the one hand is as faithful as the Tibetan translation of Indian works generally tend to be, and on the other hand is still readable and—hopefully—enjoyable for the modern reader. With the "Letter to the

Great King Kaniṣka," it was a great challenge to maintain the simplicity of the original work, which can still be felt in its excellent Tibetan translation.

During this intensive collaboration, the on-going struggle for a lucid and intelligible English revealed that in several places of both works a full understanding had not yet been achieved. Consequently, the two original texts—the Sanskrit of the "Letter to a Disciple" and the Tibetan of the "Letter to the Great King Kaniṣka"—were consulted and reconsidered again and again with the result that minor improvements could be arrived at in a great number of cases and major improvements in a limited number of cases. The reader who compares the rendering of Mātṛceṭa's letter as printed in this book with my previous German translation will notice the progress that was possible.

I am very glad that the translation of Nāgārjuna's "Letter to a Friend" that was published in this series twenty years ago (in *Golden Zephyr*) is now followed by the letters of two other great Buddhist masters, and that thereby all three letters belonging to the early period of Buddhist epistolary literature are available in one series. I am sure the attentive reader will agree with me that each of these letters has its own merits and that we are fortunate to have all three of them.

While expressing my heartfelt thanks to all the members of the Dharma Publishing staff, I would like especially to thank Tarthang Tulku, the founder of Dharma Publishing and Dharma Press, who made the publication of this book in its present form possible. Through his visionary energy, charisma, and zeal, a very substantial portion of the spiritual and literary treasures that Tibet preserved or discovered for mankind over the last fourteen centuries is now saved for many generations to come. At the same time Tarthang Tulku has launched a project that eventually will unlock these treasures for all who are able to appreciate them: the Tibetan Translation Series. With Tibetan culture endangered, this is a pressing task. Nevertheless, taking into consideration that it took one thousand years to translate the Buddhist texts into Chinese and seven hundred years to translate them into Tibetan, my own view is that pride of place should be given to quality rather than quantity. Relying on the truth of the old Indian wisdom verse that was also included in the "Staff of Wisdom," we can be confident that this noble undertaking will continually grow over the years, decades, and centuries:

An anthill and understanding the teaching,
The waxing moon, 'til full,
The possessions of kings and beggars—
These increase by gradual accumulation.
(Staff of Wisdom 29, in *Elegant Sayings*, p. 9)

As a great admirer of Mātṛceṭa and Candragomin, I am particularly happy that their works, eighteen hundred and fifteen hundred years after they were originally composed, are finally brought to light in the shape they deserve. This again is the sole merit of Tarthang Tulku, who from the beginning saw to it that everything that leaves Dharma Publishing is prepared with both great care and elegant taste.

As a scholar I am grateful that I was permitted to include in this book—which is designed to speak to any interested reader, not only to specialists in the field of Indian and Buddhist literature—a great portion of scholarly material: analyses of Tibetan and Sanskrit vocabulary, variant readings, and a facsimile of the old palmleaf manuscript of

Candragomin's letter. The main purpose of all these additions is to enable anyone who is not fully satisfied with the interpretation presented here to form his or her own opinion. And I sincerely hope that by presenting in this book my views on the date of Candragomin, which place him in the fifth century C.E., I have not offended anyone who rather adheres to the Tibetan tradition that makes him younger by two hundred years.

In closing, I would like to dedicate my efforts on this book to my son, T. M. Hahn. May the noble ideas expressed in the "Letter to the Great King Kaniṣka" and the "Letter to a Disciple" again contribute to a more harmonious and peaceful life among beings!

Michael Hahn
Berkeley, California
October 15, 1997

Introduction

On Buddhist Epistles in General

Buddhist teachers and scholars in India made use of a great variety of literary forms in their efforts to convey the Dharma as widely as possible. Pre-existing genres often developed in their hands into something novel and original, or they created entirely new forms to meet the specific requirements of teaching.

One of the literary genres that came into being and was used exclusively in the realm of Indian and Tibetan Buddhism is the epistle, lekha in Sanskrit and sprin-yig[1] in Tibetan. The development of this genre is closely related to the origin and growth of Mahāyāna Buddhism in India and its later dissemination in Tibet.

In India none of these epistles has been preserved; in Nepal only one has survived, Candragomin's "Letter to a Disciple" (Śiṣyalekha). The only epistle to be translated into Chinese, Nāgārjuna's "Letter to a Friend" (Suhṛllekha), survives in the Chinese Canon in three different renderings, a fact that indicates the high esteem in which it was held. In the Tibetan Canon, however, we find no less than thirteen epistles. It is only through the skill and devotion of the Tibetan translators and editors that we are able today to see how the epistle genre flourished in India between the second and twelfth centuries C.E.

Structure of Buddhist Epistles

In their general structure, Buddhist epistles are not nearly as formalized and standardized as their Western counterparts, the letters that have survived in Greek and Latin literature. The latter are usually divided into three major sections (leaving aside the main body of the letter, which is not formalized): the heading (Latin praescriptio), the introductory section (exordium or prooemium), and the conclusion (conclusio). Each of these sections in turn is divided into parts. The heading is divided into three parts: the greeting (salutatio), the naming of the sender (intitulatio), and the naming of the addressee (inscriptio). The introductory section is also divided into three parts: the arousing of the attention of the addressee (attentum facere), the gaining of the benevolence of the addressee (benevolum facere), and the arousing of the curiosity to listen to the content of the letter (docilem facere). The concluding section consists of two parts: the formal conclusion of the main part of the letter (conclusio) and the benediction (valedicere).

Since there were many fewer epistles in Buddhist literature than in Greek or Roman traditions, there was little need for standardizing or formalizing. As has been pointed out by Siglinde Dietz in her monograph on the Buddhist epistolary literature,[2] the Buddhist letters if taken as a whole show many traits in common with the letters of Western classical literature, but these traits are distributed randomly, not in the strict manner prescribed by the classical textbooks on rhetoric.

As far as we know, the three letters written by Nāgārjuna, Mātṛceṭa, and Candragomin were occasioned by very specific circumstances, and in each case the need to respond to these circumstances was far more important than any need to follow an abstract literary form—especially since in the Indian context there was no abstract literary form to follow! We can assume that Nāgārjuna, in the "Letter to a Friend," oriented himself to the model of an orderly and clearly written instruction for laypeople—not too long, with a metrical form (because easy to memorize), and a simple, lucid style. In the case of Mātṛceṭa, simplicity of style was even more essential since the recipient of the letter was a very young king. Candragomin's "Letter to a Disciple" also had a specific recipient, but was obviously composed with a broad and educated readership in mind.

This book includes the Tibetan translation of Mātṛceṭa's "Letter to the Great King Kaniṣka"[3] and the Sanskrit text of Candragomin's "Letter to a Disciple," together with English translations of both letters. We will now discuss these two letters in some detail. The section entitled Other Examples of the Epistolary Genre on pp. 196–212 includes a brief discussion of Nāgārjuna's well-known "Letter to a Friend" and the nine other letters edited and translated by Siglinde Dietz in her above-mentioned monograph.

The Life and Works of Mātṛceṭa

Together with Nāgārjuna's "Letter to a Friend" and Candragomin's "Letter to a Disciple," Mātṛceṭa's "Letter to the Great King Kaniṣka" belongs to the first period of the Buddhist epistles, which encompasses the second through the fifth centuries C.E. Mātṛceṭa was one of the greatest poets of early Buddhism, second only to Aśvaghoṣa, the famed author of the "Life of the Buddha" or Buddhacarita. Mātṛceṭa most probably lived in the second century C.E., as a younger contemporary of Nāgārjuna.[4]

The fame Mātṛceṭa enjoyed in India was described by the Chinese pilgrim I-Tsing (or Yi-jing) in the record that he sent home to China from Sumatra in 692 C.E. In his words:

> When in the quiet night after an uposatha day the congregation of monks is full of melancholy, one can have a talented person recite the "Hymn in 150 Stanzas" or the "Hymn in 400 Stanzas" or all the other laudatory stanzas, and that is indeed beautiful. In India many laudatory poems are transmitted for the purpose of worship and paying homage. All people of talent praise that which they hold in high esteem, like a certain Mātṛceṭa, a man of special gifts and great virtue, who far surpassed all other excellent persons. . . .
>
> He first wrote the "Hymn in 400 Stanzas," thereafter the "Hymn in 150 Stanzas," in which he dealt with the six perfections (pāramitā) in general and described the outstanding qualities of the Buddha, the World Honored. Of these [stanzas] one can say that the fragrance of their composition equals the scent of heavenly flowers, and the lofty orientation of their content rivals in height the lords of mountains of this world. All the Indian poets of laudatory stanzas took them as their model, and even the Bodhisattvas Asaṅga and Vasubandhu admired them greatly. Accordingly, everyone in India who has left home and studied the five and ten precepts is taught

the recitation of these two hymns. This holds equally true for [the followers of] the Great Vehicle and the Lesser Vehicle.

Life of Mātṛceṭa

A little later I-Tsing writes:

> The tradition goes that in early times when the Buddha was still alive, the Enlightened One once wandered about in the world of living beings, leading the assembly of his followers. At that time a bird, a loriot [oriole], seeing that the major and minor characteristics of the Buddha were as awesome as a golden mountain, made his voice resound melodiously and beautifully in the forest, in praise.
>
> The Buddha turned to his disciples and said: "This bird is filled with joy at my sight and unconsciously bursts into song. By this meritorious deed he will be reborn, after my death, as a human being called Mātṛceṭa.[5] He will praise my qualities extensively."
>
> When this man (Mātṛceṭa) first left home, he associated with non-Buddhists and worshipped the god Maheśvara (Śiva). As long as that [god] was the object of his worship, he praised him in every respect. However, when he later realized that [his birth] had been predicted, his mind changed and he converted to Buddhism. He took robes, left worldly life, and began to praise the Buddha in order to wipe out in this way the faults of his past and to follow further the most excellent path. He was full of grief not to

have met the great teacher himself but only to see his images. Therefore he wrote wonderful compositions and praised the qualities of the Buddha in accordance with the prediction. . . .

These beautiful works have not yet been brought to China. Many people wrote commentaries on them and more than one has written a [poetic] complement to them. Bodhisattva Dignāga himself wrote such a complement. Before each stanza [of the "Hymn in 150 Stanzas"] he placed his own and called the work "Mixed Hymn" (Miśrakastotra). Moreover Śākyadeva, a famous monk from the Deer Park (Mṛgadāva) placed his own stanza before those of Dignāga and called this the "Doubly Mixed Hymn;" this counts 450 stanzas. In this manner all poets take [the works of Mātṛceṭa] as their model.

I-Tsing wrote this account approximately five hundred years after the death of Mātṛceṭa, at a time when the memory of a great man was entirely dependent on the oral transmission of both his works and the facts of his life. Yet apart from the legendary portions of his record, almost all the facts mentioned by I-Tsing are corroborated by external evidence. The two hymns he refers to under their secondary titles are still available, as we shall see below. The shorter one has indeed been expanded by Dignāga to a "Mixed Hymn" whose Tibetan translation can be found in the Tanjur. And the existence of the "Doubly Mixed Hymn" is confirmed by a reference to it in Nandipriya's commentary on Mātṛceṭa's hymn.[6] That the "Hymn in 400 Stanzas" was Mātṛceṭa's first Buddhist work and that he had composed verses in praise of Hindu gods before can be deduced from the first two stanzas of that very hymn:

Because I, not knowing what is a field [of merit]
and what not, following only the ways of tradition,
in former times stupidly spoke the praise
of that which is not praiseworthy;

Therefore have I begun this act of washing away the dirt
resulting from that muddy speech
by entering into you,
a living holy bathing-place.

Some of the details of I-Tsing's record can also be found in the Mañjuśrīmūlakalpa in the context of a prophecy of the Buddha:

> At that time there will be monks of mine, very learned. One bearing the name Mātṛcīna (Tib. Ma-khol = Mātṛceṭa), having made a hymn in my praise, described me as I am, pointing out my virtues in their true form. Having made wholly serene his mind, rejoicing in the teaching of the Buddhas, he will be accomplished in your spells, oh Mañjughoṣa, hard to apprehend, virtuous, of good conduct, an expounder of the Law, of great learning.
>
> Formerly when born among animals he spoke this hymn. I dwelt happily in the lovely city called Nṛpa (Rājagṛha), in the wood called Khaṇḍa (Veṇuvana), along with a multitude of disciples. There he lived as a crow and made serene his mind towards me (?). Having made serene his mind with faith in me, his body fell asunder and he went to heaven.
>
> Having fallen from among the gods he will be born among men and when reborn among men he will forsake the world as a follower of my teaching.

> Having forsaken the world that great-souled one, the pious Mātṛcīna, will then praise me even as I am. He will put forth an offering of true praise with various instances and reasons, well-spoken for the good of all beings. Devoting himself to exhortation by means of hymns for the benefit of living creatures he will live at that time, at the close of the aeon ill reputed among men. His body being split, having gone to heaven through the ripening of his *karma* and enjoyed varied happiness, that wise one will in due course attain *bodhi*, omniscient, the highest aim, beyond thought.[7]

A little later the Mañjuśrīmūlakalpa adds the following, somewhat puzzling, passage about Mātṛceṭa:

When the teaching of the master on earth
and the world at the end of an aeon have degenerated,
there will undoubtedly appear monks
whose conduct is connected with a kingdom,
such as the one who is known under the names Mātṛcīna
and Kusuma ("flower"),
under the name beginning with Ma and Kumāra,
exceedingly fond of the Dharma.

In addition to I-Tsing and the Mañjuśrīmūlakalpa, the two oldest sources to mention Mātṛceṭa, there are two short passages in Bu-ston's famous *History of Buddhism* and a comparatively long biography in Tāranātha's *History of Buddhism in India*. In his short biography of Āryadeva, Bu-ston writes:

> The (spiritual) son of Nāgārjuna was the teacher Āryadeva. The latter was miraculously born in the island Siṁhala in the petals of a lotus-flower and

was adopted by the king of that country. When he grew up, he went to a place where the teacher Nāgārjuna was residing, entered his school, and became proficient in all the branches of science and all the heterodox and orthodox philosophical systems.

At that time there lived a heretical teacher called Mātṛceṭa who had propitiated the god Maheçvara [sic] and was exceedingly powerful, so that no living being could match him. This teacher, having caused great harm to the Doctrine of Buddha and seduced the greater part (of the people) to the heretical teachings, came to Nālanda. The Nālanda monks sent a message to Nāgārjuna who was residing on the Śrī-parvata. The teacher Āryadeva (who was abiding with him) said that he would subdue (the heretic) and went (to Nālanda). On the way there the goddess of a tree begged him to grant her an eye, and he accordingly presented her with one of his eyes. Thereafter, as he had vanquished the heretic, (the monks said): 'Who is this one-eyed?' Āryadeva replied:

The Terrific One, though he has 3 eyes,
Cannot perceive the Absolute Truth;
Indra, though endowed with 1000 eyes,
Is likewise unable to see it.
But Āryadeva, who has only one eye,
Has the intuition of the true Essence
Of all the 3 Spheres of Existence.

(The heretical teacher) was vanquished by (the words of) the Doctrine, was converted to Buddhism, and became a great Paṇḍit. . . .

> Āryadeva's pupil Mātṛceṭa has likewise composed a great number of treatises and has acted for the sake of the Doctrine. We do not however give his biography, for fear that it would take too much place.[8]

The most comprehensive biography of Mātṛceṭa is that of the Tibetan historian Tāranātha, who composed his work in the beginning of the seventeenth century C.E. Apart from the facts already known from the earlier records, it adds a few details of a more legendary character and introduces some new names of places and persons in connection with Mātṛceṭa that are not confirmed elsewhere. The most important detail is Tāranātha's claim that Mātṛceṭa was known under a multitude of names—Durdharṣakāla, Śūra, Aśvaghoṣa, Mātṛceṭa, Pitṛceṭa, Dhārmika Subhūti, and Maticitra. Except for the equation of Mātṛceṭa with Aśvaghoṣa in one of the works of Atiśa (eleventh century C.E.), there is no further evidence for the authenticity of this claim. For the time being it seems best to treat the well-known authors Aśvaghoṣa, Śūra, Mātṛceṭa, and Dhārmika Subhūti as different individuals.

Works of Mātṛceṭa

Mātṛceṭa is credited with the authorship of about fifteen works, most of which are available only in Tibetan translation.[9] Apart from the "Letter to the Great King Kaniṣka," his other known works are hymns, prayers, and sermons, all of which belong, at least in a wider sense, to the so-called didactic literature of Buddhism. Fortunately the two longest and most popular of his hymns are now accessible in their original Sanskrit, at least for the greater part: "The Rise of Understanding from Faith" (Prasādapratibhodbhava) and "Praise of the Praiseworthy" (Varṇārhavarṇa).

The first of these two hymns consists of 153 stanzas[10] divided into thirteen chapters, each of which praises a different aspect of the Buddha. A trilingual edition (Sanskrit-Tibetan-Chinese), accompanied by an English translation and the Tibetan text of the commentary by Nandipriya, was published by the British scholar D. R. Shackleton Bailey.[11] Unfortunately the book is now out of print. The second hymn is divided into twelve chapters and comprises 386 stanzas.[12] It also praises different aspects of the Buddha, although in a more elaborate and linguistically refined way.

Mātṛceṭa's Style

The following two examples from the Varṇārhavarṇa demonstrate well Mātṛceṭa's skill in handling the various types of alliteration of the Sanskrit language:

sadā sadācāravidhā**yine 'yine**
kṣarākṣarāptapratisaṁ**vide vide** |
mahāmahāyāpratimā**ya te yate**
namo namo'rhāya mahā**rhate 'rhate** | | 2.70

Homage to you, ascetic, who follows the (right) path
and always practices the conduct of the good;
the knower who has the specific knowledge
of the perishable and eternal,
endowed with great might, incomparable,
the great and worthy Arhat who deserves praise!

In each line of this stanza, the first and last syllables are doubled, but in such an ingenious way that there is never a repetition of meaning. This stylistic device is very difficult to accomplish and not attested to elsewhere before the time of Mātṛceṭa.

samā**satkārasatkāraṁ** loka**satkṛtasatkṛtam** |
satkṛtya satkaromi tvā **satkārā**vanatendriyaḥ || 3.5 ||

The organs of my senses turned to worship,
I worship you again and again,
you who are indifferent to worship and lack of worship
and are worshipped by those who are themselves
objects of worship for the world.

Here Mātṛceṭa plays with the repeated use of different derivations from the verbal compound sat-√kṛ, "to worship, to honor." The effect of these repetitions is a certain intensity and solemnity. While the first example is an exceptional case, this second type of repetition is comparatively frequent and one of Mātṛceṭa's favorite means of creating verbal intensity. The device was perhaps inherited from other didactic works such as Nāgārjuna's "Necklace of Jewels," where it is also used frequently.

Above all, Mātṛceṭa's style is characterized by the deceptive simplicity with which it expresses thoughts of great value and depth. This specific combination of simplicity and profundity was the cause for Mātṛceṭa's lasting fame in the Buddhist world, both in India and beyond, and his renown as the "author of hymns" (stotrakāra) *par excellence.*

Letter to the Great King Kaniṣka

The "Letter to the Great King Kaniṣka," which contrasts slightly with Mātṛceṭa's other compositions, seems to have been composed on the specific occasion of King Kaniṣka's invitation to visit him. This is mentioned in the very first stanza of the epistle, which also discloses the fact that the letter was written at the end of Mātṛceṭa's life, as mentioned by Tāranātha:

That I, though invited, did not come to you,
one so worthy to be approached,
was not due to lack of reverence or to disrespect,
but because I am hindered by old age and illness. [1]

The third stanza too indicates that Mātṛceṭa regarded his epistle to Kaniṣka as a kind of postscript to his previous works:

What I have to teach, I have already largely taught,
and who can advise on everything?
Yet because of your many virtues,
I have become loquacious once more. [3]

Mātṛceṭa's epistle to Kaniṣka is a very personal document. An old and wise man at the end of his life is given the chance to speak to a young ruler into whose hands enormous power has been placed. Kaniṣka, heir to the kingdom of the Kuṣāṇas, will become the greatest of all the Kuṣāṇa kings, forging an empire that embraces Greeks, Indians, Kuṣāṇas, Śakas, and Parthians, and opens trade routes linking India with China and the expanding Roman Empire. Early in his rule, however, the king's youth and inexperience present a great temptation to misuse his extraordinary power.

Mātṛceṭa thus faces a certain dilemma: He wishes to raise the topics he regards as most important from the point of view of Buddhist ethics and his own lifelong experience, yet he knows that he has to keep the letter brief if he wishes to catch the king's attention. Consequently he avoids all the technicalities of the Buddhist Abhidharma that Nāgārjuna could dare to include in his "Letter to a Friend." Instead he warns against the dangers of youth:

Sense objects that give rise to pleasure,
youth swelling with pride,
and doing just as one likes without regard for others—
these are the gates to what is entirely harmful. [6]

Avoid these three things leading to ruin.
For a wise man must act to diminish these three faults
by relying upon the noble, controlling the senses,
and using the power of wisdom. [7]

He then stresses the importance of listening to and accepting good advice (stanzas 10–16), gives a number of general rules of conduct for a king (stanzas 17–40), continues with specific recommendations for Kaniṣka (stanzas 41–49), and then turns to two issues that are obviously close to his heart: Always be aware of death every moment of your life (stanzas 50–63), and avoid killing animals (stanzas 64–78). The letter ends with Mātṛceṭa's urgent request to Kaniṣka to follow his advice if he finds it useful.

The "Letter to the Great King Kaniṣka" is characterized by an utmost simplicity of style. Nowhere does Mātṛceṭa use the difficult or refined figures of speech found in his earlier works.[13] The charm of this little work lies in its simple yet well-chosen similes and its warm human tone. While the letter is written to King Kaniṣka, its content, rich with the wisdom of age and experience, appeals to any feeling human being.

The Life and Works of Candragomin

The Author

Compared to accounts of the life of Mātṛceṭa, the "writer of hymns" and the author of the "Letter to the Great King Kaniṣka," the record of the life of Candragomin in the Tibetan historical tradition is far more detailed, and many more of his works are preserved, both in the original Sanskrit and in Tibetan translation. Nevertheless, for the Western scholar it is not easy to decide which of the roughly fifty-five works in the Tibetan Tanjur were composed by the famous Candragomin, the poet and the grammarian, and which are authored by a later namesake or an entirely different person. Likewise it is by no means clear which of the many biographical details related in Tāranātha's famous *History of Buddhism in India* are historical facts and which are later accretions.

Here a very cautious attitude has been adopted. Only those details are reported that can be verified from writings incontrovertibly attributable to Candragomin or supported by independent external evidence. This yields the following picture:

There was a Buddhist poet and scholar by the name of Candra or "Moon" who also called himself Candragomin, the "honorable Mr. Moon" or "Sir Moon," or—rarely—Candradāsa, the "humble Mr. Moon." He came from the eastern part of India, probably Bengal, and lived in the fifth century C.E. His lasting fame rests on his contribution to the field of Indian grammar, perhaps the greatest achievement of classical Indian scholarship, for Candragomin replaced the undisputed standard work on the Sanskrit language, the grammar of Pāṇini, with a work of his own, and thus founded a new school of Indian grammar, the Cāndra school. Taking into consideration that Pāṇini's grammar was composed almost a millennium before Candragomin's, that it enjoyed the highest possible reputation, and that it had been commented upon by great scholars, we can only admire the courage and competence that led Candragomin to embark successfully upon such a challenging task.

The two major and several minor works that embody Candragomin's grammatical system have survived for the most part not only in their original Sanskrit but also in Tibetan translation, and were made accessible to the Western scholarly world at the beginning of this century. From his grammatical works, however, we learn almost nothing about Candragomin himself; had only they survived, he would not have earned the reputation that he enjoyed and still enjoys in the Buddhist world. But Candragomin was also a poet of great talent, and during the past twenty-five years several of his poetic works, which deal with Buddhist themes, have been analyzed by Western scholars. These works are the most reliable sources for determining his place, time, and personality, and we turn to them now.

Date of Candragomin

The date of Candragomin has been a somewhat thorny issue until recently. It has repeatedly been held that the poet Candragomin lived in the seventh century C.E. and must therefore have been different from the grammarian. Two sources support this view: the statement by the Chinese pilgrim I-Tsing that the poet Candragomin was still alive when I-Tsing came to India in 673 C.E., and the account by the Tibetan historian Tāranātha of Candragomin's debate with Candrakīrti. Tāranātha's account is not corroborated by any reliable external evidence; in the case of I-Tsing, it seems likely that his statement was based on unreliable hearsay, as in a few other cases of his otherwise trustworthy account. Stronger than the claims of the Chinese and Tibetan scholars is the evidence contained in Candragomin's own work. In stanza 6 of the prologue to his play *Joy for the World,* he says, "(Candragomin was)

"a poet who has also written a grammar of Sanskrit,
concise, abundantly clear
yet *comprehensive* in scope . . ." (see p. xliii)

These are the same words with which the grammarian Candragomin, in the introductory stanzas to some of his grammatical works, characterizes his system of grammar: "concise" (laghu), "abundantly clear" (vispaṣṭa), and "comprehensive" (saṁpūrṇa).[14] Since the date of the grammarian Candragomin is established unequivocally in the fifth century C.E., this must also be the time of the poet. Moreover, as will be argued below, the poet Candragomin seems to have been a junior contemporary of the famous fifth-century Indian poet Kālidāsa.

Joy for the World

Candragomin's most important poetic composition still extant today (in Tibetan translation) is the five-act play *Joy for the World,* or Lokānanda. It dramatizes the ancient Buddhist account of the generous king and Bodhisattva Maṇicūḍa, the "Jewel-Crested One," who by his various great and self-denying acts of generosity made great progress in his spiritual career towards enlightenment. For more details about the content of the play and its structure, the reader is referred to the present author's English translation and its introduction.[15]

The importance of *Joy for the World* lies not only in its status as the oldest complete Indian Buddhist play, but also in the perfection of its style—the flawless manner in which Candragomin combined the highly developed requirements of ancient Indian drama with the spirit of Buddhist ethics and philosophy. It is therefore not surprising that the Chinese pilgrim I-Tsing reported at the end of the seventh century C.E.—more than two hundred years after the composition of the play—that it was staged with great success "in all the five parts of India."

In the prologue, through the stage director, Candragomin gives the following information about himself:

> The poet Candradāsa has composed
> a completely new kind of play:
> the drama *Joy for the World.*
> Therefore I will now present it
> to the audience here assembled. [4]

Candragomin is certainly a poet

> Who, in answer to a wish
> directed to the goddess Tārā,[16] was born
> into the race of Jātukarṇa in the east of India,
> and who achieved great fame
> as her son and follower,
> though he was unable to bear
> the burden of rule; [5]

and who moreover

has so mastered the most magnificent means
of verbal ornament and expression
that his compositions in verse and prose,
these spacious bathing places of the learned,
are not in the least limited
to the mere description of a sole and single theme;
a poet who has also written a grammar of Sanskrit,
concise, abundantly clear
yet comprehensive in scope,
and has destroyed the great welter
of worldly passions and earthbound ignorance. [6]

The fact that he was a follower of the goddess Tārā is also mentioned by Tibetan historians.

In the concluding stanza of Act II (stanza 33) he seems to give a hint of his doctrinal affiliation, the implication of which is not quite clear to me:

For this reason did Candragomin
compose this play,
deriving its moral teaching from the school
of the vehicle of the Self-Born Svayambhū,
the Tathāgata Departed in Perfection.

It is quite remarkable that Candragomin refers to himself not only in the prologue of the play, as is customary with Indian playwrights, but also in the concluding stanzas of each of its five acts and in the formal prayer at the end of the main part of the play. He seems to have been aware of his own qualities, forthright in expressing them, and eager to stamp his literary compositions with a mark of authenticity: his name. This tendency can also be observed in the Śiṣyalekha or "Letter to a Disciple," in which the first and last stanzas contain the word candra or "moon." Moreover, the common authorship of the two works is suggested by the nine identical stanzas occurring in both the "Letter to a Disciple" and *Joy for the World*.

"Praise in Confession"

A few years ago three more works attributed to Candragomin were made accessible to the English-speaking world in Mark Tatz's book *Difficult Beginnings*:[17] "Candragomin's Resolve" (Candragomipraṇidhāna), "Twenty Verses on the Bodhisattva Vow" (Bodhisattvasaṁvaravimśaka), and the "Praise in Confession" (Deśanāstava). While the first two works are too short, technical, and general to allow any definitive conclusion about their author, the "Praise in Confession," which consists of fifty-one stanzas[18] with nine syllables per line, is penetrated by a certain poetic spirit, and its last stanza again contains the 'stamp of authenticity' in the word "moon" (zla-ba).

There is yet another feature pointing to the famous Candragomin as the author of this hymn. Stanzas 4–6 show a remarkable parallel with the beginning of *Joy for the World*. In the second stanza of the benediction to the play, Candragomin makes the daughters of Māra chide the Bodhisattva for his indifference to their temptations:

"O you whose loving character is vast
beyond all measure (apramāṇa),
you who were once so blissfully
embraced by your wife Yaśodharā—
in your great compassion
should you not show
a similar equanimity toward us as well?

But we of course must not behave as did
the noble mistress Yaśodharā!"
O, may you gain the knowledge of the Buddha
who was so addressed by the envy-drunk daughters
of Māra, the god of desire! [I.2]

Candragomin here has woven the Four Immeasurables (apramāṇa)—love (Skt. maitrī, Tib. byams pa), joy or bliss (Skt. muditā, Tib. dga' ba), compassion (Skt. karuṇā, Tib. snying rje), and equanimity (Skt. upekṣā, Tib. btang snyoms)—together with their general designation into one stanza. We also find the Four Immeasurables mentioned in stanzas 4–6 of the "Praise in Confession:"

To pacify the scorching fire of aversion,
Even if I develop the lotus pond of love
There the mind is caught by the mire of attachment
Which is (wrongly) held to be happiness by all people. [4]

To purify the stains of the mire of attachment,
If I cleanse it with the water of even-mindedness,
There even the World-Protector's compassion,
Which dispels the distress of all creatures,
would decay. [5]

O Chieftain, if I cultivate compassion,
Great sorrow is generated in me;
If I rely on gladness to pacify this,
The distracted mind grows excited. [6][19]

Other Works Attributed to Candragomin

There are twenty more poetic works attributed to Candragomin in the Tibetan Tanjur, including some repetitions. Most of these works are hymns, nine of which are related to the goddess Tārā, and three of these were translated by Martin Willson in his book *In Praise of Tārā*.[20] They are listed here with page references to Willson's book:

"The Twelve Stanzas in Praise of the Noble Tārā" or Āryatārāstotradvādaśagāthā (pp. 232–33).[21]

"The Praise of the Noble Goddess Tārā called 'A Necklace of Pearls'" or Āryatārādevīstotramuktikāmālānāma (pp. 226–31).[22]

"The Vow in the Form of a Praise of the Noble Tārā" or Āryatārāstotrapraṇidhāna[siddhi] nāma (pp. 234–35).[23]

None of these three hymns has outstanding literary merits, and none are marked by the word "moon." A fourth hymn, "The Praise of the Great Tārā" or Śrīmahātārāstotra,[24] is more ambitious. It consists of twenty-six stanzas with seventeen syllables per line. However, despite its literary qualities, its style does not display an elevated quality of thought and it also lacks the mark of authenticity.

There is a fifth hymn to the goddess Tārā attributed to a certain Candradāsa.[25] Its Sanskrit text is embedded in a commentary found in a Tibetan monastery by the Indian scholar Rāhula Sāṁkṛtyāyana. He copied the hymn and the beginning of the commentary and published his notes in an Indian journal. While the hymn, written in a rather late style with long and difficult compounds and many forced alliterations, does not offer any clue with regard to its author, the beginning of the commentary makes a very interesting remark about Candradāsa:

> [Once] this teacher Candradāsa was crossing the ocean in a ship (Skt. pota). When the ships were tossed about by the wind and other (forces of nature), [Candradāsa]

> with great devotion and (in a loud voice) made the vow to proclaim the virtues [of the goddess Tārā] which transcend those of all the three worlds, first illustrating the (i.e. his) relationship [with the goddess], the meaning (or subject matter), the purpose etc. in order to elucidate the meaning of the hymn to the Noble Tārā. Because of his extraordinary speech the water receded from that place. Since the water had receded (from that place) like a multitude of dark clouds from the disk of the moon [when driven away] by a [strong] wind, an island was created that was first called 'Candra'. . . . [26]

Compare with this the following portion of Tāranātha's description of the life of Candragomin:

> At that time he [Candragomin] took to wife a princess, Tārā by name, and the king granted him a district. On one occasion he heard a servant call her Tārā, and he thought, "It is not proper to have a marriage partner with the same name as the obligational deity (yi-dam)." So the master prepared himself to move to another land. The king came to know of this, and said: "If he will not live with my daughter, put him in a box and throw it into the Ganges." Thus he ordered, and thus it was performed. The master made an entreaty to the noble Lady Tārā and emerged at an island at the confluence of the Ganges with the sea. The island is reported to have been created magically by the noble Lady. It has been given the name Candradvīpa (Candra's Island), because Candragomin himself dwelt there. [The island] can be found nowadays, and is reportedly large enough to accommodate some seven thousand villages.[27]

Bu-ston, who reports the same incident in his *History of Buddhism in India,* adds the remarkable detail that Candragomin was saved by composing a stotra and that the island was magically created.[28] There can be little doubt that both Bu-ston's and Tāranātha's records go back, either directly or indirectly, to this commentarial passage or a common source. It can hardly be coincidence that this detail is preserved in a Sanskrit manuscript found in a Tibetan monastery.

Perhaps the following passage in Tāranātha's record is also influenced by the same anecdote in Sanskrit:

> Having thus spent his life in working for the welfare of sentient beings, he resolved, at its close, to go to Potala. From Jambudvīpa he set sail for the island of Dhanaśrī. Śeṣanāga, bearing rancour for past criticism, began to destroy the ship with tidal waves. From the midst of the sea came a voice: "Throw overboard Candragomin!" He made an entreaty to Tārā, and the chief noble came through the sky with her retinue of five, mounted on a garuḍa. The nāgas fled in terror, and the ship arrived safely in Dhanaśrī.[29]

Note the detail of the entreaty or vow and the similarity between pota, "ship," in the Sanskrit passage, and the place-name "Potala" used here. This case illustrates well how even the minutest pieces of information were collected by the Tibetan historians and used, in good faith, for their biographies of the Indian masters.

Of similarly limited value is Tāranātha's statement that Candragomin hails from the district Varendra or Vareṇḍrī in northern Bengal. This detail is probably taken from the colophon of a hymn in praise of Avalokiteśvara in twenty-five stanzas, which runs as follows:

The hymn to the Lord of the World, called "Splitter of Sins and Enticer of the Mind" and composed by Candragomin, the teacher and scholar from Vareṇḍrī in Eastern (India), is completed. It was translated by Dānaśīla, the great scholar from Jāgatala of Vareṇḍrī in Eastern India.[30]

Only a few years ago I discovered that the Sanskrit original of this hymn is not only available but has been accessible to the Western scholarly world for more than a century. It is the very same Avalokiteśvarastotra or Lokanāthastotra by Carpaṭi, which was edited by the Russian scholar Minaev.[31] This hymn was translated into Tibetan three times, obviously independently of one another, since the translations vary widely in their wording. In one case[32] the name of the author is given correctly as Carpaṭi. In the second[33] it corrupted through the intermediate form *Carpaṭi-pāda[34] to Caryadīpa, "the Lamp of Conduct," and in the third case,[35] the name was changed to Candragomin. It remains unclear whether the place name Vareṇḍrī in the last case was meant to refer to the original author of the hymn, Carpaṭi, or to Candragomin, who was wrongly credited with this work.

The majority of the works in the Tibetan Tanjur (more than thirty) attributed to Candragomin are very short and mostly elementary treatises belonging to the category of offerings to and visualizations of Tantric deities. Personally I can hardly believe that they were written by the famous grammarian and poet Candragomin, and prefer to believe that they were written by a later namesake. The only works of note are a lengthy commentary upon the "Recitation of the [One Hundred and Fifty] Names of Mañjuśrī" (Mañjuśrī-nāmasaṃgīti) and a short logical treatise, the Nyāyasiddhyāloka. According to Ernst Steinkellner,[36] the latter work was composed not earlier than the eighth century C.E., and therefore could not have been written by the grammarian, playwright, and letter-writer.

Tāranātha's Account of Candragomin

Since the information contained in the works attributed to Candragomin is so meager, we can understand that the Tibetan historians would have wished to embellish the scarce facts with more vivid details. Of them Tāranātha gives the longest record.[37] The two most important details of Tāranātha's biography are Candragomin's affiliation with the teacher Sthiramati and the Vijñānavāda doctrine, and his debates with Candrakīrti, in which he upheld the Vijñānavāda view. Apart from Tāranātha there is only one late and extremely brief independent source that brings together the names Candragomin and Candrakīrti: the "Anecdote about Candragomin," which can be found in the Tanjur editions of Derge[38] and Narthang. The Indian and Chinese sources are completely silent about the identity of Candrakīrti's opponent in these debates.

Neither in *Joy for the World* nor in any other of Candragomin's genuine poetic compositions do we find a trace of the Vijñanavāda philosophy. In fact, no philosophical work at all by the pre-eighth-century Candragomin has come down to us. Given the great competence in this field that Tāranātha attributes to him—and the great number of minor philosophical works by other authors that have survived at least in Tibetan translation—this is more than surprising. Why should such a great number of unexceptional hymns and ritual texts have been preserved, yet no trace remain of his much more important contributions to the core of Buddhist philosophy?

To conclude this deconstructive reasoning, I would like to let Candragomin speak for himself. Which of his accomplishments does he regard as worthy of mention in the prologue of his drama *Joy for the World?* He refers only to his poetic compositions and his grammar. Since the grammar was completed before the play and—by its sheer size—has to be the work of a mature scholar, we can safely assume that Candragomin was already advanced in age when he wrote *Joy for the World*. Therefore the fact that philosophy is not mentioned in the prologue and that it is virtually absent in the body of the play is a very strong indication that Candragomin had neither at this time nor later contributed anything substantial to this field of learning. In contrast, the famous Buddhist poets Aśvaghoṣa, Āryaśūra, Haribhaṭṭa, and Gopadatta did not fail to display their philosophical erudition in their respective works.

"Letter to a Disciple"

Candragomin's "Letter to a Disciple," the central text of this book, is poetically the most refined of the extant Buddhist epistles. For the general structure Candragomin could turn to two exemplary models, Nāgārjuna's "Letter to a Friend" and Mātṛceṭa's "Letter to the Great King Kaniṣka," both of which he used, as we shall see below. In his poetic technique, however, he was strongly influenced by contemporary Hindu poetry, especially the work of Kālidāsa.

In *Joy for the World,* Candragomin could not resist the influence of the peak of Indian dramatic art, Kālidāsa's drama Śakuntalā. In at least fifteen scenes, Candragomin adapts the novel dramaturgical effects of Kālidāsa's extremely successful play to his own unique purpose.

But Kālidāsa's influence on Candragomin does not end with the Śakuntalā. The famed Hindu author wrote another very successful and influential work, the "Cloud Messenger" (Meghadūta), a poem of about 115 stanzas devoted to a single theme, the separation of a lover from his beloved. The "Cloud Messenger" is the first-known work of this type, a comparatively short work of ornate poetry focusing on a single topic.

If one compares the length, content, and formal structure of the "Cloud Messenger" with that of the "Letter to a Disciple," it is difficult not to conclude that Candragomin for a second time attempted to write the Buddhist counterpart of an impressive work of Hindu poetry. Thus two streams of Indian literary tradition flow together in the "Letter to a Disciple"—the Buddhist epistle and the full-fledged poem of a limited size, the so-called Khaṇḍakāvya.[39]

In writing the Buddhist equivalent of a masterwork of Brahmanic poetry, Candragomin certainly had to change the subject of the poem. As a Buddhist he would have had no interest in describing the feelings and emotions of two separated lovers. Instead, he chose more or less the opposite topic, a description of the dangers resulting from clinging to this world and its temptations.

The person addressed in the "Letter to a Disciple" is not mentioned in the epistle. The two Indian commentaries on the Śiṣyalekha, however, contain some information on this point. Vairocanarakṣita writes in his "Glosses on the Letter to a Disciple" (Śiṣyalekhaṭippaṇa):

> This epistle by Candragomin was meant to prevent a disciple of Candra[gomin], a hero by the name of Ratnakīrti who enjoyed great fame among men, from being guided [back] to his royal duties by a minister.[40]

Prajñākaramati gives some additional information in his "Commentary on the Letter to a Disciple:"

> In order to bring back his own disciple, who had broken his monk's vow and was engaged in a love affair with a princess, he (Candragomin) sent him [this] instruction, whose first stanza, beginning with the word gang-gis,[41] contains a praise of the teacher by giving the perfect cause [of his Buddhahood].[42]

We do not know whether there is any truth behind these two records given by scholars who lived many centuries after Candragomin, but they do not contradict the content of the "Letter to a Disciple," which in stanzas 9–18 contains a strong warning against turning away from the Buddhist teachings.

Structure of the Work

It is not the strictly logical exposition of Buddhist views and convictions but the power of the images and the refinement of the language that bring the reader under the spell of "Letter to a Disciple." An analysis of the structure of the poem reveals a loose collection of some of the basic tenets of Mahāyāna Buddhism. Siglinde Dietz has structured the "Letter to a Disciple" in the following way:[43]

PRAISE OF THE THREE JEWELS: STANZAS 1–8

1–5 Praise of the Buddha: his deeds, his body, his compassion, his beneficence towards others, comparison with the moon

6–7 Praise of the Dharma, the Buddha's Teaching: comparison of the Buddha with a cloud

8 Praise of the Sangha, the Community of the Buddha

INSTRUCTIONS FOR THE APOSTATE: STANZAS 9–18

9–13 Condemnation of apostates who refuse or abandon the Teaching; who abandon the moral commandments, morality, or the virtues of a Jina

14–16 Description of the good

17–18 The consequences of turning from the Dharma

INSTRUCTIONS ABOUT THE RIGHT VIEW OF EXISTENCE: STANZAS 19–93

19–34 The suffering of human existence

19–21 The suffering of birth

22–24 The suffering of youth

25–26 The suffering of old age

27–34 The suffering of death: the approach of death, the regret of omission, the pain of death

35–40 The suffering experienced by the pretas

41–59 The pain experienced in the various hells

60–77 About right conduct in the highest form of existence, that of a human being

60–63 Future existence as determined by the deeds of the present existence

64 The way of the Buddha as inaccessible even to gods and demigods

65–67 The need for immediate action

68–72 The beatitude of the ascetic's life in the forest

73–77 Condemnation of sensual pleasures

78–83 The suffering of the god realm (because of the inevitable descent to lower forms of existence)

84–90 Condemnation of striving for worldly happiness

84–88 The relativity of the notion of happiness

89–90 The wrong notion of happiness leads to passion; passion leads to rebirth

91–93 All forms of existence have been experienced a hundred times or more

DESCRIPTION OF THE GOOD MAN WHO WORKS FOR THE WELFARE OF OTHERS: STANZAS 94–106

94–98 Why it is necessary to work for the welfare of others

94 All beings are related to one another

95–98 All friends and relatives leave us; it is cruel to leave them in the maelstrom of samsara

99–106 The highest good: to bear the suffering of others; to bring about the happiness of others; to bring about the welfare of others; to rescue the world; to enter even the hells for the sake of others

VARIOUS EXHORTATIONS AND IMPERATIVES: STANZAS 107–12

107 Exhortation to right conduct

108 Exhortation to follow the word of the Buddha

109 Exhortation to give up sensual pleasures and delusion

110–112 Exhortations to become like a great tree, a great cloud, or a large lake for those suffering in the desert of samsara

THE WISHES OF THE POET REGARDING THE EFFECT OF HIS WORK: STANZAS 113–16

113 Desire for the word of the Buddha and attainment of omniscience

114 Wish that the hells become pleasant places

115 Wish for future rebirth as Buddha

116 Wish for the spread of the Dharma and victory over the Lord of Death

Parallels between "Letter to a Disciple" and Nāgārjuna's "Letter to a Friend"

Siglinde Dietz has already pointed to the remarkable parallels between some stanzas of the "Letter to a Disciple" and similar stanzas in Nāgārjuna's "Letter to a Friend."[44] They mainly concern the exposition of the seven evils in the wheel of rebirth, which is depicted in detail in stanzas 65–102 of the "Letter to a Friend." The corresponding passages are Śiṣyalekha 35–40 and Suhṛllekha 91–97, which describe the sufferings of the pretas or hungry ghosts;[45] Śiṣyalekha 41–59 and Suhṛllekha 77–88, the sufferings experienced in the eight hot hells; Śiṣyalekha 78–81 and 83, and Suhṛllekha 70–74 and 99, the suffering of falling from rebirth in the god realm.

In most cases the styles of Nāgārjuna and Candragomin differ greatly. Nāgārjuna expounds his topics in a brief, matter-of-fact manner, relying on their immediate effect, whereas Candragomin turns them into miniature scenes and ornaments them with all kinds of embellishment. To give an example, stanza 92 of Nāgārjuna's "Letter to a Friend" reads as follows:

Some of them, having mouths the size of a needle's eye
and stomachs the size of mountains,
and being tormented by hunger,
do not possess the strength to eat
even the smallest quantity of food,
thrown away as useless filth.[46]

Candragomin, using the figure of speech called atiśayokti or hyperbole, has added to this a new feature that further enhances the vividness of the pain—the terrible burning in the throat of the preta:

That miserable being
with a mouth the size of a needle,
whose formidable belly measures many miles around,
may drink all the water in the great ocean,
but before a single drop of that water
has reached the crevass
of the huge cavity of its throat,
it dries up completely
in the heat of his mouth. [40]

In some verses, the influence of Nāgārjuna upon Candragomin is even more clearly felt, as in Suhṛllekha 72–73 and Śiṣyalekha 78–79. Here is Nāgārjuna on the pain of falling from the heavenly realms:

Having been attended by celestial maidens
and dallied in a pleasant and most beautiful grove

one will have to suffer having the feet, hands,
ears and nose being cut off
by the sword-like leaves of the Asipattravana. [72]

Having entered the heavenly river Mandākinī,
together with celestial maidens
who are adorned with golden lotuses,
one will again have to enter Vaitaraṇī,
the river of the hell,
whose boiling acid waters are impossible to bear. [73][47]

The central ideas of both stanzas, although in reverse order, are repeated in the "Letter to a Disciple:"

Having enjoyed playfully sporting
with the heavenly nymphs,
their locks disheveled
by the current of the river Mandākinī,
these beings, having fallen, again wander about,
experiencing agonizing pain
when their bodies are eaten away
by the acid waves of Vaitaraṇī, the river of hell. [78]

Having lived pleasurably
with lovely companions in the forests of the gods,
where the beds are made
of the tender buds of the wish-fulfilling tree,
these beings again wander about
in forests with sword-like leaves,
their bodies cut apart
by the falling leaves,
a flurry of sharp swords. [79]

Parallels between "Letter to a Disciple" and Mātṛceṭa's "Letter to the Great King Kaniṣka"

The "Letter to a Friend" was not the only Buddhist model for Candragomin's Dharma poem. We can find the origin of two of its stanzas—which he also used in his drama *Joy for the World*—in Mātṛceṭa's epistle to King Kaniṣka. I give first Candragomin's stanza 66:

"I will do this tomorrow, that today,
the other thing after a short while, this now."
When people think like this,
I fear that the impatient and angry Lord of Death,
whose once black club
has been stained deep crimson
by his furious sidelong glances,
will laugh at them. [66]

The same warning is expressed in stanzas 58–60 of the "Letter to the Great King Kaniṣka:"

The Lord of Death, who is no man's friend,
will descend upon you suddenly.
Therefore, turn in haste to the holy Dharma,
and do not say, "I will do it tomorrow." [58]

"I will do this tomorrow, not today"
is not good for a man to say.
Without any doubt, that tomorrow will come
when you no longer exist. [59]

When the heartless Lord of Death,
who destroys men's powers without rhyme or reason,
approaches with the intent to kill,
what wise man can remain at ease? [60]

In this instance Candragomin has condensed the wording of his source, which contains a certain repetition. In the second case he elaborates on Mātṛceṭa's verse 56:

While revolving in the circle of existence
again and again, like a rosary,
what have you not already done in the world
a hundred times, or even thousands? [56]

This forms more or less the first half of stanza 91 of the "Letter to a Disciple:"

What form and manner of existence is there
that the soul has not already lived through
in this world a hundred times before?
And what sort of happiness is there
that has not been enjoyed
on countless previous occasions?
What sort of goddesses of happiness are those,
a sweet smile on their lips,
fanned by fans made of yak-tails,
that one has not beheld many a time before?
And yet despite all this,
human desire continues to grow! [91]

Parallels between Candragomin's "Letter to a Disciple" and the two epistles by Nāgārjuna and Mātṛceṭa are easily found because these works all belong to the same literary genre and none is very long. It would be much more time-consuming to trace the influence three other great Buddhist poets might have exercised upon Candragomin: Aśvaghoṣa, Āryaśūra, and Haribhaṭṭa. The Jātakamālās of the latter two authors have much in common with the Śiṣyalekha, in particular their repeated warnings against the danger of the objects of the senses and their detailed descriptions of the tortures in the different hells. I intend to return to these relationships at another time.

Literary Merits of "Letter to a Disciple"

Literary Theory in Candragomin's Time

A few words should be said about the theoretical basis of Candragomin's poetic composition, in particular the literary principles prevailing in India at his time. The oldest available treatise that deals with the basic principles of poetry is the "Handbook of Dramaturgy" (Nāṭyaśāstra) attributed to the "sage" (muni) Bharata.[48] Scholars assume that the nucleus of this work, which was later largely expanded, took shape in the first and second centuries. It propounds the so-called rasa theory or the theory of "aesthetic relish." Originally developed for the Indian drama, it later became the most general principle for the interpretation of any literary composition.[49]

To put it in the words of V. K. Chari, the rasa (lit. "taste") is first, "the relishable quality inherent in an artistic work" and "its emotional content."[50] Second, rasa is "the relishable experience occasioned by the work in the reader or spectator."[51] The rasas are coordinated with a set of corresponding emotions (bhāva) that are meant to evoke the respective rasas. Their traditional number is eight: the erotic rasa or mood, occasioned by erotic love; the comic rasa, occasioned by amusement or laughter; the compassionate rasa, occasioned by sorrow; the furious or dreadful rasa, occasioned by anger; the heroic rasa, occasioned by dynamic energy; the terrifying rasa, occasioned by fear; the disgusting rasa, occasioned by disgust; the awesome rasa, occasioned by wonder.[52] Later a ninth, quietude or tranquility, was added, which plays and played an important role in Buddhist literature. It is not clear whether it originated from there or from the Hindu concept of deliverance, the fourth goal of life.[53] The rasa theory was later largely expanded and fraught with philosophical and religious interpretation, but in all probability this took place after the time of Candragomin.

In addition to the rasa theory, Indian literary criticism developed three more fundamental concepts for the interpretation and assessment of literary compositions. The first is that of "ornamentation," from Skt. alaṁkāra, "ornament." It is propounded in the works of the aestheticians Bhāmaha and Daṇḍin, who are generally held to have lived in the seventh century C.E. The nucleus of this concept can already be found in the work of Bharata, and therefore its full-fledged form must have been developed between the second and seventh centuries C.E. The alaṁkāra concept focuses on the figures of speech that distinguish poetry from ordinary speech. In an often quoted simile in Daṇḍin's "Mirror of Composition," the words in a literary composition are compared to the body and the figures of speech to its ornaments.[54] Figures of speech are divided into two categories: those based on sound and those based on meaning.[55] Genres of literature are also discussed by the expounders of this theory.

The second concept is that of style, Skt. rīti, "manner, usage, custom." It focuses on the arrangement of words and the qualities awakened thereby, such as sweetness (Skt. mādhurya), clarity (Skt. prasāda), and strength (Skt. ojas). This concept is discussed in detail by Vāmana, and outlined in Daṇḍin's "Mirror of Composition." Daṇḍin distinguishes between two principal styles of writing, one used by the people of Gauḍa (gauḍīya), the other by the people of Vidarbha (vaidarbha). In short, the Gauḍa style is fond of complicated ideas put into a most refined linguistic form, whereas the Vidarbha style gives more weight to elegance and clarity of both form and meaning. When measured against these standards, there can be no doubt that the "Letter to a Disciple" belongs to the latter category. The elegance and clarity of its style, bridging more than fourteen centuries, speak directly even to readers today.

The third concept is that of "suggestion" (Skt. dhvani, "tone"). Suggestion means that the essential intention of the poet lies behind figures of speech, style, and aesthetic relish, and is only suggested by the poet's words. In all probability, this concept was developed after the time of Candragomin—the fundamental treatise of this school, "Splendor of Suggestion" or dhvanyāloka, was written by Ānandavardhana in the ninth century C.E.

At an even later time, the concept of "appropriateness" (Skt. aucitya) was introduced by writers like the Kashmiri Kṣemendra. The Sanskrit language is characterized by an unusually large number of synonyms or quasi-synonyms, and Kṣemendra focused on an aspect that, although not expressly discussed before, must have been in the mind of any poet writing in Sanskrit: the selection of a word most appropriate to the specific situation and circumstance. Below I will give one illustration: the appropriateness of the word vigraha, "body," in stanza 44.

In Candragomin's "Letter to a Disciple," the concepts of ornamentation, style, and aesthetic relish can all be clearly felt. A certain emphasis is given to ornamentation, without unduly neglecting the other principles. Buddhist authors like Aśvaghoṣa, Mātṛceṭa, Āryaśūra, and Haribhaṭṭa in their respective works successively developed this aspect, mining the flexibility of the Sanskrit language and its ability to underscore a certain emotion or aesthetic aspect with appropriately chosen words. Beginning in the sixth century C.E., this flexibility became stretched to extremes in stanzas that contained only one vowel or consonant, and palindromes or various kinds of "figurative poetry" with stanzas formed along certain graphic patterns like a lotus or bow. Candragomin and his predecessors, however, deliberately avoided these extremes and maintained an almost classical balance between form and content.

Figures of Speech in "Letter to a Disciple"

ALLITERATION AND PARONOMASIA

We will now follow the Indian way and point to some of the qualities of form and meaning in the poem. Thanks to the extremely rich vocabulary of the Sanskrit language, it is not difficult for an Indian poet to make use of two literary devices, anuprāsa or alliteration (the repetition of sounds) and paronomasia (the repetition of groups of syllables). These two figures of speech are in fact so easy to use that there is always the danger of using them to excess. Candragomin's approach, however, is once again moderate. Alliteration occurs in less than half the stanzas and its use is never forced. A few examples may suffice:

saṁsā**ra**bhūdha**ra**da**rī**jaṭha**ra**p**ra**pātād
utthātum **ud**yata**parāḥ** **para**māndhakārāt | 13ab |

In the first line the consonant r(a) is used five times and in the second line the prefix ud- and the word para(ma)- occur

Table of Sanskrit Pronunciation

a	as in b**u**t	e	as in m**a**de
ā	as in f**ar**	o	as in h**o**le
i	as in b**i**t	ai	as in s**igh**t
ī	as in m**e**	an	as in l**ou**d
u	as in p**u**t	ṅ	as in si**ng**
ū	as in s**oo**n	ñ	as in pu**n**ch

ṛ as in p**re**tty (the vowel being almost inaudible)

≈ as ṛ, but of double length (occurs only rarely)

ḷ as in **cl**ip (the vowel being almost inaudible)

c as in **ch**urch

j as in **j**udge

ś as in **sh**ip

ḍ, ṇ, ṣ, ṭ pronounced like d, n, sh, t, but with the tip of the tongue touching the palate

ḥ as h(a), h(i), h(u), depending on the preceding vowel; the vowel following h is pronounced extremely short

h following the 10 **unaspirated** stops k, g, c, j, ṭ, ḍ, t, d, p, and b is pronounced as a strongly audible aspiration, e.g., khi as in ki**ck hi**m.

twice. Likewise the consonant s(a)- occurs seven times in the second half of stanza 15:

teja**s**vinaḥ **s**ukham a**sū**n api **s**aṁtyajanti
satya**s**thitivya**s**anino na punaḥ pratijñām | | 15cd | |

Other noteworthy examples are stanzas 18 (sa six times, śa seven times), 23 (ta ten times), 25 (ta eight times), 28 (ta twelve times), 36 (la seven times, śi/śī four times), 39 (vi four times), 42 (śa four times, sa five times), 43 (ta fifteen times), 44 (ta seven times, ka four times). In many cases the poetic intention of the alliteration is immediately felt. In stanza 44, for example, Candragomin describes women whose bodies are as jagged as saws. The attribute he uses is:

krakaca-karkaśa-vigrahābhiḥ
saw-jagged-body-(possessing)

To the Indian ear this jaggedness or harshness is very aptly expressed by the sounds and sound combinations of ka, ca, and śa in krakaca-karkaśa. The use of vigraha for "body"—rather than one of the more common synonyms like aṅga or kāya—is a good illustration of the principle of appropriateness. The syllable gra not only rhymes with the preceding kra in krakaca, "saw," but also imitates very aptly the sound of sawing, especially in the sequence kra - gra.

The second figure of speech, yamaka or paronomasia, Candragomin uses comparatively often, although not in the strict form prescribed by the rhetoricians. According to the rules of rhetoric, the yamaka consists of the repetition of exactly the same sound pattern, but with a different meaning. Candragomin handles this figure of speech much more freely. He is obviously content with a kind of assonance in which one or two words are repeated in varying grammatical contexts. A good example of this type of paronomasia is stanza 3:

yaḥ sarvadā *para***sukhena sukhī** babhūva
duḥkhena duḥkham agamat *para*maṁ *pare*ṣām |
atyartham āhitamahākaruṇāguṇasya
yasyātma**duḥkhasukham** antaritaṁ tad eva || 3 ||

The terms "happiness" (sukha), "suffering, sorrow" (duḥkha) and "others" (para) are each repeated three times. Here the repetition is determined by the meaning of the stanza, the figure of speech being an incidental byproduct.

Another type of unforced paronomasia is caused when two words derived from the same root or stem are placed in close vicinity. Examples of this type are:

mohitā bahala**moha**mahāmadena (9c)
blinded by the strong intoxication of massive delusion ('blindness')

viṣama**pātam** adhaḥ **patanti** (13d)
will take ('fall') a terrible plunge ('fall') downward

tair eva yānti **gurutāṁ guravaḥ** suśiṣyaiḥ (14d)
It is only through such noble disciples that teachers become real teachers.

lajjāṁ guṇaugha**jananīṁ jananīm** ivāryām (15a)
noble modesty, which produces an abundance of virtues . . . like a noble mother ('producer') . . .

akṛtāni karoti (26c)
commits ('does') outrageous deeds

Sometimes there is no etymological relationship:

arav**indam indum ind**ī**v**araṁ ca tulayanti (90ab)
(who) compare an Aravinda lotus, the moon, and an Indīvara lotus

or only pseudo-identity of the sound pattern as in:

āviśya garbha**nilayaṁ nirayaṁ** yathaiva (19c)
having entered the womb (as his dwelling-place) (nilaya) . . . exactly like a hell (niraya)

pāpa**nilayān nirayāt** (61b)
from hell, the dwelling-place of evildoers

The latter example might lead to the conclusion that Candragomin spoke a regional variety of Sanskrit where the difference between ra and la had disappeared, but this seems presumptuous. In the light of all the other paranomasias and assonances of his poem, it seems much more likely that he deliberately chose two almost identical words.

Complete Simile

Among the figures based on meaning, the prevailing category is that of simile (upamā). It is also used by Candragomin, although less frequently than by other authors. He is obviously fond of its most developed form, the so-called "complete simile" (pūrṇopamā). In its rigid form it makes use of an important feature of the Sanskrit language: the ambiguity of many of its words. The complete simile has the following structure: A, characterized by a set of attributes a, b, c, etc., resembles B. The attributes a, b, c, etc. then have to be chosen in such a manner that each of them in principle allows for two interpretations: one referring to A, the other to B. Here is an example:

sa tathāpi vijihmaceṣṭitaḥ
kuśalenāpi bhayād ivojjhitaḥ |
akṛtāni karoti mohitaḥ
śaravat svātmavadhāya puṣpitaḥ | 26 |

Nevertheless, deluded (mohitaḥ),
his gait crooked (vijihmaceṣṭitaḥ),
deserted (ujjhitaḥ) even by his own well-being (kuśalenāpi),
as if afraid (bhayād iva),
his skin mottled with dark spots (puṣpitaḥ),
a mark of being soon to die (svavadhāya),
he commits outrageous deeds (akṛtāni karoti),
just as an arrow gone astray (mohitaḥ),
wobbling in its course (vijihmaceṣṭitaḥ)
when released (ujjhitaḥ),
even by a skilled archer (kuśalenāpi) startled into fright (bhayād iva),
decorated with flowers (puṣpitaḥ)
that point to its own destruction (svavadhāya),
commits outrageous deeds (akṛtāni karoti).

There are other examples in stanzas 5, 6, 7, 8 and 19. Stanza 19 is a particularly simple complete simile, since the four attributes referring to both "womb" and "hell" were chosen in such a way that they can be translated in exactly the same manner in both cases.

Metaphorical Identification and Ascription

While the simile, according to the Indian aestheticians, always requires a particle or verb to imply resemblance, similarity, or even identity, the so-called "metaphorical identification" (rūpaka) draws on compound noun forms. Instead of saying "existence is like an ocean," "morality is like a vessel" or "the defilements are like fire," the poet uses noun compounds such as "the ocean of existence," "the vessel of morality" and "the fire of the defilements," as does Candragomin in stanzas 12 and 72. In stanza 13, three metaphorical identifications are elaborated into a complete simile: Samsara is compared to a mountain, the human being's effort to cross samsara is compared to the mountaineer's efforts to climb the mountain, and the virtues (guṇa) that assist in the effort are compared to the rope (guṇa) used to secure the mountain-climber.

Another frequently used figure of speech is that of "ascription" (utprekṣā), in which the feelings or thoughts of an animate being are attributed or ascribed to an inanimate subject. A particularly impressive illustration is stanza 27:

Then Death,
the younger brother of Old Age,
who can by no means be appeased,
as if laughing, sets out
to devour him from the head down
with his huge teeth—
the shock of white hair.

Telling the Nature of a Thing

Additional figures of speech, like hyperbole or "(mild) exaggeration" (atiśayokti), are not different from those used in Western literature, although most of them are used with stringent restrictions. All of them are subordinated, however, to one figure of speech that was not accepted unanimously by all Indian writers on poetics: the so-called svabhāvokti or "telling the nature (of a thing)." Gerow defines it as "a figure in which a natural or typical individual is characterized."[56]

As can be seen from the structural analysis of the "Letter to a Disciple," the main purport of the letter is to provide not only the addressee, but every reader of the work with an accurate view of human existence in all its negative and terrifying aspects. This requires a description "as it is," in which the comparison with something similarly terrifying can be used only sparingly, so as not to distract from the main topic. The prevailing rasa or emotional experience to be created in the reader is bībhatsarasa or the aesthetic experience of "disgust," which is evoked by the description of disgusting states, conditions, and feelings; its corresponding emotion is fear. In his description, Candragomin could draw from the meditative practice of the "evocation of unpleasant things" (aśubhabhāvanā), which was used in a similar manner by the monks and ascetics to suppress the craving for living and rebirth.

The rasa "mood of disgust" is so dominating that there is little room left for the ninth rasa, the rasa that we expect also to be part of a Buddhist poem: the śāntarasa or the aesthetic relish of "tranquility." In the section that praises the solitary life there is one such stanza (72) that expresses this experience:

The vast and vaulted mountain caves,
wondrously deep and blessed
by the presence of sages rich in austerities,
girded by verdant forest borders
and near the banks of rivers,
appear to call out to the wayfarers
in the voices of waterfalls, sweet as tambourines:

"We lie beyond all reach
of the fire of the defilements!"

"Tranquility" is obviously the main topic of the concluding section, where it is expressly mentioned in stanzas 107 (śama), 109 (śānti), 110 (praśānti and śamatha), 111 (praśamita), 114 (praśānta), and 116 (śama).

Metrical Structure

A few words should be added about the metrical structure of this short poem. I have indicated above that it might have been Candragomin's intention to compose a Buddhist counterpart to Kālidāsa's famous "Cloud Messenger." I have already pointed to the great contrast in the subject matter of the two poems; there is also a contrast in the use of meter. Kālidāsa uses only one meter, the mandākrāntā. The permanent repetition of the same meter—even without the change to another meter at the end as is customary with the greater works divided into cantos—creates a certain monotony that underscores the melancholic and elegiac mood of the yakṣa who is separated from his wife.

Candragomin could have used the same device, for monotony and disgust are related feelings, but he did not. In all he used nine different meters, deliberately avoiding the vaktra or anuṣṭubh meter, which is commonly known as śloka. The chart on the following page contains all the meters used in the "Letter to a Disciple" together with examples of their scanned structure. With the exception of puṣpitāgrā and viyoginī, all four lines of a verse have the same structure.

The main meter is vasantatilakā. It is used in 73 stanzas: 1–22, 34–53, 59–70, 73–75, 77–83, and 90–98. The other eight

Meters Used in "Letter to a Disciple"

puṣpitāgrā (2 times, 12 + 13 syllables

◡ ◡ ◡ ◡ ◡ ◡ – ◡ – ◡ – –
◡ ◡ ◡ ◡ – ◡ ◡ – ◡ – ◡ – –

pṛthvī (4 times, 17 syllables)

◡ – ◡ ◡ ◡ – ◡ – | ◡ ◡ ◡ – ◡ – – ◡ –

praharṣiṇī (4 times, 13 syllables)

– – – | ◡ ◡ ◡ ◡ – ◡ – ◡ – –

mandākrāntā (4 times, 17 syllables)

– – – – | ◡ ◡ ◡ ◡ ◡ – | – ◡ – – ◡ – –

mālinī (4 times, 17 syllables)

◡ ◡ ◡ ◡ ◡ ◡ – – | – ◡ – – ◡ – –

vasantatilakā (4 times, 14 syllables)

– – ◡ – ◡ ◡ ◡ – ◡ ◡ – ◡ – –

viyoginī (2 times, 10 + 11 syllables)

◡ ◡ – ◡ ◡ – ◡ – ◡ –
◡ ◡ – – ◡ ◡ – ◡ – ◡ –

śikhariṇī (4 times, 17 syllables)

◡ – – – – – | ◡ ◡ ◡ ◡ ◡ – – ◡ ◡ ◡ –

hariṇī (4 times, 17 syllables)

◡ ◡ ◡ ◡ ◡ – | – – – – | ◡ – ◡ ◡ – ◡ –

meters are used in 43 stanzas, forming small groups that are inserted into the flow of the main meter: viyoginī (23–33, eleven times), pṛthvī (54–58, five times), śikhariṇī (71–72 and 99–104, eight times), praharṣiṇī (76 and 84–85, thrice), mandākrāntā (86–89, four times), puṣpitāgrā (105–6, twice), mālinī (107–8, twice), hariṇī (109–16, eight times). In several cases the motive for the use of a particular meter is obvious; see the notes on stanzas 23 and 54. In other cases the reader might find his or her own explanation after repeatedly reciting the stanzas aloud.

Footnotes

1 There are various lexicographical forms in Tibetan: sprin-yig, spring-yig, phrin-yig, and 'phrin-yig, literally meaning "message letter."

2 *Die buddhistische Briefliteratur Indiens. Nach dem tibetischen Tanjur herausgegeben, übersetzt und erläutert* [The Buddhist Epistolary Literature of India. Edited, translated and explicated on the basis of the Tibetan Tanjur], by Siglinde Dietz. Asiatische Forschungen 84 (Wiesbaden: Otto Harrassowitz, 1984).

3 The "Letter to the Great King Kaniṣka" has survived only in Tibetan translation. The Sanskrit original is lost and we do not know of any other independent translation.

A Mongolian translation of the Tibetan text was done between 1742 and 1749, on the basis of the Peking (or Qianlong) edition of the Tibetan Tanjur. It was a part of the huge but inadequately executed task of translating the complete Tibetan Tanjur into Mongolian within less than eight years. During this comparatively short time the wooden blocks of this translation were also carved.

The Mongolian Tanjur has survived in a single copy belonging to the collections of the state library in Ulan Bator, Mongolia. Xerox copies of this unique print are kept in the International Academy of Indian Culture, New Delhi; the State Library at Berlin, Germany; and the Central-Asian Institute of the University of Bonn, Germany. The present writer was able to consult these copies for some of his editions of Tibetan texts, and thereby gained a first-hand impression of the rather limited value of the Mongolian Tanjur.

4 The following sketch of Mātṛceṭa's life and work is based on a German scholarly publication, the critical edition (Sanskrit-Tibetan) and copiously annotated translation of Mātṛceṭa's

longest work, "The Praise of the Praiseworthy," by Jens-Uwe Hartmann: *Das Varṇārhavarṇastotra des Mātṛceṭa* (Göttingen, 1987). In particular, the two passages from I-Tsing's record are taken from Hartmann's German rendition of the Chinese text, not from Takakusu's well-known English translation (Oxford, 1896).

5 I-Tsing notes that "mātṛ" means "mother," and "ceṭa" means "little child." This is not quite accurate, since "ceṭa" means "servant," as correctly translated by the Tibetans, i.e. khol.

6 The following stanza by Śākyabuddhi—quoted by Nandipriya in his commentary—is syntactically incomplete since it is meant to be followed first by stanza 2 of Dignāga's "Mixed Hymn" (of which only one line is quoted by Nandipriya), and then by stanza 2 of Mātṛceṭa's "Hymn in 150 Stanzas." The three stanzas together form a syntactical unit.

'di nyid spel ma'i spel mar gnas brtan Śākya blo yis bshad pa ni |

| 'bar zhing tsha ba'i 'dod chags sogs |
| me yis lus ni bsregs gyur cing |
| skye mched kun la gnod byed pa'i |
| dmyal bar yid ni skrag gyur pas |

| de ring gang la skyabs su mchi |

| zhes pa ni rgyas pa'o | |

"Exactly this has been said by the elder monk Śākyabuddhi in his 'Doubly Mixed [Hymn]' (Miśrakamiśraka):

[My] body is burnt by the fire
of burning hot lust and other [things]
and [my] mind is afraid of hell
which does harm to all spheres of life —

in whom I now take refuge because of that [= beginning line of Dignāga's Miśrakastotra 2]

With these [words by Dignāga the stanza is to be] expanded."

7 Translation quoted from D. R. Shackleton Bailey, *The Śata-pañcāśatka of Mātṛceṭa* (Cambridge, 1951), p. 6.

8 Translation quoted from E. Obermiller, *History of Buddhism (Chos-ḥbyung) by Bu-ston. Part 2. The History of Buddhism in India and Tibet* (Heidelberg, 1932), pp. 130, 136. The spelling is modernized.

9 For the most complete list of all works and stanzas attributed to Mātṛceṭa, see Jens-Uwe Hartmann's monograph *Das Varṇārhavarṇastotra des Mātṛceṭa*, pp. 22–30.

10 Hence the alternative name "(The Hymn) Consisting of One Hundred and Fifty (Stanzas)" (Adhyardhaśatikā or Śatapañcāśatka).

11 *The Śatapañcāśatka of Mātṛceṭa*. Sanskrit Text, Tibetan Translation, Commentary and Chinese Translation (Cambridge, 1951).

12 Hence the alternative name "(The Hymn) Consisting of Four Hundred (Stanzas)" (Catuḥśataka).

13 Such as the "Praise of the Praiseworthy" (Varṇārhavarṇa) or the "Hymn to the Guiltless" (Anaparāddhastotra). This latter hymn is not available in Tibetan translation; fragments of the original Sanskrit text, however, were found in Central Asia. The hymn consists of twenty-six stanzas in the long and difficult śārdūlavikrīḍita meter (nineteen syllables per line). Jens-Uwe Hartmann has published the most complete edition of the fragments, which cover stanzas 10 through 26 (none of them being complete) and the colophon in his study, *Neue Aśvaghoṣa- und Mātṛceṭa-Fragmente aus Ostturkistan* [New Aśvaghoṣa and Mātṛceṭa Fragments from Eastern Turkestan] (Göttingen, 1988).

14 There is no reason to discard the poet's own statement, and the assumption of a later insertion or forgery leads to absurd

consequences, as I have recently tried to show in two papers: "Über den indirekten Beweis bei literaturhistorischen Fragestellungen," in *Wiener Zeitschrift für die Kunde Südasiens* 36 (1992): 91–103, and "A Difficult Beginning. Comments upon an English translation of Candragomin's Deśanāstava," in *Researches in Indian and Buddhist Philosophy: Essays in Honour of Professor Alex Wayman* (Delhi, 1993), pp. 31–60. See also Roland Steiner, *Untersuchungen zu Harṣadevas* Nāgānanda *und zum indischen Schauspiel* (Swisttal-Odendorf 1997), pp. 32 ff.

15 *Joy for the World, A Buddhist Play by Candragomin.* Translated with an introduction and notes by Michael Hahn (Berkeley: Dharma Publishing, 1987).

16 The transmitted text, which is not free of mistakes, reads rgyal ma, "the Victorious One," which would correspond to Skt. *Jayā. I have emended to sgrol ma, "the Savioress" or Tārā. In Buddhism, Jayā is an almost unknown minor deity and I can hardly believe that Candragomin would have made an invocation to her at the beginning of his important play and not to one of the major figures in the Buddhist pantheon.

17 *Difficult Beginnings. Three Works on the Bodhisattva Path.* [By] Candragomin. Translated, with commentary by Mark Tatz (Boston, London, 1985).

18 Like Triratnadāsa's "Praise of the Unlimited Virtues [of the Buddha]" (Guṇāparyantastotra), consisting of fifty-one stanzas in the śikhariṇī meter with seventeen syllables per line.

19 Translation quoted from Mark Tatz, *Difficult Beginnings,* pp. 39–40. The last two lines of stanza 4 I have replaced with my own translation. The Tibetan reads as follows:

| der ni skye bo thams cad bder 'dod pa'i |
| chags pa'i 'dam gyis yid ni zin par 'gyur |

20 Martin Willson, *In Praise of Tārā* (London: Wisdom Publications, 1986).

21 Derge (D) 3668, vol. Mu, fols. 281a5–281b5; Peking (Q) 4490, vol. Du, fols. 368b6–369a8. This is perhaps identical with D 3671 and 3695 = Q 4493 and 4870, where the hymn is called Āryātārādevīstotra.

22 Q 4869. Perhaps identical with Q 4492. The work is absent in D.

23 Q 4871. The work is absent in D.

24 D 3667, vol. Mu, fols. 279a2–281a5; Q 4489, vol. Du, fols. 366a1–368b6.

25 Note that this is the same form of the name used in stanza 4 of the prologue of *Joy for the World*.

26 ayam ācā[1]ryacandradāsaḥ samudre potārūḍhaḥ samīraṇādibhiḥ poteṣu vistīryamāṇeṣu mahatyā bhaktyāryatārāyāḥ stotrārthābhidhānārtham ādau sambandhābhidheyaprayojanādy avadyotayan sakalajagattrayātiśāyināṁ [2] guṇānām abhidhānapratijñām uccacāra | tadvacanātiśayena taddeśāj jalam apasasāra | candramaṇḍalād vāyunā nīlābhravṛndam iva | jalāpasaraṇāc candrapūrvākhyo dvīpaḥ samvṛttas . . . . Text quoted from the transliteration of Rāhula Sāṁkṛtyāyana in the *Journal of the Bihar and Orissa Research Society* XXIII (1937): 51–52.

27 The translation is quoted from the paper by Mark Tatz, "The Life of Candragomin in Tibetan Historical Tradition," *The Tibet Journal* 7.3 (1982): 1–22; here pp. 9–10.

28 Obermiller, *op. cit.* (note 8), p. 132.

29 Quoted from Mark Tatz, "The Life ... ," p. 18.

30 'jig rten dbang phyug gi bstod pa yid 'phrog sdig 'joms zhes bya ba | shar phyogs ba ren ḍi'i slob dpon mkhas pa chen po tsantra go mis mdzad pa rdzogs so | | rgya gar shar phyogs ba ren ḍi'i dzā ga ta la'i paṇḍi ta chen po dā na shī las bsgyur ba.

31 In his paper "Buddijskija molitvij. I" [Buddhist Prayers. I], in *Zapiski vostoдnago otdelenija imperatorskago archeoloдeskago obπдestva* [Memoirs of the Oriental Section of the Imperial Archeological Society] 2 (1887): 125–36.

32 D 2726, Q 3546.

33 D 2724. The work is absent in Q.

34 Pāda, "foot," is used frequently after personal names as a honorific.

35 D 2722, Q 3542.

36 In his paper "Miszellen zur erkenntnistheoretisch-logischen Schule des Buddhismus," *Wiener Zeitschrift für die Kunde Südasiens* 28 (1984): 177–78.

37 The life of Candragomin can be found on pp. 199–209 of the English translation of *Tāranātha's History of Buddhism*. Trans. from Tibetan by Lama Chimpa [and] Alaka Chattopadhyaya. Ed. by Debiprasad Chattopadhyaya (Simla, 1970).

38 D 4340: Tsandra go mi'i gtam rgyud. Narthang has lo rgyus instead of gtam rgyud.

39 Khaṇḍakāvya or "poetry [consisting of only one] section" contrasts with the larger ornate epic like "The Life of the Buddha" by Aśvaghoṣa, which is called sargabandha or "composition [consisting of several] cantos."

40 | 'gro ba rnams la snyan par grags pa yi | zla bar grags pa'i slob ma dpa' bo rin chen grags pa zhes bya ba blon pos rgyal srid kyi don du khrid pa la | dpal tsandra go mi'i zhal snga nas kyi phrin yig 'dis bzlog go | (folios 114b1–2 in D, 376b4–5 in Q)

41 In its Tibetan version! The Sanskrit stanza does not begin with yasya, which corresponds to gang-gi(s).

42 rang gi slob ma dge slong gi brtul zhugs dor te | rgyal po'i bu mo dang 'dod pa bsten (rten Q) pa las slar bzlog (zlog Q) pa'i phyir de la gdams pa springs ba'i (springs pa'i Q) thog mar ston pa la bstod pa ni rgyu phun sum tshogs pa **gang gis** zhes tshigs su bcad pa gcig go | (folios 122a5 in D, 389b4–5 in Q)

43 Dietz, *Die buddhistische Briefliteratur Indiens*, 33–35.

44 Ibid., 36–37.

45 Two specific details common to both letters are the tiny mouths ("as small as the eye of a needle") of the pretas in Suhṛllekha 92 and Śiṣyalekha 40, and the impurity of the liquid they drink, Suhṛllekha 94 and Śiṣyalekha 35.

46 The Tibetan text runs as follows:

| kha cig kha ni khab kyi mig tsam la |
| lto ba ri yi gtos tsam bkres pas nyen |
| mi gtsang gyi nar bor ba cung zad tsam |
| 'tshal ba'i mthu dang ldan pa ma lags so | 92 |

47 The Tibetan text of the two stanzas runs as follows:

| mtho ris bu mos 'brongs shing dga' ba dang |
| rnam par mdzes tshal son par rtses nas slar |
| 'dab ma ral gri 'dra tshal gnas rnams kyis |
| rkang lag rna ba sna gcod 'thob par 'gyur | 72 |

| dal gyis 'bab par lha yi bu mo ni |
| gdong mdzes gser gyi padmar ldan zhugs nas |

| slar yang dmyal bar chu bo rabs med pa |
| tsha rgo bzod glags chu tshan 'jug 'tshal lo | 73 |

48 For an English translation of this work, see Manomohan Ghosh, *The Nāṭyaśāstra. A Treatise on Hindu Dramaturgy and Histrionics. Ascribed to Bharata-Muni* (Calcutta, 1950–1961).

49 For a sharp analysis of the early development of the rasa theory, see the paper by Bernhard Kölver, "Zur Frügeschichte der Rasa-Lehre" ["On the Early History of the Rasa Doctrine"], *Berliner Indologische Studien* 6 (1991): 21–48.

On the complicated textual history of Bharata's work, see Srinivasa Ayya Srinivasan, *On the Composition of the Nāṭyaśāstra* (Reinbek, 1980).

50 *Sanskrit Criticism* (Honolulu: University of Hawaii Press, 1990), pp. 9–10.

51 Ibid., p. 10.

52 See the translation of the relevant section from Bharata's Nāṭya-śāstra in the monograph by J. L. Masson and M. V. Patwardhan, *Aesthetic Rapture* (Poona: Deccan College, 1970), vol. I, pp. 43–57.

Kölver ingeniously groups the eight rasas into two sets of two opposing pairs:

Group I	*Group II*
Attractive – Revulsive	Humorous – Fearful
Heroic – Dreadful	Awesome – Pitiful

53 Recently an interesting theory has been put forward, suggesting that the tranquil mood forms the center and nucleus of the other eight rasas, out of which they first evolve and later dissolve (or merge) back into. See Kölver, *op. cit.*, 44–47.

54 "Mirror of Composition," 1.10. Cf. *Kāvyādarśa*. Edited with commentary by Pandit Rangacharya Raddi Shastri. 2nd ed. (Bhandarkar Oriental Research Institute: Poona, 1970).

55 The most comprehensive survey of the Indian figures of speech is Edwin Gerow, *A Glossary of Indian Figures of Speech* (The Hague, Mouton, 1971).

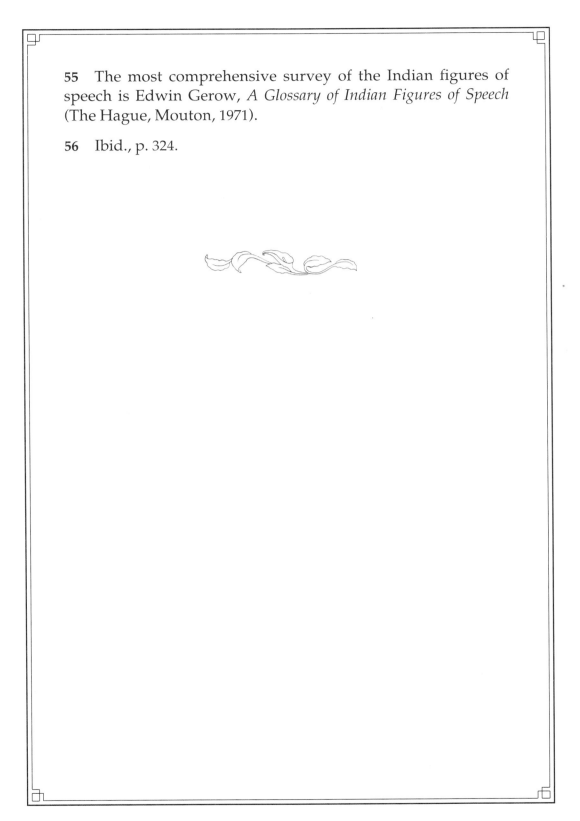

56 Ibid., p. 324.

Invitation to Enlightenment

PART ONE

The Texts and Translations

Homage to Mātṛceṭa, whose songs of praise awaken the qualities of enlightenment

महाराजकनिष्कलेख

།རྒྱལ་པོ་ཆེན་པོ་ཀ་ནིས་ཀ་ལ་སྤྲིངས་པའི་འཕྲིན་ཡིག།

Mahārājakaniṣkalekha

The Letter to the Great King Kaniṣka

།དེ་བཞིན་གཤེགས་པ་ཐམས་ཅད་ལ་ཕྱག་འཚལ་ལོ།

༡

།བསྒྲོད་པར་བགྱི་འོས་ཁྱོད་ལགས་ན། །བཀུག་ཀྱང་མ་མཆིས་གང་ལགས་དེ།
།མ་གུས་མ་ལགས་བརྙས་མ་ལགས། །རྒ་དང་ནད་ཀྱིས་བར་ཆད་བགྱིས།

༢

།བདག་ནི་སེམས་ཅན་ཐམས་ཅད་དང་། །འདྲ་བར་ཁྱོད་ལ་བརྩེ་མོད་ཀྱི།
།ཁྱོད་ཀྱི་ཡོན་ཏན་གྱིས་ཁྱོད་ལ། །ལྷག་པར་ཉེ་མགོན་ཁྱད་པར་བགྱིད།

༣

།གདམས་བགྱི་ཕལ་ཆེར་མཆིས་མོད་ཀྱི། །ཐམས་ཅད་གདམས་པར་སྤུས་རྫོ
ཐོགས། །ཁྱོད་ཀྱི་ཡོན་ཏན་གང་ལགས་དེས། །བདག་ནི་སྤྲི་བརྗོལ་སྐྱེས་པར་གྱུར།

༤

།བཟློག་པ་མེད་པའི་ཡོན་ཏན་གྱིས། །ཕྱོགས་རྣམས་ཀུན་ཏུ་བསྔོས་པས་ནི།
།མི་མཆོག་རྣམས་ཀྱང་ཐུགས་ཐུབ་པར། །མཛའ་བ་ཤེས་བཞིན་དུ་འཛེམ་པ་མེད།

Homage to all the Tathāgatas!

~1~

That I, though invited, did not come to you,
one so worthy to be approached,
was not due to lack of reverence or to disrespect,
but because I am hindered by old age and illness.

~2~

Although the love I feel for you
is similar to what I feel toward all beings,
because of your virtues,
I feel especially intimate and close to you.

~3~

What I have to teach, I have already largely taught,
and who can advise on everything?
Yet because of your many virtues,
I have become loquacious once more.

~4~

The fragrance of your irresistible qualities
has imbued every corner of the world,
so that even the greatest men,
fully confident in their own abilities,
do not shun your friendship.

༥

།དེ་ལྟས་སྨན་གཏོང་ཉིད་ཀྱི་ཚེད། །བདག་གིས་གསོལ་བ་འདི་གསོན་ཏེ།
།བསྒྲུབ་དང་བཏང་བའི་ཕྱོགས་གཉིས་ལས། །གང་རིགས་དེ་ནི་ཉམས་སུ་བཞེས།

༦

།དགའ་བར་བགྱིད་པའི་ཡུལ་རྣམས་དང་། །ཀྲུགས་པར་བགྱིད་པའི་ལང་ཚོ་དང་།
།བདག་ཉིད་རང་དབང་སྤྱོད་པ་དེ། །ཀུན་ཏུ་དོན་མེད་བགྱིད་པའི་སྒོ།

༧

།འཕྱུང་བར་བྱེད་པ་དེ་གསུམ་སྤང་། །མཁས་པས་དམ་པ་བསྟེན་པ་དང་།
།དབང་པོ་གདུལ་དང་ཤེས་རབ་ཀྱི། །སྟོབས་མཐུས་ཉམས་ནི་སྨད་ནས་སྤྱད།

༨

།ཁྱོད་ཀྱི་ཉེས་པའི་གཞིར་གྱུར་པའི། །ཚ་ནི་གསུམ་པོ་དེ་དག་རྣམས།
།ཆོས་ལུགས་དག་དང་འདུལ་བ་ཡིས། །བཅོས་ནས་ཡོན་ཏན་ཉིད་དུ་མཛོད།

~5~

Therefore, please lend me your ear and
for your own sake, listen well to what I have to say,
so that out of the two opposites—
what should be done and what should be given up—
you may take the right one to heart.

~6~

Sense objects that give rise to pleasure,
youth swelling with pride,
and acting just as one likes without regard for others—
these are the gates to what is entirely harmful.

~7~

Avoid these three things leading to ruin.
For a wise man must act to diminish these three faults
by relying upon the noble, controlling the senses,
and using the power of wisdom.

~8~

These three things have become
the foundation of your failings;
having remedied them with discipline
and lawful behavior,
turn them into virtues.

༩

།ཅི་སྟེ་རྒྱལ་པོ་སྔོན་པོ་དག །དཀྲིལ་ཆེ་སྙིང་རྗེའི་བདག་ཉིད་ནི།
།རྟག་ཏུ་ཉོན་མོངས་མེད་པ་ཡི། །ལས་ཀྱིས་རྒྱལ་སྲིད་བྱ་བར་རུང་།

༡༠

།འཇིག་རྟེན་འདི་ན་སྔོ་སྒྲོས་ཀྱི། །ཉམ་ཆུང་སྐྱུར་དང་མགོན་མེད་པ།
།བྱ་བ་མ་ཡིན་བྱེད་པ་ལ། །གདོན་མི་ཟ་བར་འཇུག་པར་འགྱུར།

༡༡

།དེ་བས་ཇི་སྲིད་ས་དེ་ལས། །སྨྱུར་དུ་མ་བཅལ་བར་དུ་ནི།
།སྔོ་མཐུ་བསྐྱེད་ཕྱིར་མཁས་པ་དག །བསྡུ་བར་དགོས་པའི་ནན་ཏན་མཛོད།

༡༢

།ཆོས་ཀྱི་བསྟན་བཅོས་གདོན་བགྲི་ཞིང་། །དེ་ཡི་དོན་གྱི་ཚུལ་གསོན་ལ།
།གསན་པའི་ཆོས་རྣམས་རྣམ་དཔྱད་དེ། །དཔྱད་པ་ལ་ནི་མཁས་པར་མཛོད།

~9~

Is it not especially appropriate for the king
and his ministers,
their hearts filled with vast compassion,
to exert their sovereign power
through deeds always free of emotional taint?

~10~

In this world, those who are weak-minded
and without a protector
will certainly become involved in doing
actions that should not be done.

~11~

Therefore, so long as you have not yet
passed beyond that stage,
cheerfully endeavor to gather wise men around you
in order to gain strength of mind.

~12~

Have the code of laws recited
and listen to the way it is explained.
Examine the laws you hear
and be wise in your judgments.

༡༣

།སྨྲ་ངན་གྱིས་ནི་མ་གདུངས་ཤིང་། །ན་གཞོན་ནད་མེད་ཡོངས་པ་ཡི།
།དངོས་པོ་དལྟར་བྱུང་བ་ཡི། །བློ་གྲོས་ལ་ནི་མི་ནུས་མེད།

༡༤

།འདིར་ནི་སྐྱེས་བུ་དམ་པ་ལས། །དུས་དུས་སུ་ཡང་ཅུང་ཟད་གསོན།
།ཅུང་དུ་བསགས་ནའང་ངེས་པར་ནི། །རིང་པོར་མི་ཐོགས་མང་པོར་འགྱུར།

༡༥

།རྟག་ཏུ་ཆུ་ཐིགས་རེ་རེའི་རྒྱུན། །བར་ཆད་མེད་པར་འབབ་པ་ཡིས།
།གང་ཞིག་གང་བར་མི་འགྱུར་བའི། །སྣོད་དེ་ཇི་ལྟ་བུ་ཞིག་མཆིས།

༡༦

།དེ་ལྟར་དཔེ་གསལ་དེ་ལྟ་བུ། །རྒྱལ་པོ་ཚད་མར་མཛད་ནས་ནི།
།དམ་པའི་ཆོས་ནི་གསན་པ་ལ། །རྟག་ཏུ་དགོས་པ་ཉིད་དུ་མཛོད།

~13~

Nothing seems impossible to a mind
free from the torment of sorrow
and characterized by
youth, health, and self-confidence.

~14~

Here in this life, whenever you can, listen
to even little things said by noble people.
Even if you accumulate knowledge a little at a time,
it will certainly not be long
before it becomes considerable.

~15~

Is there any vessel
that would not become full
when an uninterrupted chain of water droplets
falls into it constantly?

~16~

Therefore, Your Majesty, take as conclusively valid
what has been shown in this clear example,
and always take delight in
listening to the holy Dharma.

༢༧

།ཡོན་ཏན་ནོར་ནི་གཉེར་ལ་གཉེན། །མཁས་ཤིང་སྙིང་རྗེའི་བདག་ཉིད་ཅན།
།ཁྲུས་གཙོ་ཡོངས་ཚོས་མི་བགྲིད་པ། །བཟང་པོ་ཁྲོད་ཀྱི་སྨད་དུ་ཞོག

༢༨

།ཁྲོད་ཀྱིས་བླུན་དང་ཡོངས་ཚོས་ཅན། །བརྐམ་ཞིང་ཁྲུས་པ་མི་གཙོ་དང་།
།ཁ་གསག་གཏུམ་པོ་མི་བཟད་པ། །ཡུལ་ནའང་གནས་སུ་མ་སྩུལ་ཅིག

༢༩

།རྟག་ཏུ་སོ་སོའི་སྐྱེ་བོ་ཡི། །ཁྱད་པར་མཁྱེན་པར་མཛོད་ཅིག་དང་།
།དེ་ཡི་ཁྱད་པར་མཁྱེན་ཙམ་ལ། །ཕུན་སུམ་ཚོགས་པ་རག་ལས་སོ།

༣༠

།མི་གང་དཀའ་བ་སྤྱོད་བྱེད་དང་། །དོར་བར་བྱ་དཀའ་དོར་བ་དང་།
།བཟོད་པར་དཀའ་བ་བཟོད་བྱེད་དང་། །བཀུར་དཀའ་ཉམས་སུ་ལེན་པ་དང་།

~17~

For your own sake, keep around you good men
who assist you in seeking a wealth of virtue,
who are wise and full of compassion,
who show gratitude and open-handedness.

~18~

You should not allow
the stupid, stingy, greedy,
ungrateful, garrulous, cruel,
and evil even to remain in your realm.

~19~

You should always get to know
the particular merits of each individual person;
your welfare and prosperity depend solely
on knowing these distinctive qualities.

~20~

Those who accomplish difficult tasks,
who give up what is difficult to give up,
who tolerate what is difficult to bear,
who accept what is difficult to accept;

༣༡

།གནས་མིན་ལས་ནི་ཟློག་བྱེད་དང་། །གནས་སུ་འཇོག་པར་བརྩོན་པ་དང་།
།དེ་ཡི་བསམ་པ་མཐུན་གྱུས་དང་། །བདེ་བར་འདོད་ཅིང་འོ་བྱམས་པ།

༣༢

།དེ་དག་རྣམས་ནི་མཛའ་བ་ཤེས་ཏེ། །གཉེན་འདུན་གྲོགས་པོའང་དེ་དག་ལགས།
།རང་དོན་ཙམ་ཕྱིར་འབྲང་བའི་མི། །གཞན་དག་སྐྱེ་བོ་ཕལ་པར་བས།

༣༣

།གྲོགས་པོ་ཕན་པར་འདོད་པའི་ཚིག །མི་སྙན་ཡང་ནི་ཕན་པ་དང་།
།འཇམ་དང་བདེན་པ་ལགས་པ་དག །ཐུགས་ལ་བཞག་པར་མཛད་དུ་གསོལ།

༣༤

།ཚིག་སྙན་ཕན་པ་མ་ལགས་དང་། །འཇམ་ཡང་བདེན་པ་མ་ལགས་པ།
།དམ་པ་མ་ཡིན་རྣམས་ཀྱི་ཚིག །ཁྱོད་ཀྱི་ཐུགས་ལ་མ་བཟུང་ཞིག

~21~

who turn you away from what is inappropriate,
and take care to turn you toward what is appropriate;
whose devotion matches their thoughts,
who desire your happiness
and regard you with affection—

~22~

these are friends,
relatives, and allies.
Others who follow you only in their own interest
are nothing but very ordinary beings.

~23~

Please take to heart the words of a friend
who intends your benefit.
Even when not sweet to hear,
these words are useful, tender, and true.

~24~

But do not take to heart
the sweet words of wicked people,
which are harmful,
and neither tender nor true.

༣༥

།ཁྲོ་པར་སྨྲ་བ་བྲོ་ཡང་ནི། །ཁྱོད་ཀྱིས་གནང་ཆེན་དག་ཏུ་མཛོད།
།མི་ཕན་སྨྲ་བ་བསྟོད་བགྱིད་ཀྱང་། །དགྱེས་པ་དག་ཏུ་མ་མཛད་ཅིག

༣༦

།རབ་དང་མཚོལ་དང་པ་ཡི། །རྒྱལ་པོ་དང་ནི་ཆུས་འཇིག་བཞིན།
།དམ་པ་རྣམས་ཀྱིས་བསྟེན་སླ་དང་། །དམ་པ་མིན་པས་བསྟེན་དཀའ་མཛོད།

༣༧

།ཁྱོད་ཀྱིས་མཁས་རྣམས་ཚིམ་བགྱིས་པས། །འཁོར་པ་དོན་དུ་གཉེར་མི་བགྱི།
།ཡོན་ཏན་དགྱེས་ཕྱིར་ཁྱོད་ཀྱིས་ནི། །ཡོན་ཏན་རྣམས་ཀྱིས་མི་དོམས་མཛོད།

༣༨

།ལོངས་སྤྱོད་བྱེད་དམ་བདེ་བ་དང་། །སྡུག་བསྔལ་ཟད་པའམ་སྤྱོད་པའམ།
།སྤྱོད་ལམ་ཀུན་ཏུ་སྤྱོད་པ་ན། །ཁྱོད་ཀྱིས་དམ་པ་བསྟེན་པ་དང་།

~25~

May you accept with an open heart
one who gives useful advice, even if wrathful,
but take no pleasure in one
who gives harmful advice,
even though full of praise.

~26~

Just as access to a crystal clear lake should be
easy for the king of geese and difficult for flood,
let access to you be easy for the good,
and difficult for the wicked.

~27~

Consider it more important to please the wise
than to strive for wealth;
in order to rejoice in virtues,
become insatiable for virtues.

~28~

In conducting your life,
whether enjoying yourself,
or feeling happy or sad,
or being engaged in ordinary or higher pursuits,
you should adhere to the good;

༢༩

།དྲན་པའི་གྲོགས་ཀྱིས་བསྐོར་བ་ན། །བག་ཡོད་པར་ནི་གནས་འགྱུར་ཏེ།
།སྣ་ལའི་ཤིང་ལ་འཁྲི་ཤིང་བཞིན། །བཟང་པོ་དཔལ་གྱིས་འཁྱུད་པར་འགྱུར།

༣༠

།ཁྱོད་ཀྱིས་བཞམ་པ་བདེན་པ་དང་། །ཁྱད་པར་ཞིང་ལ་སྦྱིན་པ་དང་།
།དྲན་དང་བྲལ་བས་འདོད་པ་དབྱེ། །ཚད་པས་གང་དུའང་གཅད་མི་བགྱི།

༣༡

།ཡོག་པས་འཕབ་གཙུགས་བྱེད་པ་དང་། །བཀྲིན་ལ་དམན་པར་ལྟ་བ་དང་།
།ཚུལ་ཁྲིམས་ལྡན་རྣམས་མི་དགའ་དང་། །དཀའ་ཐུབ་སྨོམ་པ་འཁྲུལ་བྱེད་པ།

༣༢

།བཞི་པོ་འདི་དག་འདོད་མིན་ཏེ། །རྩ་བ་འཇོམས་པར་བགྱིད་པ་ལགས།
།རབ་བརྩོན་ཁྱོད་ཀྱི་ཡུལ་ན་ནི། །དེ་དག་གཏན་མ་མཆིས་པར་མཛོད།

~29~

when you surround yourself with mindful friends,
you will remain alert and watchful.
O good monarch,
you will then be embraced by good fortune
as the sal tree is embraced by creepers.

~30~

You should bestow gifts upon those who are mild,
truthful, and especially worthy;
examine your desires without dwelling on them;
never use punishment.

~31~

But those who use deceit to cultivate quarrels and strife,
who look down upon the poor,
who do not delight in moral beings,
and who distract ascetics from their vows—

~32~

these four types of people are not desirable.
They destroy the root of moral behavior.
Take great care to ensure that such people
do not stay here in your realm.

༣༣

།སྟོབས་དང་ལྡན་པས་སྟོབས་ཆུང་བ། །གནོང་ཆེན་གྱིས་ནི་མི་གནོང་དང་།
།མཆོད་འོས་རྣམས་ཀྱིས་མི་མཆོད་དང་། །སྨྲོས་འདྲིས་ཀྱིས་ནི་མི་བཞེས་པ།

༣༤

།གང་ཡང་རུང་བ་གང་གིས་ཀྱང་། །བརྙས་པ་མེད་པར་ཁྱོད་ཀྱིས་མཛོད།
།ཐ་སྙད་རྣམས་ནི་དག་པ་ཡིས། །ཀུན་ལ་འདྲ་བར་གཟིགས་སུ་གསོལ།

༣༥

།ཀུན་གྱིས་རང་གི་ཆོས་ཐོབ་ཅིང་། །ཆོས་ཀྱིས་ཐམས་ཅད་འཚོ་བར་མཛོད།
།མི་སྡུག་ཀྱང་ནི་ཉེས་མེད་ན། །ཐམས་ཅད་བདེ་བར་མཛད་དུ་གསོལ།

༣༦

།ཕ་ཡིས་བུ་ལ་ཇི་ལྟ་བར། །ཁྱོད་ཀྱིས་འཁོར་ལ་བྱམས་བགྱིས་ན།
།བུ་ཡིས་ཕ་ལ་ཇི་ལྟ་བར། །ཁྱོད་ལ་ཞབས་འབྲིང་དགའ་བར་བགྱིད།

~33~

You must see to it that there is no contempt or disdain
among the strong toward the weak,
among benefactors toward those
who have nothing to give,
among the honored toward the unworthy,

~34~

among intimate friends toward those they do not know,
or for anyone at all toward anyone.
Conducting all business with honesty,
may you regard everyone as equal.

~35~

See to it that everyone fulfills his own dharma,
and that all live according to the law.
May you make all happy,
even the disagreeable, if they are free from fault.

~36~

If you love your retinue
as a father loves his son,
your subjects will want to please you
as a son would please his father.

༣༧

།ཕལ་རྣམས་རང་བཞིན་བཟང་ན་ནི། །ཁྱོད་ཀྱིས་དགོངས་པ་བཞིན་དུ་འགྱུར།
།ཕལ་རྣམས་རང་བཞིན་ངན་ན་ནི། །ཁྱོད་ཀྱིས་དགོངས་པ་བཞིན་མི་འགྱུར།

༣༨

།གལ་ཏེ་གཞུང་ལུགས་བཟང་བཞེས་ན། །གོང་ནས་གོང་དུ་འཕང་བར་འགྱུར།
།ཅི་སྟེ་ངན་པའི་སྤྱོད་མཛད་ན། །འོག་ནས་འོག་ཏུ་ལྟུང་བར་འགྱུར།

༣༩

།དམ་པའི་ལས་ལ་གནས་ན་ནི། །ཁྱུ་མཆོག་དང་ནི་ཁྱུ་ལྷ་བུར།
།རྗེས་སུ་འཚོ་བའི་སྐྱེ་བོའི་ཚོགས། །འདི་ཀུན་རྗེས་སུ་འབྲང་བར་འགྱུར།

༤༠

།ཁྱོད་ནི་གྲུ་གྲུ་ལ་ཞུགས་ན། །གྲུ་གྲུ་བོ་ནའི་རྗེས་འབྲངས་པས།
།སྐྱེ་དགུ་ཁྱོད་མཛད་རྗེས་འབྲང་བའི། །སྐྱེ་དགུ་འདི་ནི་ཉམས་པར་འགྱུར།

~37~

When the general populace is good-natured,
they will become what you intend;
when the people are bad-natured,
they will not become what you intend.

~38~

If you adopt good thoughts and views,
you will be lifted higher and higher,
but if you practice bad behavior,
you will fall lower and lower.

~39~

If you abide by good works,
all the people, whose lives depend upon you,
will follow you
as a flock follows its leader.

~40~

If you become involved in duplicity,
and follow nothing but intrigue,
then all the people,
the subjects who follow your example,
will be polluted.

༨༡

།དེ་བས་བདག་གཞན་བསྲུང་སླད་དུ། །ཐུགས་ཀྱིས་རབ་ཏུ་བསྒྲིམས་ནས་ནི།
།གནའ་རྒྱལ་དྲང་སྲོང་རྣམས་ཀྱི་ལུགས། །ཉམས་པ་སར་པར་བཅོས་སུ་གསོལ།

༨༢

།གནའ་ཡི་རྒྱལ་པོའི་སྤྱོད་པ་ལས། །གང་དག་བཟང་བ་དེ་མཛོད་ལ།
།མི་རིགས་པ་ནི་གང་ལགས་དེ། །སྨད་པར་མཛོད་ལ་སྤང་དུ་གསོལ།

༨༣

།སྔོན་གྱི་བཀའ་ཁྲིམས་སྐྱོན་ཆགས་པ། །གནའ་ནས་མཆིས་ཀྱང་རྒྱུན་ཆད་ལ།
།རྒྱལ་པོ་ཀ་ནི་ཥྐ་མཚན་པའི། །ཁྲིམས་སུ་བཅའ་བ་གསར་པ་མཛོད།

༨༤

།ལྷ་ཁྱོད་ཡོན་ཏན་དོན་གཉེར་བས། །ཡོན་ཏན་ལྷ་བཞིན་ཕོ་ནར་མཛོད།
།ལྷ་ཁྱོད་སྐྱོན་རྣམས་མཁྱེན་པ་ཡིས། །ལྷ་བཞིན་ཉེས་མེད་ཕོ་ནར་མཛོད།

~41~

Therefore, in order to protect yourself and others,
please apply yourself fully
and establish anew the declining
tradition of the ancient kings and seers.

~42~

From the practice of the ancient kings,
take whatever is good and put it into practice.
But whatever is not appropriate
you must revile and abandon.

~43~

Break the hold of former laws that were enacted in error,
even when they exist as of old,
and make a new code of law
marked by the name of King Kaniṣka.

~44~

Your Majesty—you who are like a god—
intent on virtue, practice only virtues, like a god.
Your Majesty—you who are like a god—
as one who knows fault,
do only what is faultless, like a god.

༥༦

།ཟླ་བ་མར་གྱི་ངོ་བཞིན་དུ། །ཉེས་པའི་ཚོགས་རྣམས་འགྲིབ་པ་དང་།
།ཟླ་བ་ཡར་གྱི་ངོ་བཞིན་དུ། །རྟག་ཏུ་ཡོན་ཏན་གྱིས་བརྒྱན་མཛོད།

༥༧

།ཡབ་མེས་བཞིན་དུ་བདག་ཉིད་ཀྱིས། །ཆོས་ཀྱིས་ས་སྐྱོང་བསྐྱང་བ་དང་།
།ཡབ་མེས་བཞིན་དུ་ལྷ་ཁང་གི །དུས་སྟོན་འཕེལ་བར་མཛད་དུ་གསོལ།

༥༨

།ཁྱོད་ཀྱིས་མཐོ་རིས་བྱང་གྲོལ་གྱི། །ཐེམ་སྐས་མི་མཉམ་མཉམ་པའི་ཕྱིར།
།བསོད་ནམས་ལས་བྱུང་བཟོ་རིག་ཆེ། །རྟག་ཏུ་ལྷ་ཁང་དག་ཏུ་སོགས།

༥༩

།ནད་དང་འཆི་བས་བསྐྱེངས་མཛོད་དེ། །ཆོས་བཞིན་རྒྱལ་སྲིད་དཔལ་སྤྱོད་ནས།
།བགྲེས་ཀར་དགོན་པར་གཤེགས་སུ་གསོལ། །དམ་ཆོས་བསྟན་པས་འབྲས་
མཆིས་མཛོད།

~45~

Be like the waning moon,
and dim the hosts of evil;
be like the waxing moon,
and ever adorn yourself with virtues.

~46~

Like your fathers before you, wholeheartedly
rule the earth according to the law.
Like your fathers before you, increase
the ceremonies in the temples.

~47~

For the sake of (gaining) the matchless ladder
that leads to heaven and liberation,
always gather together in the temples
the great works of art that merit produces.

~48~

Be apprehensive of old age and death.
Having enjoyed the glory of lawful sovereignty,
in your old age retire into a hermitage
and let your life become fruitful
through the teachings of the holy Dharma.

༤༩

།རང་བྱུང་རྣམས་ཀྱི་རྗེས་བསླབས་པ། །ཀུ་ཤའི་རིགས་སུ་འབྲུངས་ཁྱོད་ཀྱིས།
།ཡབ་མེས་འཕགས་རིགས་ཉིད་མ་ཡི། །གདུང་རྒྱུད་ཆོས་ལུགས་མ་ཉམས་མཛོད།

༥༠

།སྐྱེ་བ་ཅན་ལ་ངེས་པར་ནི། །རྒས་དང་འཆི་དང་ན་མཆིས་ན།
།མ་བཀྲེས་མ་བསྐྱངས་མ་གྲོངས་ཞེས། །ལེགས་སྨོན་གསོལ་ཡང་ཅི་ལ་སྨན།

༥༡

།སྲིད་པ་དག་ནི་གང་ཡང་རུང་། །དེ་ཉིད་རྒས་དང་འཆི་བ་ལགས།
།ཡོངས་སུ་འགྱུར་བས་རྒ་བ་སྟེ། །སྐད་ཅིག་འཇིག་པས་འཆི་བ་ཡིན།

༥༢

།མ་རྒས་མ་ན་མ་འཆི་ཞེས། །སྨྲ་བ་དག་ནི་སྨྲ་བ་ན།
།དེ་ལྟར་འཇིག་རྟེན་ཀུན་འབབ་ར་ན། །ཡང་སྲིད་མེད་ལས་གཞན་ཅི་ཡོད།

~49~

You who were born into the lineage of the Kuṣāṇas
and instructed according to the (teaching of the)
self-arising Buddhas
must see to it that the religious system
of the solar race, your noble lineage,
does not degenerate.

~50~

Given the absolute certainty that those who are born
will grow old, fall ill, and die,
of what use is it even to pray: "May you not
become old, not become sick, not die."

~51~

Any life form whatsoever
by its very nature grows old and dies.
Gradual transformation is the nature of old age;
instantaneous destruction is the nature of death.

~52~

If people say, "May I not grow old,
not become sick, not die"—
since this world will be completely consumed by fire,
what choice is left but not to exist again at all?

༥༣

།གང་ན་མི་མཐུན་ཡོད་མ་ཡིན། །གང་དུ་འདུ་བྱེད་འཇིག་མི་འགྱུར།
།གང་ན་གཅིག་ཏུ་བདེ་བར་གནས། །གང་དུ་སོང་ན་འཆི་མི་འགྱུར།

༥༤

།སྲིད་པ་ཀུན་ནས་ཉོན་མོངས་དང་། །སྡུག་བསྔལ་འབྱུང་བཙིར་མི་མགོ།
།དེ་སླད་དེས་པ་སྲིད་པ་རྣམས། །མེད་པར་བསྒོམ་པ་བརྒྱུས་པར་མཛོད།

༥༥

།འདིར་ནི་བགྱི་བ་འདི་ཉིད་དེ། །དེ་ལས་གཞན་པ་བགྱི་མི་འཚལ།
།བགྱི་བ་དེ་ནི་བགྱིས་པ་ཡིས། །མི་བགྱི་བ་ཡི་ཚར་ཕྱིན་ནོ།

༥༦

།བགྲང་ཕྲེང་བཞིན་དུ་འཁོར་བ་རུ། །ལན་མང་ཡོངས་སུ་འཁོར་བ་ནི།
།ལན་བརྒྱའམ་ཡང་ན་སྟོང་དག་ཏུ། །འཇིག་རྟེན་དག་ཏུ་ཅིམ་བགྱིས།

~53~

Where is the place where nothing is unpleasant?
Where will composite things not decay?
Where is the place of happiness alone?
Where can you go where you will not die?

~54~

Do not defilement and suffering
inevitably arise in the phenomenal world?
Therefore, noble one, meditate extensively
on the non-existence of the phenomenal world.

~55~

This alone is what you should do here in samsara—
do not seek to do anything other than that.
Having done what you should do,
you will avoid doing what you should not do.

~56~

While revolving in the circle of existence
again and again, like a rosary,
what have you not already done in the world
a hundred times, or even thousands?

༥༧

།འདི་མ་བསྒྲིས་སྣད་བྲིས་པ་ཡིས། །ཡང་དང་ཡང་དུ་བསྒྲི་འཚལ་བས།
།ཐོག་མ་མེད་པའི་དུས་ཅན་འདི། །ད་དུང་བར་དུ་མ་ཡོག་གོ།

༥༨

།འཆི་བདག་སྲུ་དང་མི་བཞེས་པ། །གློ་བུར་དག་ཏུ་འབབ་འགྱུར་བས།
།སང་དག་བྱ་ཞེས་མ་བཞེས་པར། །དམ་པའི་ཆོས་ལ་བསྒྱུར་ཏེ་མཛོད།

༥༩

།འདི་སང་དེང་འདི་མི་བྱ་ཞེས། །བྱ་བ་མི་ལ་བཟང་པོ་མིན།
།ནམ་ཞིག་ཁྱོད་ནི་མེད་འགྱུར་བའི། །སང་དེ་གདོན་མི་ཟ་བར་འོང་།

༦༠

།འཆི་བདག་བརྩེ་བ་མེད་པ་ཅན། །སྐྱེས་རྒྱལ་དོན་མེད་གསོད་འགྱུར་བ།
།གསོད་པ་མདོན་དུ་འོང་བཞིན་དུ། །མཁས་པ་སུ་ཞིག་བག་རྗོད་སྤྱོད།

~57~

Believing that we have not done something,
we foolishly try again and again to do it.
Thus, since beginningless time,
we have not reversed direction up to now.

~58~

The Lord of Death, who is no man's friend,
will descend upon you suddenly.
Therefore, with great effort turn to the holy Dharma
and do not say, "I will do it tomorrow."

~59~

"I will do this tomorrow, not today"
is not good for a man to say.
Without any doubt, that tomorrow will come
when you no longer exist.

~60~

When the heartless Lord of Death,
who destroys men's powers without rhyme or reason,
approaches with the intent to kill,
what wise man can remain at ease?

༨༡

།དེ་སྣང་དཔག་ཆེན་བཟོད་མེད་དེས། །མདའ་ནི་མི་བཟད་འཚོར་མེད་པ།
།དེ་ནི་ཇི་སྲིད་མ་འཕངས་པ། །དེ་སྲིད་རང་གི་དོན་ལ་འབོད།

༨༢

།ནམ་སྨིན་འབྲིན་པ་སྨོན་ལམ་ཀྱིས། །ཁྱོད་ནི་ཡོངས་སུ་བཏང་གྱུར་པ།
།གསར་པའི་ལམ་དང་རྗེས་འབྲེལ་ཞིང་། །འཆི་བདག་གིས་ནི་དྲངས་པ་ན།

༨༣

།དགེ་དང་སྡིག་པ་མ་གཏོགས་པར། །འགྲོ་བ་ཐམས་ཅད་ཕྱིར་ལོག་ནས།
།འགའ་ཡང་ཁྱོད་རྗེས་མི་འབྲང་བར། །མཁྱེན་པར་མཛོད་ལ་ལེགས་པར་སྒྲོད།

~61~

Therefore, so long as that extremely impatient one
has not loosed that unbearable arrow
which cannot be avoided,
give heed to your own welfare.

~62~

When your former karma,
having brought forth its fruit, has abandoned you,
you will be dragged away by the Lord of Death,
bound to new karma.

~63~

Then all beings will turn away and
nothing at all will follow you,
save for your virtuous and evil actions.
Knowing this, conduct your life well.

༤༥

།བདག་ནི་སྙིང་རྗེས་ཟིལ་གནོན་ཅིང་། །ཡིད་མི་དགའ་བའི་སྟན་ཀྱིས་ནི།
།ཤིན་ཏུ་བསྟན་པའི་སྨྲེ་སྔགས་འདི། །རེ་ཞིག་གསན་པར་མཛད་དུ་གསོལ།

༤༦

།འགྲོ་བ་དམན་པ་ཡོག་ལྟུང་བ། །མགོན་མེད་ཉེས་མེད་ཕལ་ཆེར་ནི།
།རྩྭ་དང་ཆུ་དང་འབྲས་བུ་ནི། །ཕལ་པས་འཚོ་བ་སྒྲུབ་བགྱིད་པ།

༤༧

།བྱ་དང་རི་དགས་ཕྱུགས་དག་ལ། །རྒྱལ་པོས་གསོད་དམ་གསོད་འཇུག་པ།
།ཅི་ག་རིགས་སམ་མི་རིགས་པ། །བདེན་ལ་གནས་པ་ཁྱོད་ཉིད་གསུངས།

༤༨

།ཁྱོད་ནི་ཆེན་པོར་མི་ཁྲོ་ཞིང་། །གནོད་པ་བགྱིད་ལའང་བཟོད་ཅེས་གདའ།
།ཁྱོད་ཀྱི་ཐུགས་རྗེ་དུད་འགྲོ་ལ། །ཀྱེ་མ་སུ་ཡིས་དགག་པར་བགྱིས།

~64~

Pray listen for a while to
my lamentation, which is overwhelmed by compassion
and soaked through and through
with the moisture of melancholy.

~65~

Unfortunate beings that have fallen low,
who are unprotected and blameless,
who live mostly on plain
grass, water, and fruit—

~66~

relying on truth, you yourself should say
whether it is right or wrong
for a king to kill or be involved in killing
birds, game, and cattle.

~67~

They say that you never become very angry
and that you forgive even those
who have done you harm.
Alas, who has obstructed
your compassion toward animals?

༤༨

།གནོད་པ་བགྱིད་ལ་བཟོད་མཛད་ཅིང་། །གནོད་མི་བགྱིད་པ་འགྲུམས་མཛད་པས། །ཁྱོད་ལ་བརྩེ་དང་མི་བརྩེ་བའི། །རྒྱུ་མཐུན་པ་ནི་གཉིས་ཀ་གདའ།

༤༩

།སྔོན་ཆད་བགྱིས་པའི་སྡུག་ལས་ཀྱིས། །འདི་ལྟར་འབེན་དུ་གྱུར་པ་ལ།
།ཁྱོད་ཉིད་གནོད་པ་མཛད་ན་གོ །སྨུ་ལ་སྐྲུབས་སུ་མཆིབ་གསུངས།

༥༠

།གཞན་གྱིས་གནོད་པ་བགྱིས་ན་ཡང་། །ཉིད་ཀྱི་ཕྱུག་གིས་བཤུགས་འཚལ་ན།
།ཁྱོད་བཞེངས་མངོན་དུ་གནོད་མཛད་ན། །ཕྱོགས་ཀུན་ཁྱུན་པར་མ་གྱུར་ཏམ།

༥༡

།ཀུན་ལ་སྲོག་ནི་ཕངས་པ་སྐྱེ། །ཀུན་ལ་གསོན་པ་སྡུག་པ་ལགས།
།ཐམས་ཅད་འཆི་བའི་ཆོས་ཅན་ཏེ། །ཐམས་ཅད་སྡུག་བསྔལ་རྣམས་ཀྱིས་གདུངས།

~68~

Since you pardon those who harm you,
but put to death those who have done you no harm,
there are clearly two bases for
your kindness and unkindness.

~69~

When even someone in your position harms those
who have become a target
because of deeds committed in the past,
tell me, in whom will they take refuge?

~70~

When others harm you
but still you offer your own hand to raise them up,
and then openly harm those to whom you give shelter—
has not the whole world turned dark?

~71~

All beings take pleasure in being alive;
life is dear to all.
All are subject to death;
all are tormented by suffering.

༥༢

།འདི་ལྟར་གང་ཞིག་མི་འཚལ་བ། །དེ་ཉིད་ཀྱིས་ནི་སྡུག་བསྔལ་ཏེ།
།མཁས་པ་སུ་ཞིག་མགར་བ་ལྟར། །ཚིག་པ་ལ་ནི་ཡང་སྲེག་བཞིན།

༥༣

།ཁྱོད་ནི་སྲོག་གཅོད་མི་དགྱེས་ཤིང་། །སྲོག་གཅོད་དགྱེས་ལས་ཕྱིར་ལོག་ན།
།རྒྱལ་སྲིད་ཉམས་པར་འགྱུར་རམ་ཅི། །ལུགས་འདི་ཅི་ཞིག་ལགས་པ་གསུངས།

༥༤

།མཚོན་ཆའི་ཐབས་ལ་མཁས་ཁྱོད་ཀྱིས། །གཡུལ་ངོར་སྲོལ་བརྗོད་མཐོང་ལགས་
ན། །གཞན་དུ་ཁྱོད་ནི་རི་དགས་ལ། །ཅི་སླད་གནོད་པའི་ལས་རྣམས་མཛད།

༥༥

།རི་དགས་གཞོན་ནུའི་སྤྱན་མངའ་ཁྱོད། །སྤྱན་དང་འདྲ་བའི་རི་དགས་རྣམས།
།རྟབས་ནས་རིག་རིག་ལྟ་བ་ལ། །ཅི་ཡི་སླད་དུ་ཐུགས་མི་རྗེ།

~72~

Thus anything we do not want
leads to suffering.
What wise man would, like a smith,
put fire again on what is already burned?

~73~

If you do not take pleasure in taking life
and turn away from pleasure in killing,
will your kingdom come to ruin?
Tell me, what kind of custom is this killing?

~74~

If you, who are skilled in the use of weapons,
see with your own eyes what they can do in battle,
why do you, at other times,
commit such harm against animals?

~75~

You who have the eyes of a young deer,
why do you not feel compassion
for the deer who are like your eyes
when they are wild-eyed with fright?

༥༦

།ཁྱོད་ཀྱི་སྤྱན་དང་མིག་འདྲའི་ཕྱིར། །ཁྱོད་ལ་དགའ་བ་གང་ལགས་དེ།
།རི་དགས་ལ་ཡང་དགའ་བགྱིད་ན། །ཁྱོད་ནི་ཇི་ལྟར་དགྱེས་མི་མཛད།

༥༧

།ཡོག་པར་ལྟུང་དང་སྤྱན་འདྲ་དང་། །མགོན་མེད་ཡུལ་ན་གནས་པ་ཉིད།
།རེ་རེ་ཡང་ནི་རི་དགས་དག །མི་འགྲུམས་པ་ཡི་རྒྱུར་རུང་ངོ་།

༥༨

།མི་རྣམས་ལ་ནི་མཛད་པ་བས། །སྡུག་བསྔལ་ལྷག་པར་བརྟགས་པ་ཡི།
།དུད་འགྲོ་རྣམས་ལ་ཆེས་ལྷག་པར། །ཁྱོད་ཀྱིས་ཐུགས་རྗེ་མཛད་དུ་གསོལ།

༥༩

།ཁྱོད་ཉིད་བསྲུང་བའི་དོན་འདི་ལ། །བདག་གིས་ཐལ་མོ་སྦྱར་མི་འཚལ། །རྒྱུད་
གཞན་གསོལ་བས་གུས་བགྱིས་པར། །ལེགས་པར་ཐུགས་ཚོད་མངའ་ལགས་གྲང་།

~76~

How could you not rejoice
when you give joy even to the deer
who give pleasure to you
because their eyes are like your eyes?

~77~

That they are fallen beings,
that their eyes are similar to yours,
that they live in a place where there is no protection—
these facts, even taken singly,
should be valid reasons for not killing deer.

~78~

I entreat you to act toward animals,
who are sorely troubled by sorrow,
with even greater compassion than
you have shown toward human beings.

~79~

I do not fold my hands
in order to ask for your protection, but
to make a request on behalf of the lives of others.
Therefore, with all respect, may you consider it well.

༤༠

།ཙོ་ནས་བཟུང་སྟེ་བསྐལ་བ་སྟོང་བ། །དམ་པ་རྣམས་ཀྱི་ལུགས་སུ་གྲགས།
།དེ་ལྟར་ལགས་པས་རྒྱལ་པོ་ལ། །བུ་སྡུག་བཞིན་དུ་གསོལ་བ་ལགས།

༤༡

།གལ་ཏེ་བདག་གིས་མི་ཕན་པ། །གསོལ་ན་བདག་ལ་ཆད་པས་ཁྲུམ།
།ཅི་སྟེ་གཅིག་ཏུ་ཕན་གསོལ་ན། །བདག་གིས་གསོལ་བ་བཞིན་དུ་མཛོད།

༤༢

།གལ་ཏེ་མི་དགྱེས་མཛད་པར་མ་གྱུར་ན། །བདག་གིས་ཡང་དང་ཡང་དུ་
གསོལ་བར་འཚལ། །ཅི་སྟེ་བདག་ཚིག་ཁྱོད་དུ་འགྱུམས་མཛད་ན། །བཀའ་
མཆིད་འདི་ནི་ངེས་པར་གཏང་བར་བགྱི།

༤༣

།དགྱེས་པར་གྱུར་ན་སྣར་རྗེས་མི་འགྱུམས་ཏེ། །མི་དགྱེས་གྱུར་ན་དགོངས་པ་
གཟུང་བར་འཚལ། །གནོད་བགྱིད་ཉི་མ་ལྟར་རྗེ་མི་ཕྱོགས་པས། །ས་བདག་
སྣ་བསྣ་བ་བཞིན་དུ་མཛོད།

~80~

To refine your studies, begin with the main points—
this is known as the custom of the noble.
In light of this, I make my request to the king
as would a beloved son.

~81~

If I request what is not beneficial,
then sentence me to death!
But if I request only what has benefit,
then act in accord with my request.

~82~

If I have not displeased you,
I would repeat my request again and again.
But if you scorn my words,
please ignore what I have said.

~83~

If you are pleased, then henceforth do not kill.
If you are displeased, may you have some misgivings.
Because doing harm like the sun is something
you simply cannot do, act like the moon,
O moon among kings!

༨༤

།ས་བདག་ཚེར་མའི་ཤིང་ལས་སྦྲང་རྩི་ལྟར། །དགྲ་བོ་ལས་ཀྱང་ལེགས་པར་སྨྲས་པ་གཟུང་། །གསེར་གྱི་རི་ལས་དུག་རྒྱུན་ཇི་བཞིན་དུ། །ཡིད་འོང་སྐྱེ་བོའི་ཚིག་ངན་སྤང་འཚལ་ལོ།

༨༥

།མི་མཆོག་གལ་ཏེ་ལེགས་པར་མཛད་པའི་སྦྱོར་བས་བསྒྲུབས་གྱུར་ཏེ། །ཕ་རོལ་གནོད་པ་སེལ་བའི་དཔལ་འདི་ཡོན་ཏན་རྒྱུན་རྣམས་ཀྱིས། །ཕྱུག་པར་བགྱིས་ན་ལེགས་སྤྱོད་བརྒྱ་ལ་ཆགས་ཕྱིར་གཡོ་བའི་སྙིང་། །མི་བརྟན་པ་ཡང་རང་དབང་མེད་པར་ཡུན་རིང་ཁྱོད་ལ་ཆགས།

།སློབ་དཔོན་མ་ཏི་ཙི་ཏྲས་རྒྱལ་པོ་ཆེན་པོ་ཀ་ནིས་ཀ་ལ་སྤྲིངས་པའི་འཕྲིན་ཡིག་རྫོགས་སོ། །རྒྱ་གར་གྱི་མཁན་པོ་བི་དྱཱ་ཀ་ར་པྲ་བྷ་དང་། ཞུ་ཆེན་གྱི་ལོ་ཙཱ་བ་བནྡེ་རིན་ཆེན་མཆོག་གིས་བསྒྱུར། ཨཱ་ཙརྱ་དཔལ་བརྩེགས་ཀྱིས་ཞུས་ཏེ་གཏན་ལ་ཕབ་པའོ། །

~84~

O king, like honey from a thorny bush,
accept words well said even from an enemy,
but like a poisonous stream from the Golden Mountain,
reject the evil words of a congenial person.

~85~

Supreme among men,
if this royal splendor—achieved
by practicing good works in former lives
and having the power to ward off the harm
enemies would do—
is ornamented by virtue in this life, then such glory,
even though intrinsically fickle and unreliable,
through being somehow linked to virtuous behavior,
cannot help but be faithful to you for a long time to come.

The "Letter Sent to the Great King Kaniṣka" by Mātṛceṭa is completed. It was translated by the Indian master Vidyākaraprabha and the great reviser and translator, the Venerable Rin-chen-mchog. Later it was corrected and edited by the teacher dPal-brtsegs.

Homage to Candragomin, whose compassion illuminated the Dharma for all beings

शिष्यलेख

།སློབ་མ་ལ་སྤྲིངས་པའི་སྤྲིང་ཡིག།

Śiṣyalekha

The Letter to a Disciple

namaḥ sarvabuddhabodhisattvebhyaḥ |

~1~

pūrvāvadānacariteṣu suduṣkareṣu
gīteṣu yasya surakinnarasundarībhiḥ |
adyāpi candrakiraṇair iva saṁkucanti
mārāṅganāvadanapaṅkajakānanāni | |

~2~

saubhāgyahṛdyavapuṣaḥ paramādbhutasya
yasyālpapuṇyajanadurlabhadarśanasya |
saṁpāditābhimatalokamanorathasya
cintāmaṇer iva parārtharasaikavṛttiḥ | |

~3~

yaḥ sarvadā parasukhena sukhī babhūva
duḥkhena duḥkham agamat paramaṁ pareṣām |
atyartham āhitamahākaruṇāguṇasya
yasyātmaduḥkhasukham antaritaṁ tad eva | |

Homage to all Buddhas and Bodhisattvas!

Even nowadays,
when the beautiful goddesses and kinnaras,
the musicians of the heavens,
sing of the most difficult deeds
that the Buddha performed in his former lives,
the forests of lotuses,
the faces of Mara's daughters,
fold up, as if struck by the rays of the moon. [1]

His shape is beautiful, pleasing,
exceedingly wonderful,
and difficult to behold by those of little spiritual merit.
He has fulfilled
the most ardently hoped-for wishes of the world;
his actions have the unique flavor
of the welfare of others.
In all these ways, he is like the wish-fulfilling gem. [2]

The happiness of others always makes him happy,
while the suffering of others
plunges him into the deepest sorrow.
He has the virtue of great compassion
implanted to the utmost degree,
having completely separated happiness and suffering
from personal happiness and suffering. [3]

~4~

vicchidyamānam api yasya śiraḥ parārtham
⟨unmīla⟩*yannayanapaṅkajatām avāpa ।
svārthaṁ punar vihasadekasitātapatrā
pṛthvī babhūva niśiteva kṛpāṇadhārā ।।

~5~

lokopakāraniratapraka ṭodayena
śuklaika⟨pakṣaparipū⟩rṇaguṇojjvalena ।
doṣāndhakārabhidureṇa manoramenạ
yenoditena śaśineva jagat prakāśam ।।

~6~

cūḍāvibhūṣaṇam ivottamaratnakalpam
ūḍhaṁ śirobhir urubhiḥ phaṇināṁ (va)⟨rāṇām ।⟩
yacchāsanaṁ śubham akhaṇḍaviśuddhavṛttaṁ
pātālagarbhanilayattimiraṁ pramārṣṭi ।।

Even when his head was cut off
for the benefit of another,
his lotus-like eyes gazed openly, like blossoms.
But when, to glorify him as ruler,
the earth was shaded over with a single white parasol,
for him it was as painful
as the edge of a sharpened sword. [4]

When he appears on earth, his brilliant presence devoted
to the service of all beings,
radiant by virtue of his perfect qualities, which allow
only pure traits of character to develop,
so pleasing,
and clearing away the darkness of moral faults,
he illuminates the world just like the risen moon,
its brilliant presence devoted to the benefit of the world,
radiant by virtue of being full and bright,
so pleasing,
and clearing away the darkness of the night. [5]

His teaching,
blissful, untainted, and immaculate in nature,
clears away the darkness
pervading the world,
just as the head ornament of precious gems,
shining, unbroken, immaculate, and perfectly round,
worn on the broad hoods of the subterranean Nāgas,
expels the darkness
pervading their subterranean realm. [6]

~7~

dharmāmbuvāha iva yo 'bhyudito hitāya
dharmāmṛtaṁ jalam ivaikarasaṁ vavarṣa |
tāpā(pa)⟨hāri para⟩ni⟨r⟩(v)⟨ṛt⟩ikāraṇaṁ ca
⟨pātrā⟩ś⟨r⟩ayeṇa yad anekarasa(ṁ babhūva) | |

~8~

vistīrṇanimnavimalaprakaṭāśayeṣu
pātreṣu sarvaparimardasaheṣu yeṣu |
tat saṁsthitaṁ bhavati sarvajanopabho⟨gyaṁ
tasmai namaḥ puruṣarūpamahāhradāya⟩ | |

Having appeared for the welfare of the world,
like a cloud of the holy Dharma,
he poured down like a life-giving rain
the nectar of his teaching,
its unique flavor clearing away pain and sorrow,
bringing about complete liberation,
and taking on various flavors
depending on the disposition of those who hear it.
In the same way, the water of rain clouds,
having appeared for the welfare of the world,
with its uniform taste drives away heat,
brings complete refreshment,
and takes on various tastes
depending on the condition of the vessel
in which it is collected. [7]

This nectar of the holy Dharma,
ready to be enjoyed by all beings,
is retained in recipients
who can bear hardships of all kinds,
and whose basic natures are broad,
deep, immaculate, and clear,
like vessels that can withstand all kinds of rough water,
and have a body that is spacious, deep, clean, and clear:
Homage to Him who is linked to a great lake of human beings,
the followers and recipients of His teaching! [8]

~9~

tajjāmṛtaṁ maraṇajanmajarāpahāri
ye nāpnuvanti na pibanti na dhārayanti |
te mohitā bahalamohamahāmadena
⟨dī⟩(r)⟨ghārtava na ca mahau⟩ṣadham ādriyante ||

~10~

cakṣur yad ekam amalaṁ jagato 'khilasya
sādhāraṇa⟨s⟩ tribhuvanasya yad ekadīpaḥ |
tac chāsanaṁ samadhigamya yad utsṛjanti
mohasya tad vilasitaṁ paramādbhutasya ||

~11~

śikṣā⟨padeṣu⟩ viditeṣv iva bodhisaudha-
sopānapaddhatipadeṣu padaṁ dadhānāḥ |
tuṅgāṁ prayānti padavīm *anuvartamānā
bhūmiṁ nijām avataranti vivartamānāḥ ||

Those who do not receive or drink or preserve
that nectar, the holy Dharma, produced by him,
which banishes old age, death, and rebirth,
are blinded
by the strong intoxication of massive delusion;
they are like people
who suffer from a protracted disease
yet refuse to take an effective medicine. [9]

His teaching is the only immaculate eye
for all living beings
and the sole common light
for the triple world.
For someone to first adopt,
and then discard that very teaching
is the most amazing manifestation of delusion! [10]

Those who take a firm hold on the moral precepts,
which resemble the well-prepared steps of the staircase
leading up to the palace of enlightenment,
will reach a high level of attainment
if they continue on and on.
But should they ever turn back,
they will tumble down
to their original position. [11]

~12~

janmārṇavaṁ paramadustaram uttitīrṣuḥ
śīlaplavaṁ ka iha hastagataṁ jahāti |
kāntāramadhyapatitaḥ katham āryasārthād
bhraṣṭo na śocati ciraṁ supathānabhijñaḥ | |

~13~

saṁsārabhūdharadarījaṭharaprapātād
utthātum udyataparāḥ paramāndhakārāt |
muñcanti ye nijaguṇāvalim antarāle
vegena te viṣamapātam adhaḥ patanti | |

~14~

ekākino 'pi manasā niyamaṁ prakalpya
ye karmaṇā samuditena samunnayanti |
te sādhavo bhuvanamaṇḍalamaulibhūtās
tair eva yānti gurutāṁ guravaḥ suśiṣyaiḥ | |

Desiring to cross the ocean of existence,
so very difficult to cross,
who would abandon the vessel of morality
once he has taken hold of it?
Would not someone
who has been separated from his caravan
and forced to wander in a wilderness
suffer for a long time,
not knowing the right way? [12]

Those who endeavor most diligently
to raise themselves up
from the utterly dark depths of the steep crevasses
in the mountain of samsara,
into which they have fallen,
and who, midway, let go of the garland-like rope
of their innate virtuous qualities,
will take a terrible plunge downward,
with ever increasing speed. [13]

Those who, in complete solitude,
conceive a vow in their hearts
and integrate it with every action
are great, and they will become
head-ornaments of the whole globe.
It is only through such noble disciples
that teachers become real teachers. [14]

~15~

lajjāṁ guṇaughajananīṁ jananīm ivāryām
atyantaśuddhahṛdayām anuvartamānāḥ ।
tejasvinaḥ sukham asūn api saṁtyajanti
satyasthitivyasanino na punaḥ pratijñām ॥

~16~

tiṣṭhantu tāvad iha sarvajanāpavādāḥ
sarvāś ca pāpagatayo nirayāś ca ghorāḥ ।
sadyo jahāti sahajāṁ prakṛtiṁ yad eṣa
duḥkhaṁ tataḥ kim aparaṁ bhuvi sajjanasya ॥

~17~

yaḥ prāpya nāvam iva dharmamayīṁ viśālāṁ
bhūyo jahāti padavīṁ munibhiḥ praklṛptām ।
saṁsārasāgaravivartananartaneṣu
cetaḥspṛhā taralitā niyamena tasya ॥

Heroic people pursue noble modesty,
which produces an abundance of virtues
and indicates a completely pure heart,
just as if they would follow their noble mother,
who brings forth an abundance of virtues
and possesses a completely pure heart.
They easily give up even their own lives
in their endeavor to be truthful and constant—
but never their vow. [15]

What matter all the abuses of the people here,
all the sinful states of existence,
and all the dreadful hells—
what worse suffering could there be on earth
for a virtuous man
than suddenly to abandon his original nature? [16]

He who finds
the broad path of the Dharma
established by the seers—
which is like a spacious ship—
and then abandons it again,
will certainly have
his heart's desire thrown about here and there
during the tossing and dancing
in the ocean of samsara. [17]

~18~

saṁsāracakram aniśaṁ parivartamānam
āruhya yaḥ sukham avaiti vivartamānaḥ |
so 'vaśyam eva vivaśaḥ śataśaḥ krameṇa
sarvāḥ samāś ca viṣamāś ca gatīḥ prayāti ||

~19~

atyugragandham aśuciprakaroparuddham
atyantasaṅkaṭam upoḍhaghanāndhakāram |
āviśya garbhanilayaṁ nirayaṁ yathaiva
duḥkhaṁ mahat sa sahate paripiṇḍitāṅgaḥ ||

~20~

kālakrameṇa sa tato dṛḍhatailayantra-
ni⟨ṣpī⟩ḍyamāna iva yāti bhuvaṁ kathaṁ cit |
sadyas tathāpi yad ayaṁ na jahāti jīvaṁ
duḥkhopabhogagatidurlalitaṁ tad eva ||

He who mounts
the ever-revolving wheel of samsara
and enjoys being tossed about,
will most certainly undergo,
successively and helplessly,
all the pleasant and unpleasant states of existence,
hundreds of times. [18]

Having entered the womb,
with its exceedingly horrible stench,
full of impurities,
extremely narrow,
and utterly dark,
exactly like a hell,
with its exceedingly horrible stench,
full of impurities,
extremely narrow,
and utterly dark—
the body is squashed into a ball,
and one endures great pain. [19]

Then, in the course of time,
as if squeezed by a sesame oil press,
with great effort he comes into the world.
That despite all this,
he does not immediately throw his life away
is the waywardness of a form of existence
destined to experience suffering. [20]

~21~

tatra sthitaṁ tam aśucau parivartamānam
ārdrolbaveṣṭitatanuṁ ba⟨ha⟩logragandham |
pūrvasmṛti⟨r⟩ vraṇam ivolbaṇadoṣapākaṁ
bhinnaṁ jahāti ghṛṇayeva nipīḍyamānā | |

~22~

sarvopacāravivaśaṁ śithilākulāṅgam
utsṛjya bālyam upajātakaṭhorabh⟨āvaḥ |⟩
tuṅgeṣu yauvanagirīndradarītaṭeṣu
mohāyate viṣayadṛṣṭiviṣālayeṣu | |

~23~

sa tato 'pi pataty acetanaḥ
patito naiva jahāti vikriyām |
ajarāmaram ātmavigrahaṁ
la⟨l⟩i⟨taṁ⟩ manyata eva bāliśaḥ | |

At the moment of birth, wallowing in filth,
his body enveloped in a slimy membrane,
stinking horribly—
like an open abscess,
the result of a great internal disturbance—
memories of past lives,
as if repressed in disgust,
leave him. [21]

In childhood,
he is not yet master of the body's behavior,
and his limbs are weak and uncoordinated.
Leaving childhood behind,
his heart now hardened,
he roams about bewildered
in the high slopes and deep caves
of the great mountain Youth,
the dwelling place of the poisonous snakes
called objects of the senses. [22]

Lacking understanding,
he falls down even from there;
fallen, he still does not give up the excesses of youth,
foolishly thinking
that his handsome, healthy body
will never become old and die. [23]

~24~

sa vihāya munīndrasevitaṁ
supathaṁ yāty apathena mohitaḥ |
rabhasena parān vicūrṇayan
gajavaj jātamado niraṅkuśaḥ ||

~25~

atha tasya balā⟨d a⟩nicchataḥ
śirasi nyastapadā sunirdayam |
niśitaṁ palitāṅkuśaṁ jarā
kariṇo hastipakīva yacchati ||

~26~

sa tathāpi vijihmaceṣṭitaḥ
kuśalenāpi bhayād ivojjhitaḥ |
akṛtāni ⟨karo⟩ti mohitaḥ
śaravat svātmavadhāya puṣpitaḥ ||

Having left the good path
practiced by the seers,
deceived, he proceeds on the wrong path,
recklessly crushing others
like an unchecked elephant in rut. [24]

Old age,
forcibly and without an iota of compassion,
then puts its feet on his head, against his will,
and makes him feel the sharp goad
of his grey hair,
just as an elephant-driver,
forcibly and without an iota of compassion,
puts his feet on the head of an elephant, against its will,
and makes it feel the sharp goad. [25]

Nevertheless, deluded,
his gait crooked,
deserted even by his own well-being, as if afraid,
his skin mottled with dark spots,
a mark of being soon to die,
he commits outrageous deeds,
just as an arrow gone astray, wobbling in its course
when released even by a skilled archer startled into fright,
decorated with flowers
that point to its own destruction,
commits outrageous deeds. [26]

~27~

atha taṁ prahasann ivāntakaḥ
palitaughair daśanair ivolbaṇaiḥ ।
śirasi grasituṁ pravartate
nirupāyapraśamo *jarānujaḥ ।।

~28~

vidalanti ⟨tato⟩ 'sya saṁdhayo
matir utkrāmati hīyate gatiḥ ।
kṣayam eti vapuḥ pariślathaṁ
niyataṁ vardhata eva *jīvitā ।।

~29~

kramaśaś ca nimīlitendriyo
hataśaktir viṣayeṣu lālasaḥ ।
upa⟨ga⟩cchati yām ayam daśāṁ
narake sā yadi bhīma eva saḥ ।।

Then Death,
the younger brother of Old Age,
who can by no means be appeased,
as if laughing, sets out
to devour him from the head down
with his huge teeth—
the shock of white hair. [27]

His joints begin to crack,
his mental capacity diminishes,
his ability to move comes to an end,
the utterly weakened body decays—
and yet his hope to live increases. [28]

Gradually the sense-organs close down,
and the abilities deteriorate;
still craving for the objects of the senses,
he falls into a state so horrible
that even in hell
he would be absolutely terrifying. [29]

~30~

katham evam idaṁ mayā kṛtaṁ
katham evaṁ na kṛtaṁ hatā gatiḥ ।
katham evam ayaṁ mayāntakaḥ
śirasi nyastapado na lakṣitaḥ ।।

~31~

iti (ce)⟨ti ca⟩ cittamāthibhiḥ
*kuliśaiḥ śokamayair upadrutaḥ ।
vyathitena sabāṣpavāriṇā
karuṇaṁ bandhujanena vīkṣitaḥ ।।

~32~

vinipīḍitamarmabandhanas
timiraṁ ghorataraṁ viśann iva ।
vijahāti ⟨nijaṁ⟩ kaḍevaraṁ
dayitaṁ yatnapareṇa rakṣitam ।।

"How could I have done it like this,
why didn't I do it like that?
I have wasted my life!
How could I not have seen
that Death was putting his feet
upon my head!" [30]

As he is attacked
by all these mind-crushing thunderbolts of grief,
his shaken relatives
look at him mournfully
with eyes veiled with tears. [31]

Joints and sinews aching fiercely,
he somehow finds himself
in a very terrible darkness
where he must give up his own body,
which he has cherished and cared for
with so much effort. [32]

~33~

sa virauti gṛhītamūrdhajo
yamadūtair dṛḍhapāśasaṁyataḥ ǀ
na śṛṇoti jano 'sya bhāṣitaṁ
svakṛtākrandaravād ivākulaḥ ǀ ǀ

~34~

prastāraśailasaridantaradurgameṣu
mārgeṣu tīkṣṇatarakaṇṭakasaṅkaṭeṣu ǀ
ghoraiḥ kṛtāntapuruṣaiḥ samadaṇḍaghātam
ākṛṣyate galaniveśitakālapāśaḥ ǀ ǀ

~35~

dūrān nirīkṣya vimalaṁ salilaṁ pipāsur
abhyeti gāḍhatṛṣito yad ayaṁ tad eva ǀ
keśaughaśaivalavimiśritapūtipūya-
paṅkāṅkitaṁ kṣatajavijjalatāṁ prayāti ǀ ǀ

Seized by the hair by the messengers of Yama
and fettered with strong chains,
he screams.
His mourners, as if distracted by the noise
of their own lamentations,
do not hear his cries. [33]

On roads terrible to travel,
winding through thickets, rocks, and rivers
and hemmed in by piercing thorns,
he is dragged along
by the dreadful servants of the Lord of Death,
steadily beaten by rods,
a black rope around his neck. [34]

From afar he sees pure water
and yearns to drink,
but when he moves toward it
with an increasing thirst,
it turns out to be full of filth, pus,
and mud mixed with masses of hair and weeds,
as slimy as blood. [35]

~36~

velānilākulitaśīkaraśītasānum
ānīlacandanatarum̐ malayam̐ prayāti |
so 'py asya caṇḍavanadāvaśikhāvalīḍha-
śīrṇolmukaprakaradanturatām̐ prayāti ||

~37~

yady eti vārinidhim uddhatabhīmalola-
kallolabhedajanitolbaṇaphenahāsam |
so 'py asya taptaviṣadāruṇasaikatābhra-
vibhrāntakarkaśamarunmarutām̐ prayāti ||

~38~

tatra sthitasya jaladāgamaśam̐sino 'sya
sām̐gāradhūmakuliśopalavisphulim̐gam |
vidyullatākanakarājipiśam̐gam am̐ge
nārācavarṣam abhivarṣati vārivāhaḥ ||

When he approaches the Malaya mountain range,
whose ridge is cooled by mists
scattered by coastal winds,
and whose slopes are bedecked with
dark-blue sandalwood trees,
this too changes
and becomes jagged peaks
covered with masses of smoldering splinters
licked by the tongues of a fierce forest fire. [36]

As he approaches the ocean,
its dense foam seeming to reveal a smile
in the breaking
of the high, impressively rolling waves,
this too changes
and becomes a desert
with whirling harsh winds and clouds of red-hot sand,
harsh and pitiless like poison. [37]

While he stands there
and gives thanks for the arrival of rain clouds,
they pour down upon his body
a shower of iron arrows,
reddish-gold like rows of lightning streaks,,
mixed with sparks and coal-black smoke
from thunderbolts and meteorites. [38]

~39~

tāpārditasya dahanas *tuhinānilo 'pi
śītārditasya dahano 'pi karoti śītam |
atyugrakarmapariṇāmavimohitasya
viśvaṁ tadāsya viparītam idaṁ vibhāti ||

~40~

sūcīmukhasya bahuyojanabhīmakukṣer
ārtasya vāri pibato 'pi mahāsamudre |
aprāpta eva pṛthukaṇṭhadarīprapātam
*āsyoṣmaṇā jalalavaḥ pariśoṣam eti ||

~41~

cañcaj*jaṭānikara*pīvarasārameya-
daṁṣṭr*āṅkuśāgrakuliśakṣatacūrṇitāṅgaḥ |
kṣārāmbupūrṇataravaitaraṇītaṭeṣu
niṣkṛṣyate viṣamakoṭiśitopaleṣu ||

While he is tortured by heat,
even a cold wind burns him;
while he is tortured by cold,
even fire freezes him;
thus, confused
by the consequences of extremely fierce karma,
each and every thing appears reversed to him. [39]

That miserable being
with a mouth the size of a needle,
whose formidable belly measures many miles around,
may even drink all the water in the great ocean,
but before a single drop of that water
has reached the crevass
of the huge cavity of its throat,
it dries up completely
in the heat of the mouth. [40]

He whose limbs are smashed and rent
by the goad-like fangs, sharp as Indra's thunderbolts,
of the massive watchdogs of Yama,
with their fluttering manes,
is torn into pieces
on the banks of the hell river Vaitaraṇī,
which overflow with acid
and are strewn with
jagged-edged sharp rocks. [41]

~42~

dhāvañ javena niśitakṣurasaṁstareṣu
vicchinnamūrtir asipattralatāvaneṣu |
kūpe pataty aśaraṇaḥ śitaśūlaśakti-
prāsāsihāsa*nicitāntakavaktrarandhre ||

~43~

tīvrātapakvathitaduḥsahakhinnadeho
vṛkṣān nirīkṣya ghananīladalān upaiti |
tatpattraśastraśatapātavibhinnamūrtis
tatraiva tiṣṭhati ciraṁ virutaikabandhuḥ ||

~44~

paryantanirgataśikhāśatavisphuliṅga-
mālākulajvalitamaṇḍanamaṇḍitābhiḥ |
premottarapraṇayanirdayam aṅganābhir
āliṅgyate krakacakarkaśavigrahābhiḥ ||

His body slashed and torn,
he runs quickly through forests
whose creepers are made
of the edges of swords,
and where the beds of leaves
are sharpened razors.
Unprotected, he falls into a well,
the chasm-like mouth of Yama,
grinning with sharp spikes,
spears, lances, and swords. [42]

Exhausted and racked with unbearable pain,
his body burnt by fierce heat,
he sees trees with thick green leaves
and approaches them;
by the downpour of hundreds of their leaves,
sharp as weapons,
his body is cut and pinned to that very spot
for a long time,
his screams his only companions. [43]

He is unmercifully embraced by women
obsessed by uncontrollable lust,
whose bodies are as jagged as saws,
and who are adorned with blazing ornaments
full of sparks
from the hundreds of flames
shooting out on all sides. [44]

~45~

śailābhabhīṣaṇavisaṅkaṭameṣa*yugma-
saṁghaṭṭacūrṇitaviśīrṇasamastagātraḥ |
āpātavātalavaśaityasamarpitāsuḥ
saṁcūrṇyate punar asau śataśas tathaiva ||

~46~

uttrāsitaḥ śvakharakhaḍgaśivāsahasrair
ārohati drutapadaṁ punar eva raudrām |
tāṁ kūṭaśālmalim adhomukhakaṇṭakaugha-
nirbhidyamānavapur arpitagāḍhaśalyaḥ ||

~47~

mṛtyoḥ karāntagalitair iva kālapāśair
āśīviṣair dhṛtaphaṇair dṛḍhasaṁyatasya |
utpāṭayanti ⟨naya⟩ne sphurataḥ prasahya
tatra sthitasya bakavāyasakaṅkagṛdhrāḥ ||

His shattered body is totally ground to pieces
by the crashing together of a pair of rams
as massive as mountains,
dreadful, and extremely dangerous.
Then his spirits are revived
by the coolness of the tiny bursts of wind
caused by their impact;
in precisely this way, again and again
he is ground to pieces
hundreds of times. [45]

Terrified by thousands of dogs,
mules, rhinoceroses, and jackals,
with intense speed he once again climbs
that fierce kūṭaśālmalī tree;
as he climbs, his body is torn open
by the masses of thorns pointing down
and he experiences intense pain. [46]

Tightly enveloped and held
by poisonous snakes with erect hoods,
which are like the black ropes
hanging down from the fingers of Death,
he wriggles and writhes
while grey baka herons, crows,
white kaṅka herons, and vultures
violently tear out his eyes. [47]

~48~

teṣāṁ mukhaiḥ kuliśakoṭinibhaiḥ prasahya
*nirdāryamāṇavapur eṣa kṛtārtanādaḥ |
lohonmukhapracurapīvaratīkṣṇaśaṅku-
nirbhinnamūrtir avarohati naṣṭacetāḥ ||

~49~

ādīptaśūlaśitaśalyavibhinnadehās
tatraiva ke cid avaroḍhum aśaknuvantaḥ |
ghorair yadā niśitaśastramukhair ayobhir
ākṛṣyamāṇavisaradgalitāntrasūtrāḥ ||

~50~

ke cit patanti viṣameṣu gires taṭeṣu
ke cit parikvathitatailakaṭāhakukṣau |
uttaptavālukabhuvaṁ visṛtasphuliṅgām
anye viśanti padasaṅgam anāpnuvantaḥ ||

While his body is savagely torn open
by their beaks,
which resemble the tips of lightning bolts,
he screams out in pain;
stupefied, he descends,
his body ripped open
by rows of huge iron barbs,
pointing up and razor sharp. [48]

At that very place there are some,
their bodies pierced by blazing lances
and sharpened arrows,
who are not able to descend
when the coils of their intestines,
bulging out and hanging down,
are pulled out by dreadful iron instruments
with sharpened blades at their tips. [49]

Some fall down onto the rugged slopes of mountains,
some into cauldrons filled with boiling oil;
others proceed to places
covered with hot sand and emitting sparks,
where they find no place to put their feet. [50]

~51~

eke punaḥ simisimāyitasūkṣmajantu-
saṁghātajarjaritaśūnavipūtikāyāḥ |
saṁcālamātram api *kartum aśaknuvanto
jīvanti karmamayapāśanibaddhajīvāḥ ||

~52~

asthīny api *pralayatā rahitopamena
śītena jarjaritavepitapiṇḍitāṅgāḥ |
utpannabhinnapiṭakāśatajātajantu-
jagdhakṣatasrutasamajjavasālasīkāḥ ||

~53~

saṁdaṣṭalagnadaśanās tanulomakeśāḥ
saṁghaṭṭitavyathitalocanakarṇakaṇṭhāḥ |
ā cetaso jaḍataratvam upetakāyās
tiṣṭhanti śītanarakeṣu bhṛśaṁ nadantaḥ ||

Still others,
their bloated stinking bodies
gnawed by millions of swarming tiny insects,
are incapable of even the smallest movement.
Yet they continue to exist,
fettered to their lives
by the chains of karma. [51]

In the incomparable cold
that seeps even into their bones,
their bodies are split,
made to tremble and roll into a ball.
Their wounds,
gnawed by the worms
born in the hundreds of boils
that arise and split open,
drip pus mixed with marrow and fat. [52]

Their teeth tightly clenched and locked together,
the hair of their bodies and heads standing on end,
their eyes, ears, and throats convulsed in pain,
total numbness penetrating their whole being,
from body to mind,
they abide in the cold hells,
screaming in torment. [53]

~54~

vikīrṇabahalogragandhakaṭudhūmadhūmrāntaraṁ
vijṛmbhitaśikhākaraprakararuddhadigmaṇḍalam ।
sitāsthi*śakalāvalī*racitabhūṣaṇaṁ bhīṣaṇaṁ
pravṛttam iva bhairavaṁ *sagaja*carmahāhāravam ।।

~55~

caṭaccaṭaditi kva cit sphuradurusphuliṅgākulaṁ
chamacchamaditi kṣaṇasthagitajṛmbhitaṁ medasi ।
kaṭatkaṭaditi kvaṇantam uraso 'sthirandhrāntare
patanti narakānalaṁ vijitakalpakālānalam ।।

~56~

purāṇatṛṇajarjarajvalitaparśukāsaṁcayāḥ
sadhūmagalatālavo dhagiti vāntadīptārciṣaḥ ।
sphurajjaṭharaniḥsṛtaprasaradantrasaṁtrāsitā
vimuktagurughargharadhvanitamātraśeṣakriyāḥ ।।

Some fall into the fire of hell,
murky at its center, filled
with dense, horribly stinking acrid smoke,
its numerous all-pervading tongues of fire
encircling the whole world.
It resembles the frightful god Bhairava,
clad in an elephant's hide,
wearing a garland of tiny white pieces of bone,
and roaring Ha-ha. [54]

The flames of hell,
surpassing even the fire at the end of the world,
are full of huge sparks that dart here and there
with a crackling sound;
dying down, they flare up again at short intervals,
hissing in the fat falling from the bodies of beings,
producing in the cavities of their rib cages
a popping sound. [55]

These beings,
their ribs worn thin and burning like old dry grass,
their smoke-filled throats and palates suddenly
spewing forth hot flames,
terrified because their intestines
protrude and bulge out of their twitching bellies,
are capable only of emitting an extended gurgling sound
as their last act. [56]

~57~

nirīkṣya vivarāntaraṁ muhur apāvṛtaṁ dūrataḥ
prayānti katham apy amī pratataduḥkhamokṣāśayā |
yadā tad api *ghāṭitaṁ bhavati karmapaṭṭair dṛḍhais
tadā viphalavāñchitāḥ kim api yānti duḥkhāntaram ||

~58~

jvalanniśitatomaraprakaravarṣaṇānantaraṁ
dravīkṛtam ayorasaṁ dahanaraśmimālākulam |
pibanti galadaśravo narakapāladaṇḍāhatā
mukhaśravaṇanāsikāvivaralabdhadhūmodgamāḥ ||

~59~

ādagdhavisphuṭitanetraśiraḥkapāla-
mastiṣkadīpitapiśaṅgaśikhākalāpaḥ |
śuṣkendhanaprakaranirdayatām upaiti
śokāgnikopa iva gātracayeṣu teṣām ||

Seeing from afar
the entrance to the netherworld open repeatedly,
they desperately rush toward it
in their hope to escape
their prolonged suffering.
But when the aperture is closed
by the massive door-panels of karma,
their desire is in vain,
and they go on to some other kind of suffering. [57]

Immediately after a rain
of blazing sharpened arrows
falls down upon them,
they are beaten with clubs by the hell guardians.
Tears stream down and
smoke pours forth
from their mouths, ears, and noses
as they drink molten iron
surrounded by a halo of fire. [58]

The tongues of the blazing red flames, fed
by their singed and burst-open
eyes, skulls, and brains,
leap mercilessly upon all of their limbs
like the wrath of the fire of grief,
as if they were heaps of dried firewood. [59]

~60~

te jantavo girinadījalalolajīvā
auṣṇyaṁ tad eva narakeṣu sa eva cāgniḥ ।
karmāṇi tat khalu tathā pariṇāmayanti
sarvaṁ yathā paramadāruṇam āvibhāti ।।

~61~

ātmīyakarmavivaśākulaceṣṭitasya
muktasya pāpanilayān nirayāt kathaṁ cit ।
lokeṣv anantagatibhedabhayākuleṣu
mānuṣyakaṁ paramadurlabham eva jantoḥ ।।

~62~

mlaccheṣu vā narakapālasamavrateṣu
tiryakṣu vā kṛtaparasparabhakṣaṇeṣu ।
jātiṁ labheta yadi tatra tad eva śīlam
āsevate patati yena punaḥ prapātam ।।

The life of these beings
is as restless as the water of mountain streams.
Such is the heat to be found in hell;
such is the fire to be found there!
It is their deeds that transform everything
into manifestations extreme in their cruelty. [60]

Even if these beings,
whose conduct is determined
by their deeds and is therefore erratic,
somehow escape from hell,
the dwelling place of evildoers,
it is still extremely difficult
for them to be reborn as a human being
in those worlds that are frightening
in the variety
of their innumerable states of existence. [61]

If they are born in the world of mankind,
it is among barbarians
who follow the same way of life
as the guardians of hell,
or among animals
that devour one another;
thus they take up the same kinds of actions,
whereby they will fall down again. [62]

~63~

yat prāpya janmajaladher api yānti pāram
*āropayanti *śivam uttama*bodhibījam |
cintāmaṇer api samabhyadhikaṁ guṇaughair
mānuṣyakaṁ ka iha tad viphalīkaroti | |

~64~

| bde gshegs lam bsten 'gro ba 'dren par chas gyur cing |
| sems kyi stobs chen mi yis rnyed pa gang yin pa'i |
| lam de lha dang klu yis mi rnyed lha min dang |
| mkha' lding rig 'dzin mi 'am ci dang lto 'phye min |

~65~

atyantadurlabham upetya manuṣyabhāvaṁ
yad vāñchitaṁ tad abhivāñchitam eva kuryāt |
caṇḍānilākulitadīpaśikhācalasya
na hy āyuṣaḥ kṣaṇam api sthitiniścayo 'sti | |

Having attained
the state of a human being,
which enables one to cross the ocean of existence
and plant the auspicious seed of supreme enlightenment,
which by its multitude of virtues
is superior even to the wish-fulfilling gem—
who on earth would spoil this state? [63]

The path taught by the Buddha
and practiced by him in order to guide the world
is within the reach of human beings
endowed with great spiritual power,
but cannot be attained
by gods, nāgas, asuras, garuḍas,
Vidyādharas, kinnaras, and uragas. [64]

"Having attained the state of a human being,
so extremely difficult to attain,
I can do what I like,
following any impulse that enters my mind,
because life is as fickle as the flickering flame
of a lamp blown by a fierce wind,
and is not certain to last
for even a single moment! [65]

~66~

śvaḥ kāryam etad idam adya paraṁ muhūrtād
etat kṣaṇād iti janena vicintyamāne |
tiryagnirīkṣaṇapiśaṅgitakāladaṇḍaḥ
śaṅke hasaty asahanaḥ kupitaḥ kṛtāntaḥ ||

~67~

āyāti phullakusumaḥ kusumāgamo 'yam
eṣā śaśāṅkatilakā śarad āgateti |
sarvaḥ prahṛṣyati jano na punar mamaitad
āyuḥ prahīṇam iti yāti paraṁ viṣādam ||

~68~

āsannapīnaśaśimaṇḍalamaṇḍanāsu
viśrāntavāriguruvāridamekhalāsu |
niḥsaṁgamāsu giriśṛṅgavanasthalīṣu
dhanyā nayanty anilacañcalaśīlam āyuḥ ||

I will do this tomorrow, that today,
the other thing after a short while, this now."
When people think like this,
I fear that the impatient and angry Lord of Death,
whose once black club
has been stained deep crimson
by his furious sidelong glances,
will laugh at them. [66]

"Spring is here! the flowers are in bloom;
autumn has arrived, with the bright moon
as its beauty mark!"
Saying this, everyone rejoices,
but no one sinks into deepest despair,
reflecting, "My life is wearing out." [67]

In forests on the tops of mountains—
adorned with the nearby orb of the full moon,
girded with water-laden clouds
that settle there to rest—
solitary and free from encounters with others,
human beings spend their lives,
by nature as mobile as the wind,
blissfully and happily. [68]

~69~

kiṁ sā ratir bhavati nandanabhūmikāsu
divyāṅganājaghanapṛṣṭhaśilātalāsu |
yā mugdhamugdhahariṇīgaṇasevitāsu
niḥsaṅgacārusubhagāsu vanasthalīṣu | |

~70~

divyāṅganāparimalāvilaveṇibhinna-
saṁtānakastabakahāsaviḍambinīṣu |
kiṁ sā ratiḥ surasaritsu viviktaramya-
tīrāsu yā śucijalāsu vane nadīṣu | |

~71~

| rtsa ba 'bras bu shun pa lo ma phun sum tshogs pa'i ljon shing ldan | | nags tshal bltos med ri bo'i chu rgyun bsil 'bab chags pa med pa'i gnas | | chu klung yangs pa'i mtha' ru 'bras bu me tog lhung bas brgyan pa yi | | nyams dga'i bas mthar ci zhig med de dmyal stong khyim gyis bslus te sdod |

Could that same joy then rule supreme
in the precincts and quarters
of the heavenly Nandana grove,
where the slates and rock slabs are as soft
as the buttocks of the goddesses—
joy such as is felt in woodlands,
lonely, lovely, and blessed,
where droves of gazelles dwell and romp
in their abundant innocent charm? [69]

Could that same joy then rule supreme
near the rivers of the gods,
which seem to smile
with the clusters of fully opened santānaka blossoms
in the perfume-laden locks of the goddesses—
joy such as is felt near the rivers in the forests
with their pure water and their lovely, lonely banks? [70]

Are there no forests,
with trees abounding in roots, fruits, bark, and leaves;
with places free of passion
where streams of cool water pour down continuously;
with lovely remote areas adorned with flowers and fruits
that drop down onto the banks of wide rivers—
are there no forests,
that we are deceived by the householder's life,
worse than thousands of hells,
and remain in the house? [71]

~72~

viśālāḥ śailānāṁ viratajanasaṁpātasubhagā
guhā gāḍhābhogā haritavanalekhāparikarāḥ |
sarittīrāsannā murajamadhurair nirjhararavair
na gamyāḥ kleśāgner vayam iti vadantīva pathikān ||

~73~

māyāmarīcidakacandrataraṅgakalpāḥ
kāmā jinena gaditā vibhavāḥ striyaś ca |
svapnāntadurlalitavibhramavipralabdhā
bālāḥ patanti nirayeṣv api yeṣu saktāḥ ||

~74~

āpātamātramadhurā viṣayā viṣaṁ ca
ghorā vipākakaṭukā viṣayā viṣaṁ ca |
mohāndhakāragahanā viṣayā viṣaṁ ca
durvāravegacapalā viṣayā viṣaṁ ca ||

The vast and vaulted mountain caves,
wondrously deep and blessed
by the presence of sages rich in austerities,
girded by verdant forest borders
and near the banks of rivers,
appear to call out to the wayfarers
in the voices of waterfalls, sweet as tambourines:
"We lie beyond all reach
of the fire of the defilements!" [72]

The Buddha has said
that desire, wealth, and women
are like the wavering image of the moon
in the water of a mirage brought about by illusion.
Fools cling to them
as if deceived in a dream by roguish tricks,
and fall even into the hells. [73]

The pleasures of the senses
are like poison—both are sweet
but in the first moment of their tasting;
in their aftermath, when digested,
both are terrible and full of torments.
The dense darkness of delusion is common to both,
and both bring a body to trembling
by their inevitable effect. [74]

~75~

*kāmaṁ viṣaṁ ca viṣayāś ca nirūpyamāṇāḥ
śreyo viṣaṁ na viṣayā viṣamasvabhāvāḥ |
ekatra janmani viṣaṁ viṣatāṁ prayāti
janmāntare 'pi viṣayā viṣatāṁ prayānti ||

~76~

saṁsṛṣṭaṁ vrajati viṣaṁ viṣeṇa śāntiṁ
sanmantrair agadadharaiś ca sādhyamānam |
yuktaṁ vā bhavati viṣaṁ hitāya n≈ṇāṁ
na tv evaṁ viṣayamahāviṣaṁ kadā cit ||

~77~

yadvad vṛṣo viṣamakūpataṭāntarūḍho
dūrvāpravālalavalālasamānasaḥ san |
śvabhre pataty atha ca *nāsthita eva lābhaṁ
tadvat sukhānvitamatiḥ khalu jīvalokaḥ ||

Should one take a closer look, however,
at poison and the pleasures of the senses,
then poison proves to be the better thing
when weighed against
the dangerous sensual pleasures.
For poison's bane is perilous
but in a single round of existence,
while sensual pleasures poison a being
in the incarnation to come as well. [75]

When poison is mixed with poison
and prepared with the proper mantras and antidotes,
it is rendered ineffective.
What is more, when properly used,
poison even becomes beneficial to beings.
But never does the strong poison
"objects of the senses"
act in such a way. [76]

Just as a young bull,
having wandered to the edge
of a dangerous precipice near a water-hole,
intent upon the tiny shoots of dūrvā grass,
falls into the chasm and gains nothing,
so living beings,
their minds craving the pleasures of the world,
plummet down
without attaining what they desire. [77]

~78~

mandākinījalarayākulitālakābhiḥ
krīḍāvihāram anubhūya sahāpsarobhiḥ |
bhūyo bhramanti kharavaitaraṇītaraṅga-
saṁparkajarjaritadāruṇaduḥkhabhājaḥ ||

~79~

āstīrṇakalpatarupallavasaṁstareṣu
kāntāsakhāḥ suravaneṣu sukhaṁ vihṛtya |
bhūyo bhramanti niśitākulaśastrapāta-
vicchinnagātram asipattravanasthalīṣu ||

~80~

sparśe sukhāsu padapātanatonnatāsu
meror nitambapadavīṣu ciraṁ vihṛtya |
uttaptasaikatakukūlakṛśānurāśi-
saṁśīryamāṇacaraṇorubhujā bhramanti ||

Having enjoyed playfully sporting
with the heavenly nymphs,
their locks disheveled
by the current of the river Mandākinī,
these beings, having fallen, again wander about,
experiencing agonizing pain
when their bodies are eaten away
by the acid waves of Vaitaraṇī, the river of hell. [78]

Having lived pleasurably
with lovely companions in the forests of the gods,
where beds are made
of the tender buds of the wish-fulfilling tree,
these beings again wander about
in forests with sword-like leaves,
their bodies cut apart
by the falling leaves,
a flurry of sharp swords. [79]

Having strolled about for ages
on the paths on the slopes of Mount Meru,
so pleasurable to walk upon,
springing gently beneath the feet,
they now wander about
on heated sands,
their feet, thighs, and arms
completely withered away
by the huge fire of the hell Kukūla. [80]

~81~

gatvā divaṁ mukharabhāsurakiṅkaṇīka-
hārāvalīnikaradanturitair vimānaiḥ ।
ghoraṁ *nirāśrayam ameyam anantapāram
andhaṁ tamaḥ punar adhaḥśirasā patanti ।।

~82~

śakro 'pi yatra surakinnaranāgayakṣa-
mauliprabhāprakarapiñjarapādapīṭhaḥ ।
karmānilākulagatiḥ kugatīḥ prayāti
ko nāma tatra puruṣo na bhayaṁ bhajeta ।।

~83~

pramlāyamānakusumāḥ srutagharmadigdhā
mlānāmbarāḥ karuṇavīkṣitabandhuvargāḥ ।
duḥkham paraṁ yad amarā maraṇe vrajanti
tan mānavā na jalabudbudalolajīvāḥ ।।

Having traveled in heaven
in celestial chariots
adorned with strands of pearls
and small bells, sparkling and jingling,
they again fall headlong
into a blinding darkness
without any protection,
immeasurable and boundless,
truly dreadful. [81]

What being could possibly
remain fearless in that divine state
wherein even the god Indra—
whose gleaming footstool reflects
the great golden radiance of the head ornaments
of the gods, kinnaras, nāgas, and yakṣas—
is himself afflicted by the wind of karma,
and will fall to the lower forms of existence? [82]

Human beings,
whose lives are as unsteady as drops of water,
are not so severely stricken with grief
at the time of their death
as are the gods, who,
their flowers withering away,
their bodies smeared with trickling sweat,
their garments fading,
are mournfully observed by all their companions. [83]

~84~

duḥkhāgniprakaranirodhabhairave 'smin
yal loke vahati janaḥ sukhābhimānam |
tan mṛtyor vadanam apāvṛtaṁ viśālaṁ
tad bījaṁ punar api janmapādapasya ||

~85~

tat tṛṣṇāmayadṛḍhadīrghatantubaddhaṁ
paryastapraṇihitabhīmakāladaṇḍam |
sattvānāṁ bhavajaladhau pariplutānāṁ
matsyānāṁ baḍiśam ivāntakena dattam ||

~86~

kumbhīpākakvathitakalilād uṣṇasaṁrambhavegāt
kṛtvodgrīvaṁ kṣaṇam api sukhaṁ labdhaniśvāsamokṣāḥ |
krodhāpūrṇaiḥ subahubhir ayomudgarais tāḍyamānā
manyante taṁ param iva sukhaṁ nārakā yadvad eva |

The arrogant notion developed by human beings
that happiness is possible
in this terrifying world
walled in by the numerous fires of suffering:
That is the wide-open mouth of the Lord of Death;
that is, once more, the seed of the tree of rebirth. [84]

It is the hook,
fixed with the long, strong cord of greed,
and swung around and cast by his black club—
dreadful in its perverse aspirations—
that the Lord of Death
presents to the beings swimming around
in the ocean of existence,
just as a fish hook is presented to the fish
swimming around in the sea. [85]

Just as the inhabitants of hell,
stretching their heads out
of the hot and fiercely churning boiling brew
in the cauldron-like Kumbhīpāka hell—
even though they are beaten upon
with a hail of iron maces
by those brimming with wrath—
enjoy for a short moment
the relief of breathing easily,
and regard this as the greatest happiness, [86]

~87~

tadvad duḥkhair aniśam avaśo dāruṇaiḥ pīḍyamānas
tāvatkālaṁ jananamaraṇakṣobhamuktaḥ kathaṁ cit |
mandībhūte kṣaṇam api nije duḥsahe duḥkhavahnau
sarvo lokas tanusukhalavagrāmatṛṣṇāṁ karoti ||

~88~

yāvad yāvaj jagati sakale jāyate saukhyasaṁjñā
tāvat tāvad bahalataratām eti mohāndhakāraḥ |
yāvad yāvaj jagati sakale jāyate duḥkhasaṁjñā
tāvat tāvat taralataratām eti mohāndhakāraḥ ||

~89~

yāvad yāvad visarati śubhā bhāvanā bhāvyamānā
tāvat tāvad bahutaraśikho jāyate rāgavahniḥ |
yāvad yāvan niyatam aśubhā bhāvanā yāti vṛddhiṁ
tāvat tāvat tanutaraśikho jāyate rāgavahniḥ ||

just so, every human being
who has been tormented incessantly
by terrible pain, powerless to stop it,
and then, somehow, for just a short time,
is freed from the agitation of birth and death,
develops a vulgar greed
for the tiniest bits of happiness,
the inborn unbearable fire of suffering
having died down for a short while. [87]

To exactly the same degree
that the notion of happiness arises
throughout the world,
the darkness of delusion grows thicker and thicker;
to exactly the same degree
that the notion of suffering arises throughout the world,
the darkness of delusion grows lighter and lighter. [88]

To exactly the same degree
that the contemplation of pleasant things
is practiced and developed,
the flames of the fire of passion
grow stronger and stronger;
to exactly the same degree
that the contemplation of unpleasant things
continuously increases,
the flames of the fire of passion
grow weaker and weaker. [89]

~90~

durgandhipūtivikṛtair aravindam indum
indīvaraṁ ca tulayanti yad aṅganāṅgaiḥ |
tasyānṛtasya phalam ugram idaṁ kavīnāṁ
tāsv eva garbhanilayaṁ yad amī viśanti | |

~91~

kāsau gatir jagati yā śataśo na yātā
kiṁ tat sukhaṁ yad asakṛn na purānubhūtam |
kās tāḥ śriyaś capalacāmaracāruhāsāḥ
prāptā na yās tad api vardhata eva rāgaḥ | |

~92~

nadyo na tā na vihṛtaṁ pulineṣu yāsāṁ
sthānaṁ na taj jagati yatra kṛto na vāsaḥ |
vyomno 'pi tan na padam asti na yatra yātaṁ
duṣpūraṇas tad api vardhata eva rāgaḥ | |

Such is the terrible fruit of the lies of the poets:
Those who wrongly compare an aravinda lotus,
the moon, and an indīvara lotus
to the bodies of women—
which are ugly with stinking secretions—
enter the dwelling place of the womb
in these very bodies. [90]

What form and manner of existence is there
that the soul has not already lived through
in this world a hundred times before?
And what sort of happiness is there
that has not been enjoyed
on countless previous occasions?
What sort of goddesses of happiness are those,
a sweet smile on their lips,
fanned by fans made of yak-tails,
that one has not beheld many a time before?
And yet despite all this,
human desire continues to grow! [91]

There are no rivers on whose banks
we have not already enjoyed ourselves;
there is no place on earth where we have not already dwelt;
there is no rank even in heaven
that we have not already attained.
And yet, despite all this,
human desire, so difficult to fulfill, continues to grow. [92]

~93~

duḥkhaṁ na tad yad asakṛn na purānubhūtaṁ
kāmā na te jagati yair iha tṛptir āsīt |
sattvo na so 'sti jaṭhare śayitaṁ na yasya
saṁsāriṇas tad api nāsti kathaṁ virāgaḥ ||

~94~

atyāyate jagati janmaparigrahe 'smin
duḥkhe sukhe ca bahuśaḥ parivartamānaḥ |
nāsau jano jagati yo na babhūva bandhur
dveṣoragas tad api tiṣṭhati bhīmabhogaḥ ||

~95~

yaiḥ sārdham etya hasitaṁ lalitaṁ pragītam
ekatra pītam aśitaṁ ca kṛtāś ca goṣṭhyaḥ |
kālakrameṇa gamitāḥ *kati ke 'pi ramyā
nītāḥ samāś ca viṣamāś ca daśāḥ kathaṁ cit ||

There is no suffering
that we have not experienced many times before;
there are no objects of desire
that have ever satisfied us here on earth;
there is no being
in whose womb we have not already dwelt.
How is it possible that despite all this,
beings in samsara have not freed themselves
from passionate attachment? [93]

There is no one on earth who,
revolving many times
through happiness and suffering
in this very extensive world where we take rebirth,
has not been our relative;
and yet the snake of hatred
continues to raise its dreadful hood! [94]

Of those with whom
we used to laugh, play, sing,
drink, eat, and converse
in company with one another,
many who were dear to us
have, over time, been forced to depart,
and were then somehow led
into good and bad conditions. [95]

~96~

tān ājavaṁjavavivartanadṛṣṭanaṣṭān
āvartamadhyapatitān iva vīkṣamāṇaḥ |
saṁsārasāgaragatān apahāya bandhūn
ekaḥ prayāti yadi nāsti tataḥ kṛtaghnaḥ | |

~97~

aṅkasthitena śiśunā vivaśena yāsāṁ
pītaḥ payodhararasaḥ praṇayānuyātaḥ |
tā vatsalāḥ pracuradurlalitaikabhājaḥ
ko nāma dasyur api hātum ihotsaheta | |

~98~

yāsāṁ sthito 'yam udare 'pi kṛtāvakāśo
yāḥ snehaviklavadhiyaḥ ślatham enam ūhuḥ |
tā duḥkhitā aśaraṇāḥ kṛpaṇā vihāya
ko nāma śatrur api gantum ihotsaheta | |

If we were to see our dear ones
fallen into the ocean of samsara
as if into a whirlpool,
swiftly whirling around,
emerging, and then again disappearing
in the cycles of birth and death,
and if we were to ignore them and go away alone—
how could there be anyone more shameless? [96]

Who on earth, even the lowest of the low,
could force himself to abandon
those beings who were once his mother,
whose milk,
joined with their affectionate love,
he drank as a helpless infant on their lap,
and who sustained their tender love,
although they received from him in return
nothing but his many naughty pranks? [97]

Who on earth, even an enemy,
could possibly bear
to go away and leave behind
those suffering, unprotected, miserable beings
in whose womb he found an occasion to stay,
and who bore him when he was weak,
their hearts overcome with love? [98]

~99~

vikīrṇe duḥkhaughair jagati vivaśe 'sminn aśaraṇe
parārthe yad duḥkhaṁ tad iha sukham āhuḥ supuruṣāḥ ।
kṣaṇaṁ kṣuttṛṣṇoṣṇaśramavigamaramyānanarucaṁ
paraṁ kṛtvā teṣām yad iha ka ivāsya pratisamaḥ ॥

~100~

⟨na yānaiḥ⟩ (kṣemair) naiva ca nṛpatilakṣmīparikarair
na dārair nāpatyair na surabhavane nāsuragatau ।
kathaṁ cit *sā prāpyā* viṣayasukha⟨sa⟩ṁbhogaparamair
labhante yā⟨ṁ⟩ prīti⟨ṁ⟩ parahitasukhādhānaniratāḥ ॥

~101~

svayaṁ ghāsagrāsaṁ paśur api karoty eva sulabhaṁ
yadṛcchālabdhaṁ vā pibati salilaṁ gāḍhatṛṣitaḥ ।
parasyārthaṁ kartuṁ yad iha puruṣo 'yaṁ prayatate
tad asya svaṁ tejaḥ sukham idam aho pauruṣam idam ॥

The suffering
experienced for the benefit of others
in this helpless and unprotected world
swept by squalls of sorrow
is called happiness by the good men of this world.
For what could match the happiness they feel
in having brought to light, even if only briefly,
the beauty of another's face,
its loveliness revealed when freed from
hunger, thirst, heat, and weariness? [99]

Not by comfortable vehicles,
and not by the luxury of royal status,
not by wives or children, not in the palace of the gods,
or in the state of existence as a demigod—
not by any of these means
can those for whom enjoyment of the objects of the senses
is the greatest good attain, even through their greatest
efforts, a happiness that parallels the joy of those
who devote themselves to creating happiness
and welfare for others. [100]

By and for themselves, even the beasts of the field
eat that grass which is easy to find
or drink water which happens to be at hand
when plagued by a strong thirst.
The specific dignity of man, on the other hand,
consists in this: that he is able to care
about the welfare of others.
Yes, this alone is true happiness and true humanity! [101]

~102~

yad ālokaṁ kurvan bhramati ravir aśrāntaturagaḥ
sadā lokaṁ dhatte yad agaṇitabhārā vasumatī ǀ
na sa svārthaḥ kaś cit prakṛtir iyam e<ṣai>va mahatāṁ
yad ete lokānāṁ hitasukharasaikāntarasikāḥ ǀ ǀ

~103~

avidyādhūmrāndhabhramaparigataṁ vyākulagati
pradīpte duḥkhāgnau patitam avaśaṁ vīkṣya bhuvanam ǀ
sphuradvahnijvālāpramathitaśiroveṣṭananibhā
yatante ye trātuṁ ta iha puruṣās te sukṛtinaḥ ǀ ǀ

~104~

avīciṁ gāhante hutavahaśikhāpūritam api
prasarpadromāñcā himanikaracandrāṁśuśiśiram ǀ
parārthe ⟨svārthe tu⟩ sphuṭanalinahāsāpi nalinī
karoty eṣāṁ tāpaṁ hutavahaśikhāsaṁhatir iva ǀ ǀ

The sun, drawn by tireless steeds,
crosses the heavens, giving light to man,
and the "Bearer of Treasures," this earth,
constantly bears its burden of human beings,
without counting their numbers. In all of this
there is not a scintilla of selfishness:
It is precisely the nature of great men
that their sole and distinguishing
trait of character is this desire
for the benefit and happiness of other human beings. [102]

Those who see that the beings of the world—
erring in the smoky darkness of ignorance
and completely bewildered in their course—
have helplessly fallen into the blazing fire of suffering,
and then become eager to save them,
resemble firefighters
whose headbands are scorched by the quickening flames:
They are the true human beings in this world;
they are virtuous and wise. [103]

For the sake of others, the hair on their bodies
quivering with joy, they enter even the Avīci hell,
which is as cold as masses of snow
or the rays of the moon, although it is full of fiery flames.
Anything enjoyed for their own sake, however,
even a lotus pond adorned with the laughter
of lotuses in full bloom,
arouses in them a feeling of painful heat
like a blazing bonfire. [104]

~105~

parahitakaraṇāya baddhakakṣāḥ
sukham asipattravane vasanti santaḥ |
na punar amarasundarīsahāyāḥ
kṣaṇam api nandanakānane ramante ||

~106~

aśaraṇajanataraṇāya tīrṇāḥ
punar api vaitaraṇīṁ taranti dhīrāḥ |
na tu gaganasarittaraṅgabhaṅga-
vyatikarasaṅgasukhaṁ svayaṁ bhajante ||

~107~

iti sucaritaratnaṁ bhūṣaṇaṁ bhūṣaṇānāṁ
śivam amṛtam udāraṁ bhāsuraṁ bhāsurāṇām |
asulabham akṛtajñair nandanaṁ nandanānāṁ
bhaja śamasukhahetuṁ maṅgalaṁ maṅgalānām ||

The good, intent on creating
the welfare of others,
live happily in the forest
with sword-like leaves,
but not a single moment
do they enjoy in the heavenly Nandana grove
in the company of beautiful goddesses. [105]

The wise, who are resolved
to protect helpless beings,
will cross Vaitaraṇī,
the river of hell, again and again,
although they have crossed it already.
But not once will they enjoy for themselves
the pleasure of contact
with the sparkling waves
of the heavenly river Gaṅgā. [106]

Therefore you should honor him
who is the jewel of good conduct,
the ornament of ornaments,
the noble and wholesome nectar of tranquility,
the most radiant of radiant beings,
not easy for the ungrateful to attain,
the most delightful of all that is gladdening,
the source of the bliss of tranquility,
the most auspicious of all that is auspicious. [107]

~108~

sugatavacanapuṣpaṁ sarvadā sevanīyaṁ
phalati phalam udāraṁ puṣpam eva drumāṇām |
sugatavacanapuṣpād artharāśir niṣevyo
madhuni madhukarāṇāṁ paśya vāñchāprakarṣam ||

~109~

visṛja viṣayān *nityākīrṇān kṣaṇavyayasaṅgino
bhaja śamasukhaṁ *śā⟨ntye⟩kāntaṁ kṛtāntabhayojjhitam |
vikira timiraṁ mohavyājaṁ vimokṣapathārgalaṁ
na khalu suciraṁ nidrāyante sadaśvakiśorakāḥ ||

~110~

vinayavisaro vīryaskandhaḥ kṣamādamapallavaḥ
śamathakusumaḥ prajñāśākhaḥ pradānaghanacchadaḥ |
praṇidhiśikharaḥ śīlacchāyaḥ praśāntiphalaprado
⟨bhava⟩ bhavamarau tāpārtānāṁ tvam ekamahādrumaḥ ||

The flower of the Buddha's word
is always to be revered;
only the blossoms on those trees bring forth a noble fruit.
The richness of meaning
produced from the flower of the Buddha's word
is also to be revered—
observe the intense desire for honey among the bees! [108]

Abandon the objects of the senses,
which constantly spread out before you
yet perish in the next instant.
Solely devoted to peacefulness,
yearn for the bliss of tranquility,
devoid of the threat of the Lord of Death.
Dispel the darkness of delusion,
which bolts the door to salvation,
for the colts of noble horses do not sleep for very long. [109]

In the desert of existence, may you become—
for those afflicted by the heat of sorrow—
a unique tall tree
whose height is discipline,
whose trunk is striving,
whose buds are forbearance and self-restraint,
whose flowers are calmness,
whose branches are wisdom,
whose canopy of leaves is charity;
whose top is the vow, whose shadow is morality,
and which offers tranquility as its fruit! [110]

~111~

bahujanahito mābhairvādapradānamahāsvaraḥ
pṛthutarayaśodhārāsāraḥ kṛpānilacoditaḥ |
praśamitarajāḥ śīlacchāyāvibhūṣitabhūtalo
bhava bhavamarau tāpārtānāṁ tvam ekamahāghanaḥ ||

~112~

prakaṭavipulaḥ prahvāgādhaḥ prasannatarāśayaḥ
satataśiśiro jālavyāla*pramāda*vivarjitaḥ |
prakṛtisubhagas tṛṣṇācchedo vimardabharakṣamo
bhava bhavamarau tāpārtānāṁ tvam ekamahāhradaḥ ||

In the desert of existence, may you become—
for those afflicted by the heat of sorrow—
a unique huge rain cloud
that benefits many beings,
which produces great thunderous sound
while emitting the words, "Have no fear,"
which pours down torrents of renown,
which is driven by the wind of compassion,
which causes the dust of passion to settle,
and which adorns the earth
with its shadow of morality! [111]

In the desert of existence, may you become—
for those afflicted by the heat of sorrow—
a unique great lake,
clear and spacious,
as gently sloping and deep
as you are gently bowing down and profound,
as crystal clear a receptacle
as your mental dispositions are perfectly calm,
always cool,
as free from the danger of poisonous water-snakes
as you are free of negligence toward the serpent of greed,
pleasant and fortunate by its very nature,
a lake that ends the thirst of craving,
and is able to bear the pounding waves of samsara! [112]

~113~

iti nigadatā *puṇyaṁ ⟨svalpaṁ⟩ mayā yad upārjitaṁ*
sugatacarite kṛtvā śraddhām anena jano 'khilaḥ |
satatasukhito ramyābhogaḥ samṛddhamanorathaḥ
parahitarataḥ sarvajñattvaṁ prayātu tataḥ śanaiḥ ||

~114~

karatalasamāḥ spaṣṭālokāḥ praśāntakṛśānavaḥ
sthalakamali⟨nī⟩pattracchannā bisāṅkuradanturāḥ |
śucisurabhayaḥ phullāmbhojair vibhūṣitabhūmayo
dadhatu narakāḥ sphītāṁ śobhāṁ saśīkaravāyavaḥ ||

~115~

*vijitavirutā mārānīkāḥ kṛtābhayaghoṣaṇā
gaganasalilakrīḍāramyāḥ sametanarāmarāḥ |
jananamaraṇakleśāyāsaprabandhavighātino
diśi diśi sadā buddhotpādā bhavantu samīhitāḥ ||

Through the small merit that I have acquired
in composing these stanzas,
may all mankind develop faith
in the life and acts of the Sugata, Lord Buddha,
and may they then gradually
proceed to the state of omniscience,
always happy, supplied with a wealth of enjoyments,
their wishes fulfilled, devoted to the welfare of others! [113]

May thereby the hells display abundant beauty!
May they be made as even as the palm of the hand;
may they be filled with bright splendor,
their fires extinguished.
May they be covered with the leaves of
sthalakamalinī lotuses,
and may many lotus sprouts spring forth.
Permeated with pure fragrance,
may their floors be adorned with lotuses in full bloom.
May they be pervaded by pleasantly cool winds. [114]

May thereby the armies of Māra,
bitterly crying after their defeat,
be granted the proclamation of safety.
May the gods together with human beings
be gladdened by sporting in the heavenly waters.
And may the Buddhas,
who conquer the endless succession
of birth, death, defilements, and toil,
appear in answer to prayers, always and everywhere! [115]

~116~

bhavatu jagatāṁ dharmāmodaḥ prabandhamahotsavaḥ
suciraguṇitā mṛtyor vandhyā bhavantu manorathāḥ |
munijanakathāgoṣṭhībandhaiḥ śamāmṛtavarṣibhiḥ
śiśirasubhagaś candrālokaḥ prayātu kṛtārthatām ||

|| iti śiṣyalekhanāmadharmakāvyaṁ samāptam ||

|| kṛtir ācāryacandragomipādasya ||

May all living beings rejoice
in hearing the holy Dharma—
may it provide for them the joy and delight
of a festival never-ending!
May the desires of the Lord of Death,
which have long waxed ever stronger,
be without fruit and of no avail!
May the radiance of the moon,
as well as that of Candragomin,
which is cool and rich in blessings
through its display of words and tales of holy sages,
showering down the nectar of tranquility,
bring success! [116]

Herewith is completed the Dharma poem entitled,
"The Letter to a Disciple,"
composed by the venerable teacher
Candragomin.

Notes

Notes to Letter to the Great King Kaniṣka

Stanza 2 The expression nye mgon is difficult. The *Zang-Han Dacidian* (ZHD) offers the following two explanations: brtse sems kyis rogs ram byed pa / (p. 959), "to help with a loving mind" and phru gu rnams la bsam blo dang 'tsho ba sogs gang ci'i nye mgon byed pa / (p. 959), "to care for children and to help all living beings." Since Mātṛceṭa was an old man when he wrote this letter, it is not unlikely that he expresses some paternal feeling toward the young king Kaniṣka. Another possibility would be to regard mgon as a vocative, "O Protector," but this would be a very unusual and ambiguous placement, and is therefore much less likely.

Stanza 3 The dictionaries give "shameless, impudent, impertinent" as the meaning of spyi brtol. The Tibetan translation of stanza 9 of Mātṛceṭa's "Hymn in 150 Stanzas" (Śatapañcāśatka), however, uses it as an equivalent of Skt. mukhara, "talkative, loquacious." The content of that stanza is very similar to this one: The virtues of the Buddha [make] Mātṛceṭa talkative. I have therefore translated spyi brtol here as "loquacious."

Stanza 4 The expression thugs thub par is difficult to translate and to construe. ZHD explains thugs thub tu spyad pa as rang dbang du longs spyad pa (p. 1166); Sarat Chandra Das offers the following English translation of this expression: "to work with self-reliance, being confident of one's own abilities (A. 75)" (p. 579b). I follow his interpretation.

Stanza 7 Nyams smad, literally "to lower with regard to strength," is an equivalent of Skt. (pari)karśay, "to emaciate, to diminish." See stanza 30 of the "Hymn in 150 Stanzas."

Stanza 9 The second line literally means: "(who are) the very essence of vast compassion." This makes good sense. However, I suspect that the underlying Sanskrit compound *udāra-karuṇātmānaḥ was to be understood as an 'exocentric' or Bahuvrīhi compound: "(the kings and ministers) whose hearts (ātman) are filled with vast compassion." Since this type of Bahuvrīhi compound ending in ātman is very common in Sanskrit, I translate accordingly.

Stanza 11 The Tibetan text literally means, "Therefore, so long as you have not quickly (myur du) passed beyond that stage (described in the preceding stanza) . . . ." Since "quickly" sounds too strong, I have replaced it with the weaker "yet."

Stanza 12 Chos kyi bstan bcos renders here Skt. dharmaśāstra, "code of law," not "religious books," as the Tibetan might suggest.

Stanza 13 Longs pa is, according to ZHD (p. 2818), a word belonging to the "old language" (rnying skad) that means "pride, arrogance" (rgyags). "Characterized by" is a free translation of "where the state (dngos po) of . . . is present (da ltar byung ba)."

Stanza 18 The placement of the concessive particle yang after yul na—literally "not even in your country"—implies the continuation, "much less admitting them to your court."

Stanza 19 The Tibetan text repeats "particular merits" (khyad par) in the fourth line, where I have rendered it as "qualities."

Stanza 21 'O byams pa is, according to ZHD (p. 2526), equivalent to gces par bya ba, "to hold dear, to love, to esteem."

Stanza 22 Bas means "only, nothing but." See the examples referred to in Lokesh Chandra's *Tibetan-Sanskrit Dictionary* (LC), such as: de ni skye bo'i bka' mchid 'ba' zhig tu bas so = Skt. kevalaṁ tv ayaṁ janapravāda iti, "this is nothing but common gossip," where it is more or less a synonym of zad. See also the examples quoted in ZHD under bas pa (p. 1826).

Stanza 25 For gnang chen, see the dictionary of Chos-grags (CG): **gnang chen** / dgongs pa'i gnang ba chen po, "a great bestower of wished-for things." gNang ba usually renders Skt. adhivāsana, "endurance, consent," or anujñāna, "permission, consent."

As for phan par smra ba and mi phan smra ba, they seem to go back to Skt. hitavādin and ahitavādin, "he who gives useful advice" and "he who gives harmful advice," rather than to Skt. hitavacana and ahitavacana, "useful speech, advice" and "harmful speech, advice."

Stanza 26 In its transmitted form the first half of the stanza is somewhat difficult to understand. Literally the received text means: "As if frightened of the king of geese and of water in a crystal clear lake." This can hardly be correct. I suspect that 'jigs is to be emended as 'jig; see the entry in Das, p. 423: "**chus 'jig pa**, [Skt.] apaḥ-saṁvarttanā [sic] destruction or devastation from water." This entry is taken from Mahāvyutpatti 8286: apsaṁvartanī = chus 'jig(s) pa, a fact that proves two things: chus 'jig pa is not an ad-hoc invention, and it had a very specific meaning to the compilers of the Mahāvyutpatti. The predicate of the first half of the stanza is to be supplied from its second half.

The underlying Skt. equivalents of bsnyen sla and bsnyen dka' most likely were susevya and duḥṣevya. The root sev has the two meanings "to attend, to adhere to, to approach" and "to worship." Mātṛceṭa plays here with the two meanings of sev.

Stanza 28 The interpretation of spyod pa as "ordinary pursuits" and spyod lam as "higher pursuits" is highly tentative.

Stanza 29 I regard bzang po, "good," as vocative. As an attribute of dpal, "good luck, welfare," it would require the genitive particle.

Stanza 30 bZham seems to be a cognate of 'jam po, "mild, soft." See G, p. 745: **gzham pa** / 'jam por bya ba'i don, and ZHD, p. 2435: **bzhams pa** / bzhams po dang 'dra / and **bzhams po** / 'jam po / . . . tshig bzhams pos slob gso byas pa /.

An alternative interpretation of dran dang bral bas 'dod pa dbye is also possible: "Break your desires by not thinking about them." Chad pas gcad (gcod) pa is a well-attested equivalent of Skt. nigraha, "checking; suppression; imprisonment; punishment; rebuke, blame."

Stanza 31 Log pas most likely renders Skt. mithyā, "wrongly, improperly, deceitfully."

Stanzas 33 and 34 These two stanzas contain some difficult words and expressions. The first is gnang chen, which we have already come across in stanza 25b. I tentatively translate "great with regard to the power to bestow" as "benefactor;" mi gnang, as the antonym of gnang chen, then has to mean "one who has nothing to give, a poor person."

The second difficult expression is smos 'dris, obviously an alternative reading of smos 'drin (this is the reading of CD!), which CG (p. 666) explains as yun ring du 'dris pa'i grogs po, "a friend of old acquaintance;" likewise ZHD, p. 2176: 'dris che ba'i grogs, "a closely acquainted friend." Assuming that this meaning is by and large correct, then the following mi shes pa, the reading of the blockprints, cannot be correct, but has to be emended as mi bshes pa, "not related, not acquainted." This would be a suitable antonym of smos 'drin, as required by the structure of the stanza.

The last difficult or at least ambiguous expression is tha snyad. Usually it renders Skt. vyavahāra in all its meanings, such as "designation, conventional truth, behavior, practice, business, transaction, lawsuit," and so on. It is difficult to decide which of these meanings is most appropriate in this context. Moreover, the construction of the last two lines of stanza 34 is not quite clear. Hence my translation is only tentative.

Stanza 35 Chos, Skt. dharma, here means "law" and "law, custom of one's caste."

Stanza 38 In this stanza gzhung lugs does not mean "government." It renders Skt. mata, "thought, opinion, belief, view; doctrine, creed, tenet, principle."

Stanza 40 The repetition of skye dgu sounds somewhat strange. I assume that Matṛceṭa used the same word (Skt. jana) in two different ways, one in apposition to the other.

rJes su 'brang ba frequently renders Skt. anusāra, "going after, following; conformity to, accordance with; custom, usage, established practice." The latter meaning seems quite suitable here.

Stanza 47 Byang grol renders Skt. apavarga, "completion, fulfillment; absolution, final beatitude, liberation." It frequently occurs in the stock phrase svargāpavarga, "heaven and liberation." Byang, as in byang chub, is a derivative of 'byang ba, "to become clean, purified." Hence the literal meaning of byang grol is "purified and liberated."

Mi mnyam mnyam pa'i, a well-attested canonical expression, renders the Skt. compound asama-sama, "not having an equal peer (match), unequaled." Monier Williams records an example from the Lalitavistara in his dictionary.

bSod nams las byung literally means "resulting from (religious) merit." Here, however, we expect something like "producing religious merit." Perhaps an ambiguous Skt. compound like *udbhūtapuṇya, which can mean both "religious merit that has arisen" and "that by which religious merit has come into being," accounts for the Tibetan wording.

Stanza 48 If we accepted the reading bsten pas (N_2Q_2), the translation would be : "through adhering to the holy Dharma."

Stanza 50 Legs su smon pa means, according to Das, p. 1219, "benediction, blessing."

Stanza 52 Even if one managed not to die, it would not help, since death will come anyway in the painful conflagration at the end of the eon.

I am not sure whether 'jig rten kun 'bar na, "when the world is completely consumed by fire," indeed alludes to the all-consuming fire at the end of an eon. Since 'jig rten goes back to Skt. loka, "world, inhabitant of the world, being," the expression could also hint at the cremation of a dead person.

Stanza 55 bGyi ba, "what should be done, proper, appropriate, right." Likewise, mi bgyi ba means "what should not be done, improper, inappropriate, wrong." The meaning of the second half of the stanza is simply: If one always does only the right things, one will automatically avoid doing anything wrong.

Stanza 57 The "direction" is obviously that toward rebirth.

Stanza 58 bZhes par is probably a variant spelling of bzhed par (= gsungs pa, Das), "to speak, to say."

Stanza 65 Log ltung ba, "fallen down, sinful," seems to mean "fallen into a lower form of existence."

Stanza 68 rGyu mthun pa is a Buddhist technical term. It renders Skt. upaniṣad, "cause, basis;" see the *Buddhist Hybrid Sanskrit Dictionary*, s.v. It also occurs in Mātṛceṭa's hymn, "Praise of the Praiseworthy" (Varṇārhavarṇa) 8.10.

Stanza 69 Sug las is, according to CG (p. 906), a synonym of phyag las, "deed."

Stanza 70 bShugs (or bshug CD_1, shugs D_2) is not quite clear to me. It has to be a verb. According to Das, shugs is an equivalent of bslang ba, "to raise, erect;" however, it also means "to sell; to barter, exchange." bZhengs, "to raise, erect," is also difficult.

Stanza 72 I interpret bzhin as "nature," as if it were rang bzhin. However, it could also be the noun functioning as formative of the present participle: sreg bzhin (pa), "burning."

Stanza 79 The expression thugs tshod cannot be found in the dictionaries available to me. I take it as an equivalent of thugs dgongs.

Grang is an old modal auxiliary meaning "might, should." It can also be found in the "Hymn in 150 Stanzas" 151d, in the "Praise of the Praiseworthy" 7.21d and 11.31d, and in the Bodhicaryāvatāra 6.84d. The Skt. original has an optative, a future of the verb arhati, "shall, should."

Stanza 80 For the meaning of co nas bzung ste, see ZHD s.v. co (p. 733), where it is explained as a word belonging to the old language [rnying] and meaning mgo, "head."

Stanza 82 Khyad du 'gums mdzad na is, of course, the respectful form of khyad du gsod pa, "to despise."

Stanza 83 Or: "act like the full moon, O king!" if we adopt the reading zla ba nya pa instead of zla ba zla ba.

Stanza 84 The Golden Mountain is Mount Meru, the axis of our world system in Buddhist cosmology.

Stanza 85 We regard snying (po) as the translation of Skt. garbha, "womb; interior," which at the end of a compound usually means "having in its interior, full of, filled with, containing."

For rgya la, brgya la or brgya lam na "(once) in a hundred, occasionally, rarely" see, for example, Bodhicaryāvatāra 1.5. It usually renders Skt. kadā cit, "at some time, occasionally." See also ZHD s.v. rgya la (p. 538), where it is explained as nam zhig gam / lan 'ga', "at some time, occasionally." I do not think that brgya here has its ordinary meaning of "one hundred," although the whole expression legs spyad brgya la chags phyir is ambiguous, because chags pa can mean "to be begotten, produced" or "to love, to be attached, to cling to." My translation is therefore only tentative.

Notes to Letter to a Disciple

Stanzas 1–8 The first eight stanzas of the poem form a coherent construction of a series of relative clauses that are resolved only in the last line of verse 8:

Homage to Him who is linked to a great lake of human beings,
the followers and recipients of His teaching!

The reader is deliberately kept in protracted suspense, imagining the resolution, but unsure when and how it will occur. In English, the syntax of the lengthy, multiple relative clauses becomes confusing, so I have changed the construction to a series of sentences, all of which are aimed at the concluding line of stanza 8.

Stanzas 1 through 8 offer praise to the Buddha (1–5), his teaching, the Holy Dharma (6–7), and the Sangha of his followers (8). The brief description of the Buddha's followers is deliberately given in very general terms that include both monks and lay people.

Stanza 1 It is no coincidence that the first stanza mentions the moon, Skt. candra, which is also the name of the author of the poem, Candragomin, gomin being an honorary title.

Candragomin's poem is particularly rich in the figure of speech called "concatenation," the deliberate repetition of the same word within a few lines or stanzas. Line d of the first stanza contains the word paṅkaja, "mud-born," one of the numerous Sanskrit words for "lotus." It occurs again in line b of stanza 4.

According to Prajñākaramati, author of the commentary Śiṣyalekhavṛtti, this stanza illustrates the "perfect cause" (rgyu phun sum tshogs pa, Skt. hetusaṁpad), that is, of Śākyamuni's Buddhahood.

Stanza 2 In this comparison of the Buddha to the wish-fulfilling gem (cintāmaṇi), the attributes used to describe the Buddha, as required by the laws of Sanskrit poetics, also apply to the wish-fulfilling gem.

The word paramādbhuta, "exceedingly wonderful," in line a occurs again in line d of stanza 10, although with a rather negative connotation, as an attribute of moha, "delusion." The two words rasa, "flavor," and eka, "unique," in line d are used again, in reverse order, in line b of stanza 7, while parārtha, "welfare of others," reappears in line a of stanza 4.

According to Prajñākaramati, this stanza illustrates the "perfect fruit" ('bras bu phun sum tshogs pa, Skt. phalasaṁpad). He establishes an interesting connection between the three attributes "beautiful" (saubhāgya), "pleasing" (hṛdya), and "wonderful" (adbhuta) and various triads of Buddhist teachings, such as the doctrine of the three Kāyas:

Beautiful (saubhāgya)	Nirmāṇakāya	Mind (manas)
Pleasing (hṛdya)	Saṁbhogakāya	Speech (vāc)
Wonderful (adbhuta)	Dharmakāya	Body (kāya)

This connection is clearly established by the use of vapus, "body, shape," in line a.

Stanza 3 While worldly people understand the terms "happiness" (sukha) and "sorrow" (duḥkha) to mean "one's own happiness" and "one's own sorrow," to the Buddha they mean "the happiness of others" and "the sorrow of others." The diction of the stanza is very condensed and at the same time impressive because of the alliteration in sukhena sukhī, duḥkhena duḥkham, and para . . . paramaṁ pareṣām.

According to Prajñākaramati, this stanza illustrates the "perfect compassion" (snying rje phun sum tshogs pa, Skt. karuṇāsaṁpad) of the Buddha.

Stanza 4 The general description of the Buddha's altruistic mind is illustrated by an allusion to an act of self-sacrifice during one of his previous existences. As Prajñākaramati points out, the stanza refers to the account of the Buddha's past life as King Candraprabha, which runs as follows:

Once the Bodhisattva was born into a royal family and because of the beauty of his face, was named Candraprabha, "Possessing the Splendor of the Moon." When he became king, he promised to fulfill the wishes of every supplicant. One day a vicious brahmin by the name of Raudrākṣa appeared and demanded the king's head. Despite his ministers' desperate attempts to save his life, Candraprabha himself took Raudrākṣa to a lonely spot in the royal park and requested the brahmin to behead him. When the brahmin became afraid to commit this crime, Candraprabha cut off his own head. Even at the moment of dying, the king's lotus-like eyes looked full of love at the brahmin who had caused his death.

Numerous versions of this account in Buddhist literature have been described by the Japanese scholar Hisashi Matsumura in his unpublished dissertation, "Four Avadānas From the Gilgit Manuscript" (Canberra, 1980), lxxii-lxxvi, and by Jens-Uwe Hartmann in his paper, "Notes on the Gilgit Manuscript of the Candraprabhāvadāna," *Journal of the Nepal Research Centre*, vol. 4 Humanities (1980), 251–66.

The white parasol mentioned in the second half of the stanza symbolizes the power and glory of kingship.

According to Prajñākaramati, this stanza illustrates the "perfect deeds" (phrin las phun sum tshogs pa, Skt. karmasaṁpad) of the Buddha.

Stanza 5 As the play on words in this comparison—in which all the attributes of the Buddha also apply to the full moon—cannot be fully maintained in a single translation of the stanza, I have translated it twice, a common practice in rendering double meanings from Sanskrit. Prajñākaramati takes great pains to explain all the words of the stanza which have two meanings (see chart on the following page). The eighth example points to

The Moon	The Buddha
1. greatly waxes from the day of the new moon	greatly increases in the ten spheres of action
2. has a brilliant radiance	is brilliant (in all branches of knowledge)
3. becomes full	reaches perfection (in Buddhahood)
4. dispels darkness	dispels the darkness of sin and ignorance
5. wanders alone	is unique (in one Buddhahood)
6. is pleasant	is pleasant
7. is wholesome to behold	is devoted to the benefit of the world
8. cools the body	cools the three fires of those about to become disciples
9. rises (in the sky)	appears (in the world)

a variant whose meaning was "cooling," which is also found in the Tibetan version of the Śiṣyalekha. Vairocanarakṣita's Ṭippaṇa, however, reads prakāśam, "illuminating" (rab tu gsal ba), which supports the Sanskrit manuscript.

According to Prajñākaramati, this stanza illustrates the "perfect virtues" (yon tan phun sum tshogs pa, Skt. guṇasaṁpad) of the Buddha.

Stanza 6 The illuminating property of the Buddha's teaching is compared to that of the jewels which adorn the hoods of the Nāgas, semi-divine, serpent-like beings who live in the netherworld. Prajñākaramati explains "excellent jewels" (uttamaratna) as "cat's eyes gem" (vaiḍūrya). Five of their properties are described in the stanza: They are good (śubha), unbroken (akhaṇḍa), and pure (viśuddha); they are the head-ornaments of the Nāgas (cūḍāvibhūṣaṇa); and they dispel the darkness of the netherworld (pātālagarbhanilayattimiraṁ pramārṣṭi). With regard to the Buddha's teaching, he gives a more detailed interpretation: "blissful" (śubha) alludes to concentration (samādhi); "untainted" (akhaṇḍa) to morality (śīla); "immaculate" (viśuddha) to wisdom (prajñā); "broad" (uru) to the three lineages (Śrāvaka, Pratyekabuddha, Bodhisattva); "worn" (ūḍha) to oral instruction; "pervading the world" (pātālagarbhanilayat) to the hearts of those practicing the nine forms of contemplation; and "darkness" (timira) to the two forms of ignorance.

Stanza 7 This stanza contains one internal concatenation—"uniform taste/unique flavor" (ekarasa) and "many tastes/ many flavors" (anekarasa)—as well as two external concatenations: "driving away" (apahāri) is repeated in 9a, and pātra recurs in 8a.

Stanza 8 This stanza poses a certain grammatical problem because its last line is lost. As mentioned in the notes to stanzas 1–8, this very line resolves the antecedent relative clauses of stanzas 1 through 8c. It is not at all difficult to translate the corresponding line of the Tibetan version, mtsho chen mi yi gzugs can de la phyag 'tshal lo, which at first sight seems to mean: "Homage to that great lake which has the form of human beings!" We can even retranslate this line into Sanskrit as *tasmai namaḥ puruṣarūpamahāhradāya (in the vasantatilaka meter of the preceding three lines). This text, however, would refer to the followers of the Buddha, not to the Buddha himself. How then could we connect this line with the seven preceding relative clauses, all of which clearly refer to the Buddha: yasya 1b, yasya 2b, yaḥ 3a, yasya 4a, yena 5d, yac 6b, and yo 7a?

There is a way out of this dilemma offered by the nature of Sanskrit compounds. It is possible to analyse puruṣarūpamahāhradāya in a twofold way: as a so-called determinative compound (karmadhāraya), "a 'man-shaped' great lake" (here lake is determined by "great" and "man-shaped") and as a possessive or exocentric compound (bahuvrīhi), "(he) who has a 'man-shaped' great lake" (in this case the referent "he who has" is outside the compound, hence the term "exocentric"). Yeṣu in 8b then has to be understood as yeṣu puruṣeṣu, "in which human beings," referring to puruṣarūpamahāhrada.

It has to be admitted that the syntactical structure of this relative pronoun is somewhat different from that of the preceding pronouns, as it does not refer to the whole expression tasmai . . . puruṣarūpamahāhradāya, but just to one part of the compound. Yet it is the only possibility of forming a coherent construction from lines 1a to 8d, and it is certainly inappropriate to assume that an author like Candragomin, a poet and grammarian of the highest order, neglected the construction of the preceding stanzas when he reached stanza 8. In this connection it might not be out of place to point to stanza 112, in which the Buddha is compared to a large pond (mahāhrada).

Since the wording of the Sanskrit original as proposed above is ambiguous, its correct interpretation requiring some reflection, we cannot exclude the possibility that the Tibetan translators intended to maintain the ambiguity of the original in their translation and therefore deliberately chose a word order that does not expressly exclude the second interpretation of the Sanskrit compound.

Prajñākaramati again devotes a detailed explanation to the simile used in this stanza, summarizing the properties shared by the ocean and the followers (see chart on the following page). Prajñākaramati further elaborates the meaning of the four dispositions of mind of the Sangha:

a) "broad disposition of mind" refers to the Four Immeasurables (apramāṇa): love (maitrī), compassion (karuṇā), joy (muditā), and equanimity (upekṣā);

Skt/Tib	The Great Ocean	The Sangha
pātra, snod	is the receptacle of rain water	is the receptacle for the virtues of the worthy
vistīrṇa, yangs	its size is vast	its mental disposition is vast
nimna, zab pa	it is deep	its mental disposition is deep
vimala, dri ma med pa	its water is clean	its mental disposition is immaculate
prakāśa, gsal ba	its bottom and surface are clearly visible	its mental disposition is clear
sarvaparimardasaha, khur kun bzod pa	it bears its burden* (e.g. ships)	it does not weary of helping others*
sarvajanopabhogya, skye bo kun gyis nye bar spyad bya	it can be used by everybody (e.g. bathing & drinking)	being part of it leads to heaven and renunciation
āśaya, gnas	animals (e.g. fish and turtles) stay in it	it has the four mental dispositions described above

*This is a very unusual interpretation of parimarda!

b) "deep disposition of mind" refers to the absence of a self (pudgala-nairātmya) and the non-existence of the constituents of the phenomenal world (dharma-nairātmya);

c) "immaculate disposition of mind" refers to being free of the following six defilements: deception (māyā, sgyu), guile (śāṭhya, g.yo), arrogance (mada, rgyags pa), envious rivalry (pradāśa, 'tshig pa), hatred (upanāha, khon 'dzin), and doing harm to others (heṭhana, rnam 'tshe);

d) "clear disposition of mind" refers to the lack of obscuration caused by the defilements.

According to Prajñākaramati, the stanza illustrates the "perfect disposition of mind" (bsam pa phun sum tshogs pa, Skt. āśayasaṁpad) and the "perfect connection" (sbyor ba phun sum tshogs pa, Skt. yoga° or yojanasaṁpad) between the Buddha and his disciples.

Stanza 9 With this stanza the main part of the Śiṣyalekha begins. Stanzas 9 and 10 immediately mention one of the central topics of the letter, the great danger of becoming an apostate—entering the Buddhist order and then leaving it. This topic is continued until stanza 18. See the introduction (p. liii), where the relevant portions of the two commentaries are translated.

In this stanza Candragomin effectively uses alliteration, the repetition of one letter, in a**m**ṛta, **m**araṇa and jan**m**a in line a, and **m**ohita, **m**oha, **m**ahā and **m**ada in line c. The term moha, "delusion," is used again in 10d.

Prajñākaramati states that the three verbs—"receive" (āpnuvanti), "drink" (pibanti), and "preserve" (dhārayanti)—successively hint at three sets of interpretations, as outlined in the chart on the following page.

Stanza 10 Only the enormously attractive and enticing power of delusion (moha) can account for the actions of an apostate. Otherwise why would anyone abandon the only eye and only light of the world? Prajñākaramati explains "eye" as the Buddha Dharma: "because it makes one see what is the way and what is not."

Stanza 11 Great is the reward, says Candragomin, if one determinedly sets out to climb the staircase which has enlightenment as its ultimate goal. But never turn back, because those

Receive	Drink	Preserve
by hearing	by thinking over	by contemplating
relating to morality (adhiśīla)	relating to mind (adhicitta)	relating to wisdom (adhiprajñā)
relating to the 3 joys	relating to the 3 joys	relating to the 3 joys
relating to the Hīnayāna	relating to the Mahāyāna	relating to the Vajrayāna

who do will inevitably end up at the very place from which they started. Prajñākaramati explains the high rank as "heaven" (mtho ris, Skt. svarga) and "liberation" (thar pa, Skt. apavarga), while the "original position or stage" is specified as the (eight) unfavorable conditions of rebirth (mi khom pa, Skt. akṣaṇa) from which it is impossible to attain enlightenment.

The present stanza is obviously influenced by verse 47 of Mātṛceṭa's Mahārājakaniṣkalekha:

For the sake of (gaining) the matchless ladder
that leads to heaven and liberation,
always gather together in the temples
the great works of art that merit produces.

Candragomin has embellished this stanza by using five derivations from the verbal root pad, "to go:" pada (thrice), in the three meanings of "basis," "step," and "foot;" paddhati, "way to go," and padavī, "path; rank." In lines c and d, *anuvartamānā, "continuing on and on," is contrasted with vivartamānāḥ, "turning back." Here I adopt *anuvartamāna, "continuing on and on," as read by the Tibetan translators (rjes su sgrub pas), instead of anivartamānā, the reading of the Sanskrit manuscript. The same form (anuvartamānāḥ) occurs again in 15b. In 18ab we find parivartamānam and vivartamānaḥ, which connect this stanza with 11cd; and finally, prayānti in 11c has its correspondence in prayāti in 18d.

Stanza 12 The comparison between rebirth or life in samsara and an ocean is one of the standard similes of Buddhist (and Hindu) literature. Hence the frequent use of the metaphor "ship," which can apply to the Buddha himself, his teaching in general, or to single parts of his teaching.

A frequently used simile for one who is lost and alone, without help or protection, is that of a member of a caravan who has been separated from his companions in the middle of a wilderness or desert.

Stanza 13 Samsara is compared to a ragged mountain range, full of precipitous crevasses into which the renegade has fallen and will plunge even deeper if his determination to hoist himself up by holding onto the rope of his inborn virtues slackens. The raggedness of the mountain is aptly expressed by the frequent repetitions of the letter r. One should also note the sequence °parāḥ paramā° and viṣamapātam . . . patanti, "they fall a terrible fall."

In line c I have altered the transmitted Sanskrit text jinaguṇāvalim, "the garlands of the virtues of a Jina (Buddha)," to *nijaguṇāvalim, "the garland of one's own, inborn virtues," because of the Tibetan testimonies that have gnyug ma "innate, inborn" or its (rare) alternative spelling smyug ma. *Nija also occurs in 11d, rendered by the same Tibetan equivalent gnyug ma.

Prajñākaramati points out that the term āvali, "garland," may hint at a rope used as a lifeline in mountain climbing.

Stanza 14 Instead of further frightening the apostate by vividly depicting the consequences of his deeds, Candragomin here confines himself to an appraisal of the good and steadfast disciple.

The attentive reader will observe not only the frequent occurrences of the letter m in this stanza but also the two paronomasias: samuditena samunnayanti and gurutāṁ guravaḥ. Paronomasia is a technical term used to define a very specific and frequently used figure of speech of Sanskrit poetry. Its main characteristic is the repetition not of single sounds—this is what we would call alliteration—but of groups of one or more syllables. In its most sophisticated form the repetition is done in such a manner that the two sequences of syllables produce a different meaning.

The following anonymous poem, "London, sad London," quoted by Gerow, p. 223, gives an idea of what can be done in Sanskrit with a much higher degree of refinement:

What wants thee, that thou art in this sad taking?
A King.
What made him first remove hence residing?
Siding.
Did any here deny him satisfaction?
Faction.
Tell me whereon this strength of Faction lies?
On lies.
What did'st thou do when the King left Parliament?
Lament.
What terms would'st give to gain his company?
Any.
But how would'st serve him, with thy best endeavor?
Ever.

Candragomin most often uses the simpler variety of this figure of speech, similar to the poem above. The Indian term for this figure of speech is yamaka, "doubled" or "restraint."

Stanza 15 Candragomin here appeals to the two opposite but complementary virtues "modesty" (lajjā) and "energy" (tejas), in order to inspire his addressee to abide by the Buddhist vows, and he even mentions his noble mother (jananīm . . . āryām) to soften his feelings. The softness of line 15a is enhanced by the repetition of the soft sound j in lajjā and jananīm. The second half of the stanza conveys the feeling of energy and sharpness through the repeated occurrence of the letter s: teja**s**vinaḥ **s**ukham a**s**ūn (api) **s**aṁtyajanti **s**atya**s**thitivya**s**anino.

Prajñākaramati elaborates the comparison between modesty and a mother by attributing ten terms used in the stanza to a mother, as in the chart on the following page. Here Prajñākaramati has perhaps carried the construction too far. Only the first five terms were intended by the poet to have a double meaning. The last five terms have been selected at random from the stanza.

Stanza 16 Prajñākaramati states: "If it is objected, 'What harm is done if someone actually breaks his vow,' then [Candragomin answers him] with [the lines] '[What matter] all the abuses of the people here, for [they indicate] that friends [and] enemies as well as neutral persons would make public the fault [of the broken vow], or [he answers with the words] 'sinful states of existences', i.e. the [three] bad forms of existence, for [they] result from evil [deeds]. 'To abandon one's original nature' means to defile the enjoyments of one's previous rank, dharma, and material possessions. 'For a virtuous man on earth' means: that very spoiling of morality is a great sorrow; apart from that, what other sorrow can there be?"

Stanza 17 After one has already entered "the broad path of the Dharma," it is the fickleness of the mind and its being bound by longing and desire (spṛhā)—explained in the commentaries as "desire, lust" ('dod pa, Skt. kāma) and "attachment, passion" (rjes su chags pa, Skt. anurāga)—that can cause one to break his or her vows. According to Prajñākaramati, the "path of the

TERM	A MOTHER:
jananī, producing	'produces' the body of her son
ārya, noble	is of noble descent
śuddha, pure	is without deceit towards her son
hṛdaya, heart	has a loving heart toward her son
anuvartamāna, following	follows her son
satya, truth	speaks the truth to her son
sthiti, constancy	gives important guidelines to her son
vyasanin, endeavoring	endeavors to protect her son
tejasvin, energetic	is energetic in guiding the maidservants
asūn api saṁtyaj, to give even one's own life	would give her own life for her son

Dharma" is the triple vehicle because it is entered by the members of the three lineages: Hīnayāna, Mahāyāna, and Vajrayāna (see his notes on stanza 9). It is qualified as "broad" because of its extraordinarily great benefit; there may also be a hint at the "Great Vehicle."

The Tibetan translation and Prajñākaramati's commentary seem to understand the last line differently. The Tibetan has:

| dga' bas nges par de yi sems bslus 'gyur ba snyam |
His mind is certainly deceived by joy.

This is commented upon by the Vṛtti as follows:

| **dga' ba** ni rjes su chags pa'o | | **bslus pa** ni mtho ris dang thar pa las nyams pa'o | "'Pleasure' is to be understood as passion. 'Deceived' means that [he has] spoiled [his chance to attain] heaven and liberation."

The Ṭippaṇa has:

| **dga' ba** ni 'dod pa'o | | des na klong 'khyil te g.yob pa'o | "'Joy' means desire. That is whirling [him] around; it moves [him] around."

This translation presupposes the following Sanskrit: cetaḥ spṛhā taralitā niyamena tasya. Here cetaḥ and spṛhā are split up into the subject spṛhā and the object cetaḥ, which is, of course, possible. For the object cetaḥ a predicate is needed and this the Tibetan translators find in taralitā. They do not interpret it as the past participle of taralayati, "causes to shake, waves, moves to and fro," but take it as the periphrastic future of this verb. However, the periphrastic future, which in its third person is identical with the nomen agentis, would be taralayitā, not taralitā; therefore, this interpretation is not tenable. While dPal-brtsegs, obviously following Prajñākaramati, assigns to taralayati a meaning so far not attested to, Vairocanarakṣita's interpretation refers to the established meaning of this verb.

Stanza 18 Prajñākaramati explains the pleasant states of existence as those of gods and men, and the unpleasant ones as those of animals, pretas (miserable ghosts suffering from hunger and thirst), and hell-beings.

The stanza presents a Buddhist version of an old gnomic saying from the Indian national epic Mahābhārata (12.168.18), which can also be found in "Staff of Wisdom" (Prajñādaṇḍa), the collection of moral maxims attributed to Nāgārjuna, as stanza 64:

sukhasyānantaraṁ duḥkhaṁ duḥkhasyānantaraṁ sukham |
sukhaduḥkhe manuṣyāṇāṁ cakravat parivartate | |

Immediately after happiness follows sorrow,
immediately after sorrow follows happiness;
for men, happiness and sorrow
revolve like a wheel.

In the third and fourth lines, an alliteration of the letter ś occurs six times, as well as two derivations from the root vaś: avaśyam and vivaśaḥ. In the first two lines, the present participle vartamāna, "turning," occurs twice, with two different verbal prefixes. Candragomin is obviously very fond of this participle, as it is also used in 11c, 11d, 15b, 17c, 20a, 94b, and 96b.

Both the Tibetan Śiṣyalekha and the Prajñākaramati commentary seem to have read *virāmamātram (or similarly), instead of vivartamānaḥ, as the Tibetan rendering bsti ba tsam la, "only in (the state) of resting" shows. Prajñākaramati explains it as "attaining the five objects of desire" ('dod pa'i yul lnga thob pa'o, Skt. pañcakāmaviṣayalābha). This hints at a variant reading which also makes good sense: "He who has mounted the ever-revolving wheel of samsara and regards a mere resting place as happiness . . ."

Stanza 19 Prajñākaramati states: "It might be said, 'Well, even if I might wander [in samsara], what harm is there in that?' While pointing [to the fact] that one will be tormented by sorrow [Candragomin begins with the stanza] '[with its] exceedingly horrible [stench],' which [illustrates] the suffering in the womb after one has adopted the form of a human being."

Candragomin makes a nice play on words in comparing the dwelling-place 'womb' (garbhanilayaṁ) with the hell (nirayaṁ). The two words nilayaṁ and nirayaṁ are practically identical from the phonetic point of view, especially if one considers that in many parts of India little distinction is made between the sounds of r and l. Candragomin is obviously fond of the word garbhanilayaṁ, which he also uses in 6d and 90d.

Stanza 20 The expression "as if squeezed by a sesame oil press" has a slight parallel in Nāgārjuna's "Letter to a Friend," stanza 78: "Some are pressed like sesame seed." (*Golden Zephyr*, p. 66) To an Indian reader, the image evokes the utmost pressure. The suggestion that a newborn being, after such an experience, should be inclined to give up life voluntarily of course underlines the extreme pain of birth.

Stanza 21 Until the moment of birth, a human being is said to have the ability to recall his former births; this now leaves him. Candragomin's pūrvasmṛti, "memories of the past," is a poetically condensed expression of the more technical term pūrvanivāsānusmṛti (Pāli pubbenivāsānussati), "remembrance of one's former state of existence," which is well attested to in Buddhist literature in Sanskrit and Pāli. By adding "in disgust" (ghṛṇayā), Candragomin uses the figure of speech called "ascription" (utprekṣā), "a figure in which a property or mode of behavior is attributed to a subject literally incapable of sustaining that property, whereby an implicit simile is suggested whose subject (upameya) is the subject receiving the attributed property and whose object (upamāna) is the real basis of that property." (Gerow, p. 131)

The order of stanzas 20 and 21 poses a problem. In Vairocanarakṣita's Ṭippaṇa, the glosses on stanza 21 precede those on stanza 20, and "there" (tatra) in 21 is explained as "in the womb" (mngal-du'o, Skt. garbhe). However, we follow the Sanskrit manuscript, the Tibetan Śiṣyalekha, and Prajñākaramati's Vṛtti. "There" (tatra) would then refer to "world" (bhuvaṁ) in stanza 20. This is in accord with the idea that remembrance of previous existences is lost at the moment of birth, not in the womb. In both cases a strict concatenation among stanzas 19, 20, and 21 can be established: duḥkha (19, 20), niṣpīḍyamāna (20) and nipīḍyamānā (21), or ugragandha (19, 20), nipīḍyamānā (20) and niṣpīḍyamāna (21).

Stanza 22 The change from the innocence and softness of early childhood to the rashness and recklessness of adolescence is also expressed by phonetic means: the consonants va, śa, and la in the two attributes of "childhood" in the first line are regarded as soft, while the "harsh" letters ṭa, ṭha, and ta underline both the rashness of youth and the raggedness of the mountains with which it is compared. Finally, the fourfold occurrence of the letter ṣa in the fourth line is the acoustical representation of the hissing of the snakes symbolizing the objects of the senses.

The Vṛtti explains the expression "not yet master of the body's behavior" as "not able to perform perfectly the actions of the three spheres of life (i.e. body, speech, and mind)." The verb mohāyate, "errs, wanders around bewildered" is translated as "behaves heedlessly, carelessly" and explained in the Vṛtti as "without shame and fear."

Stanza 23 The rashness of youth is now further expressed by a change of meter. The new meter, called viyoginī, contains more short syllables and is therefore faster. Its structure is:

∪ ∪ – ∪ ∪ – ∪ – ∪ –, ∪ ∪ – – ∪ ∪ – ∪ – ∪ – |

Note the frequent use of the "harsh" letter ta in the first two lines.

"Even from there" is explained as "from the mountain ravines (into a bad form of existence)" in the Ṭippaṇa and "from youth (into old age)" in the Vṛtti. "Lacking understanding"—"of what is wholesome" adds the Vṛtti. "He does not give up the excesses of youth" means "he does not act in a tranquil manner in the three spheres of activity because he does not see old age and death." (Vṛtti) The expression "excesses" can also mean "physical deformation," a connotation well suited to the image of falling down a mountain.

Stanza 24 According to the Vṛtti, "the good path" means "charity etc. because it produces a good fruit;" "wrong way" means "unwholesome things like killing etc. because it produces an unpleasant fruit." "Crushing" means "crushing of heaven and salvation and wandering around in a bad form of existence."

Stanza 25 This stanza is connected with the preceding one by the word "goad" (aṅkuśa), which is contained in "unchecked (by a goad)" in stanza 24.

Stanza 26 According to the Vṛtti, the first half of the stanza illustrates the reduction of the wholesome factors, the second half the growth of the unwholesome factors. Unfortunately there is no further explanation of this stanza, whose second half is somewhat problematic.

Its literal translation is: "In his ignorance he commits wrong deeds, decorated with flowers for his own death like an arrow (or: white reed)." The Tibetan translates:

| rmongs pa bya ba min byed bdag skyes pa |
| smyug ma 'bru chags lta bur brlag par zad |
"(Mentally) obscured, committing wrong deeds, self-born (= independent?), [he] will only be destroyed like bamboo (reed) with its seed grown."

bDag skyes pa formally corresponds to Skt. svātma. The Tibetan translator did not read svātma as the first part of the compound svātma-vadhāya, "for his own death (or destruction)," but instead translated it as an independent expression, like mohitaḥ. Did the translator read *svāj-ja or *svôttha, "born from oneself," instead of svātma?

I believe that the stanza was composed as a "complete simile" or pūrṇopamā. Its main structure is sa . . . śaravat . . . "He (i.e. the old man) . . . (being) like an arrow (made of bamboo) . . . ." The rest of the stanza is to be interpreted as referring to both the old man and the arrow.

The predicate akṛtāni karoti, "commits outrageous deeds (of shamelessness and killing)," and the two attributes vijihmaceṣṭita, "whose gait (or flight) is crooked" and svātmavadhāya puṣpita, "[his skin] mottled with dark spots, a mark of being soon to die" (when referring to the old man) and "being decorated with flowers that point to its own destruction" (when referring to the arrow) are not so difficult to interpret. The flowers or blossoms of the reed (of which the arrow is made) are indeed an indicator of its imminent destruction, because after blossoming, the cane dies and is then most likely to be cut for use as arrows.

The other two attributes are a little more difficult. I take mohita as "in his delusion" (referring to the old man) and "inadvertently made to go astray, in the wrong direction" (referring to the arrow). I take kuśalenāpi bhayād ivojjhita as "deserted, as if afraid, by his well-being, i.e. his health (which is shocked about the old man's impudent behavior)" and "when released, i.e. shot, in some state of fear, even by a skilled [archer]." In the latter case the fear is the reason why the arrow is inadvertently sent astray, thereby hurting or killing someone.

Stanza 27 "The stanza illustrates the decay of one's good fortune and well-being. . . . 'Laughing': As white teeth become visible when a man laughs, so white hair becomes visible through old age." (Vṛtti) "Younger brother," literally "born after, younger" (anuja) is our conjectural reading; the Sanskrit manuscripts read jarābhujaḥ, "devouring old age." This is also confirmed as an alternative reading in the Ṭippaṇa: "Or, devouring old age" (yang na dga' [read: rga] ba nyid za ba zhes bya ba'o). The main reading, however, is explained in the following way: dga' [read: rga] ba nyid kyi rjes su skyes pa gang zhig nu bos so, "By him who is born after old age, by [its] younger brother." That this reading is correct is suggested by Sanskrit grammar (jarānujaḥ is the nominative case required in the stanza, whereas jarābhujaḥ would be the genitive case, which cannot be construed) and by the Tibetan translation, which has nu bo, "younger brother."

The first line of the Tibetan translation has been mutilated beyond recognition in the course of transmission. The block-print editions read: | de nas de ni 'chi bdag rga [dga' in several xylographs] ba'i spun | . As 'chi bdag rga ba'i spun has to correspond to palitaughair daśanair ivolbaṇaiḥ, "by the shock of white hair, resembling [his] huge teeth," it seems appropriate to emend the Tibetan text to mche bdo rga ba'i spus, "by [his] huge teeth, the (white) hair of old age." With the Sanskrit text at hand, one can surmise that the corruption was caused by the similar expression rgas pa'i nu bo 'chi bdag, "the younger brother of old age, the god of death." Support for this emendation of bdag as bdo is given by the Ṭippaṇa: | bod pa [read: bdo ba] ni chen pos so | , "'Huge', that means 'great', thereby."

Stanza 28 Vṛtti*:* "The stanza illustrates how body and mind degenerate. . . . 'His ability to move comes to an end' means that he is not able to go from one place to another without a staff or a vehicle. As it is said:

Who is this feeble man, charioteer,
with so little strength, whose flesh and blood
are so dried up, whose muscles sag in his wrinkled skin?
Who can this be whose head is so white,
whose teeth chatter together,
whose body and limbs are so thin,
who leans on a cane and stumbles,
walking with such difficulty?"

The Voice of the Buddha, pp. 285–86

The stanza is quoted from the Buddha biography Lalitavistara xiv.1. It is spoken by the Buddha to his charioteer on the occasion of his first excursion from the palace grounds, when he sees an old and frail man. The cracking of the joints is phonetically underlined by the frequent use of the "harsh" letter ta, about a dozen times.

Stanza 29 "The first line illustrates the decay of the sense organs, the second the decay of the attachment to lust, the third and fourth how fear is caused. Youth will be transformed into the state of old age." (Vṛtti) "By this (stanza) the state of great sorrow is illustrated." (Ṭippaṇa)

Stanza 30 "After the illustration of the sorrow of death the sorrow of repentance is illustrated." (Vṛtti) Both the Tibetan translation and the Vṛtti presuppose a slightly different Sanskrit text in the first two lines: katham evam idaṁ mayākṛtaṁ katham evaṁ tat kṛtaṁ hatā gatiḥ, "Why didn't I do (akṛtaṁ) this [wholesome deed] in such a way as I did that [sinful deed]? Destroyed is my [present good] form of existence!" However, akṛtaṁ instead of na kṛtaṁ would be very unidiomatic Sanskrit, and the second line contains a metrical fault.

The expression "has put his feet on my head" (śirasi nyastapadā) is taken over from stanza 25b, where it refers to old age.

Stanza 31 "The arising of grief hits the mind as the blows of a thunderbolt (a vajra) would hit the body." (Vṛtti) The Sanskrit manuscript reads kukṛtaiḥ, "by (thoughts of) repentance," instead of kuliśaiḥ, "by vajras, thunderbolts." The translation would then run: "by mind-crushing (thoughts of) repentance full of grief." This is also possible; however, the conjectural reading kuliśaiḥ is confirmed by the Tibetan translation and the Vṛtti, which both have rdo rje, "vajra." Moreover, the expression cittamāthibhiḥ, "mind-**crushing**," seems to fit better with "thunderbolt, axe" than with "repentance."

Stanza 34 "The stanza gives an answer to the question: 'May he be seized by the Lord of Death, what harm is thereby done?'" (Vṛtti) The Tibetan translator and the Vṛtti interpret kālapāśa, "black rope or chain," as "rope (or chain) of time" (dus kyi zhags pa), and the Vṛtti specifies that "'rope of time' means 'the moment of dying'." The Ṭippaṇa, however, also understands the ambiguous kāla simply as "black," as we do: nag po zhes pa ni gnag pa'o.

With this stanza the meter changes back to vasantatilakā, the central meter of the poem. We see that the "swift" meter viyoginī, chosen for stanzas 23 through 33, aptly illustrates the rapid passage of human life from birth to death.

Stanza 35 "After the description of the sorrow of existence as a human being, the present stanza now describes the suffering of a yakṣa, obstructed from eating [sic], as an illustration of the suffering in a bad form of existence." (Vṛtti)

The expression "as slimy as blood" (kṣataja-vijjala-tāṁ) is somewhat difficult. The word vijjala is not so frequently attested to in Sanskrit literature, but seems very apt in this context. The Tibetan translator (khrag dang phyi sas gang ba'i chur) and the Ṭippaṇa (khrag dang mi gtsang ba'i chu nyid), on the other hand, clearly had the same variant reading: kṣataja-viḍ-jalatāṁ, "the state of water which (actually consists of) blood and feces." It seems unlikely, however, that Candragomin would have chosen the clumsy expression "water becomes water (which is actually blood and feces)," so I have remained faithful to the reading of the Sanskrit manuscript. Note the alliteration in keśaughaśaivalavimiśrita and **pū**ti**pū**ya**p**aṅkā.

Stanza 36 "The top of the mountain is cool because it has been sprinkled with the water of the big waves agitated by the wind." (Vṛtti) The softness of the mountain slopes sprinkled with cool water is phonetically underlined by the frequent use of la and śa in the first two lines.

The Sanskrit text contains one difficult word, ulmuka, which usually means "firebrand." The Tibetan translation and the Ṭippaṇa both have mgal dum, "splinter of firewood." This is a more suitable meaning in the context of the stanza and I have therefore adopted it.

Stanza 37 The reading viṣadāruṇa, "pitiless like poison," is not confirmed by the Tibetan translation, which has khu ba dmar rtsub pa, "a very pungent liquid," and the Ṭippaṇa, which has khug rna . . . dmar rtsub pa, "a very rough . . . fog (?)." The Ṭippaṇa expressly mentions viṣadāruṇa as a variant reading.

Stanza 39 Here Candragomin leaves the delinquent and inserts a stanza of a more general character. His model was the "Letter to a Friend," stanza 95, where Nāgārjuna describes the suffering of the hungry spirits (pretas):

To the spirits, even the moon seems hot in summer
And the sun feels cold in winter.
A tree in paradise becomes fruitless,
And if they should even so much as look at rivers these dry up."
—*Golden Zephyr*, p. 73

The Tibetan rendering bu yug, "snowstorm," was very helpful in restoring the correct Sanskrit *tuhinānilo. The manuscript has tuhitānilo, which was wrongly separated as tu hitānilo, "however a wholesome wind" by Minaev and Vaidya, the first and second editors of the "Letter to a Disciple." This reading could not have been that of the Tibetan translators, since hita, "useful, wholesome," is usually translated as phan pa or sman pa. The Tibetan translators have aptly rendered "tortured by cold" as "tortured by a cold wind."

Stanza 40 According to the Vṛtti, the first half of the stanza describes "the suffering of those whose souls ('inner parts') are obscured."

Candragomin now continues to describe the suffering of the deceased delinquent. He is tortured by thirst, yet unable to quench it, even at the shore of the ocean. His pains are those of a preta or hungry ghost. The whole stanza is influenced by stanza 92 of the "Letter to a Friend:"

Because some have mouths the size of a needle's eye
And stomachs the size of a mountain, they are tormented,

But they do not have the energy to eat
Even a morsel of food thrown on miserable filth."
—*Golden Zephyr*, p. 72

The meaning and wording of the passage "in the heat of the mouth" (āsyoṣmaṇā), which are not quite clear in the original manuscript and are corrupted in its two copies (B reads śleṣmoṣmaṇā, "in the heat of its bile" and C mārgoṣmaṇā, "in the heat on its way down to the precipice . . ."), are confirmed by the Tibetan translation: kha yi dugs kyis, "by the heat of [his] mouth." The Ṭippaṇa reads asya, "its, i.e., of the mouth," instead of āsya.

Stanza 41 "Having described the suffering of a hungry ghost, (he now) illustrates the suffering of a hell-being." (Vṛtti) For a detailed description of the suffering experienced in the eight hot and eight cold hells see, for example, the "Letter to a Friend," stanzas 77–88, or *Path of Heroes*, pp. 148–64. The latter work contains many quotations from both canonical and non-canonical works, including the "Letter to a Disciple."

Various descriptions of the hells and the sufferings experienced there are found in Buddhist literature. In the Pāli canon of the Theravādins there are three loci classici: Aṅguttaranikāya I, 138–42, and Majjhimanikāya III, 163–67 and 178–87 (quoted according to the editions of the Pali Text Society). In the Mahāvastu, a biography of the Buddha belonging to the school of the Lokottaravādins, the first chapter, entitled Narakaparivarta or "The Chapter of Hells," consists of a detailed description of Maudgalyāyana's visit to various hells. An English translation can be found in *The Mahāvastu*, vol. I, translated from the Buddhist Sanskrit by J. J. Jones (London 1949, 1973): 6–21. Another old description is contained in Āryaśūra's Jātakamālā, legend No. 29 (Brahmajātaka), stanzas 20–45. For English translations, see *Once the Buddha Was a Monkey*, Ārya Śūra's *Jātakamālā*, translated from the Sanskrit by Peter Khoroche (Chicago, London 1989), and *The Marvelous Companion: Life Stories of the Buddha* (Berkeley: Dharma Publishing, 1983).

For other descriptions of the Buddhist hells, see Edward Joseph Thomas, "State of the Dead (Buddhist)," *Encyclopedia of Religion and Ethics* 11 (1971): 829–33, and Daigan and Alicia Matsunaga, *The Buddhist Concept of Hell* (New York, 1972).

The dogs with their fangs also occur in Nāgārjuna's "Letter to a Friend," stanza 80: "Some are thrown to the ground by [fierce] dogs with iron fangs / And lie with outstretched arms." (*Golden Zephyr*, p. 66)

Stanza 42 From here on, the Vṛtti offers little more than a very brief description of what is depicted in the stanzas (and what even the dullest reader will understand without such commentary). Therefore we will not repeat what is self-evident.

The Asipattravana or "the forest whose leaves consist of swords" is briefly described in Majjhimanikāya III, 185 where it forms one of the four or five minor hells (ussada). In the Mahāvastu it is part of the hell Kumbha (I.7 and 11). This stanza might also allude to one of the Neighboring Hells, the Plain of Spears; see *Path of Heroes*, p. 154.

The sharpness of the various weapons mentioned in the stanza is linguistically enhanced by the the frequent use of the three sibilants: ni**ś**ita, k**ṣ**ura, sa**ṁ**stare**ṣ**u, **ś**ita**ś**ūla**ś**aktiprā**s**ā**s**ihā**s**a.

Stanza 43 The idea that in hell the delinquent is accompanied only by his own screaming is also expressed by Āryaśūra in his Jātakamālā, stanza 31 of the Brahmajātaka (no. 29) : "Others taste the fruit of their actions on large heaps of live coals, the color of molten gold, and are powerless to do anything but writhe and scream." (Khoroche, p. 209) Vicchinnamūrtir (42b) and vibhinnamūrtis (43c) form a quasi-concatenation between stanzas 42 and 43.

Stanza 44 For a possible source of Candragomin's image, see the note on stanza 46. Candragomin uses a nice linguistic pun in order to underline the sharp contrast expressed in this stanza. In classical Sanskrit literature, the labials, especially the letter m, are thought to express the idea of sexual desire and pleasure. This letter is used three times in the second line. The saw-like sharpness of the women's bodies, on the other hand, is illustrated by the sequence of the four k's in **k**ra**k**aca**k**ar**k**aśa.

Premottarapraṇayanirdayam is difficult. It literally means "merciless because (their) longing exceeds (ordinary) love."

Stanza 45 In the word saṁghaṭṭa, "crashing together," Candragomin alludes to the Mass-Crushing Hell. Note the bold iteration of the retroflex sounds ṭa, ṇa, and ṣa, which are meant to illustrate the impact of the rams clashing together.

Stanza 46 This and the following stanza give Candragomin a welcome opportunity to list the wild animals and birds that torture the hell-beings. Candragomin seems to have known the following stanzas from Verses of Mindfulness of the Holy Dharma:

Those who rape and ravish will find themselves
in the forest of shalmali trees that have burning,
iron-tipped leaves sixteen inches long.
Pierced by the leaves they cry out
as they climb the trees in terror.

Horrifying women torment them
with sharp teeth and burning bodies:
Having ravished the women of others,
they will now be seized and eaten.

Those who harm the harmless and cheerful
will find themselves in the forest of razor-sharp knives;
cut apart, they will cry out and be devoured
by vultures, dogs, owls, and crows.

Those who disrupt the stability of the Dharma
and those who preach what is not right
will travel on the plain spiked with sharp spears.

—1.19-21; quoted from *Path of Heroes*, pp. 155–56

The following stanzas are concatenated by a number of repetitions that enhance the continuity of the various forms of torture: ārohati 46b; avarohati 48d; avaroḍhum 49b; prasahya 47c, 48a; bhidyamāna 46d; bhinna 48d, 49a, 52c; mukha 48a, 48d, 49c; jarjarita 51b, 52b.

Stanza 47 In the word kālapāśa, "black rope," Candragomin seems to allude to the Hell of Black Lines (kālasūtra). The tormenting by birds can also be found in stanza 80cd of the "Letter to a Friend:"

Others suffer helplessly, being clawed by crows,
With sharp iron beaks and intolerable claws."

—*Golden Zephyr*, p. 67

Stanza 50 Now follows a description of the Hot Hells. See *Path of Heroes*, p. 151.

Stanza 51 In the words jīvanti, "live, continue to exist," and jīva, "life," Candragomin certainly alludes to the Hell of Revival (saṁjīva). The image of worms and insects eating one's body is taken from stanza 81 of the "Letter to a Friend:"

Some wail and roll about, while various worms and beetles,
And myriads of bluebottles and bees with long stings
Open up wounds painful even to the touch,
And begin to feast on them."

—*Golden Zephyr*, p. 67

See also *Path of Heroes*, p. 155.

Stanza 52 "Having thus shown (the sufferings to be experienced in) the Hot Hells, (Candragomin) is now going to show those of the Cold Hells . . ." (Vṛtti). The repetition of the letter ja in **jā**ta**ja**ntu**ja**gdha enhances the image of the continuously gnawing insects.

Stanza 53 In line a the Sanskrit manuscript has a reading that is hardly convincing: tanulomakeśāḥ, "the hair of their bodies and heads being (or: having become) thin." The Tibetan translates: skra dang spu rnams g.yengs gyur pa, "the hair of their bodies and heads having become agitated, (stirred, mixed, shaken)." I suspect that Candragomin is thinking of gooseflesh and translate accordingly. It is not clear to me which Sanskrit word is translated by g.yengs gyur pa, which usually renders vikṣipta, "agitated, confused." Was it tata or stṛta ?

Stanza 54 "Now (Candragomin) is going to illustrate the special types of very hot (hells) . . ." (Vṛtti) This hell, with its mixture of dark smoke and the white pieces of bones, is compared by Candragomin to the fearful god Bhairava. "The complexion of Bhairava is dark as the rain-cloud and his garment the elephant's skin; he should have several arms carrying several weapons." From T. A. Gopinatha Rao, *Elements of Hindu Iconography* (Madras,1914; New York, 1968), p. 177.

For the next five stanzas, 54 through 58, Candragomin uses the meter pṛthvī, which consists of seventeen syllables per line and is characterized by its seemingly irregular and therefore hectic structure. It aptly underlines the atmosphere of agitation in the Intensively Hot Hell.

Stanza 55 This stanza is a feast for the grammarians among the Sanskritists, for Candragomin here very ingeniously illustrates how to form full-fledged onomatopoeic adverbs from their root syllables. Each of these root syllables and adverbs—such as caṭ-ac-caṭ-ad-iti, formed from caṭ—represents a very specific sound. The first root syllable, caṭ, illustrates the crackling of the sparks; the second, cham, the hissing of boiling fat; and the third, kaṭ, the cracking or popping of breaking ribs.

In the Tibetan translation, the first onomatopoeic is rendered by 'ur sgra, "a blowing, humming or buzzing sound" (which is not so fortunate), the second by chil chil, "hissing," and the third by lhag lhag, "a sharp noise." The second expression is also found in "Entering the Bodhisattva Path" 10.12, where scented water extinguishes the fire of hell.

Stanza 61 "Having thus illustrated the suffering [to be experienced] in the hell, [Candragomin, briefly,] pointing to the suffering of animals, [tells us] how difficult it is to find the opportune moment [of attaining the state of a human being]." (Vṛtti) This theme is fully elaborated in the first chapter of Śāntideva's "Entering the Bodhisattva Path."

The "frightening variety of innumerable states of existence" refers to the great variety within each of the six classes of beings into which one can be born.

Stanza 62 Candragomin very briefly alludes to three of the eight unfavorable states (Skt. akṣaṇa, Tib. mi khom pa) within which liberation is difficult or impossible to attain. The eight states are: hell-being, hungry ghost, animal, wild tribe living in a border country, barbarian, god, a being whose sense-organs are mutilated, and heretic. They are enumerated in full in stanzas 63 and 64 of the "Letter to a Friend:"

To entertain an erroneous view, to be born among
The animals, spirits and denizens of the hell,
To be born a savage in a far-off place where there is no Dharma,
To be born a dumb person or a long-living god—

Any one of these births is unsatisfactory.
These therefore comprise the eight obstacles.
After having encountered a satisfactory juncture free of them,
Endeavor to avert the possibility of rebirth.

—*Golden Zephyr*, *p. 56*

Stanza 63 "Having thus given the instruction on how one accomplishes the path of the Ordinary Vehicle, [Candragomin now] gives the instruction on how one accomplishes the path of the Great Vehicle, telling us what its basis is." (Vṛtti) In explaining the planting of the auspicious seed of supreme enlightenment, the Vṛtti gives the following quotation: "O son of a noble family, the thought directed toward the attainment of enlightenment (Skt. bodhicitta, Tib. byang chub kyi sems) is like the seed of the whole Dharma of the Buddha."

Stanza 64 This stanza is not available in the Sanskrit manuscript. Both the Vṛtti and the Ṭippaṇa comment upon it, however, so we know that it was found in other sources. By its content it is difficult to judge whether the stanza is genuine or not. It is certainly not indispensable to Candragomin's train of thought; it also does not disturb or spoil his presentation. The number of syllables is identical with that of stanzas 63 and 65, both of which were composed in the vasantatilakā meter in the original Sanskrit, so most likely it was composed in this meter.

Stanza 65 "At the very beginning of entering the path [leading to enlightenment], one should meditate on impermanence; the simile of the flame [illustrates] the momentariness [of life]." (Vṛtti) Syntactically, stanzas 65 and 66 belong together. The hypothetical thought begins with atyantadurlabham (65a) and ends with etat kṣaṇād (66b). Neither the Vṛtti nor the Ṭippaṇa make this fully clear.

Stanza 66 As pointed out in the introduction, this stanza repeats, in a poetically condensed form, the idea expressed in stanzas 58 through 60 of the "Letter to the Great King Kaniṣka." In Indian literature, fury is regarded as red because the eyes redden in rage. In the case of Yama, the Lord of Death, the gaze of his angry red eyes is so intense that it reddens even his dark black club. The stanza occurs again in *Joy for the World* (Act II, 21; p. 36 of the English translation).

Stanza 67 It is very likely that this stanza is the poetical expansion of a thought already expressed in folk literature. Only recently an apparently old collection of popular sayings composed in the Middle-Indic language Prakrit, the Chappaṇṇayagāhāo or the "Sayings of the 56 Wise Men," has come to light. Its stanza 19 runs as follows:

Human beings are happy
about the arrival of the agreeable festival of Indra.
The poor fellows do not realize
that arrows in the form of years have hit them.

We find still another version of this idea in an old Indian one-act farce, "The Saint and the Courtesan," which was composed not later than the middle of the seventh century A.D. It contains the following stanza:

'Spring, bedecked with tender shoots, has come,
Autumn, adorned with masses of lotuses, has arrived'—
With these words fools rejoice
At the arrival of a new season in the world;
For them that is indeed pleasant
which actually takes away their lives.

I tend to believe that the author of this play knew Candragomin's stanza. A detailed discussion of these two stanzas together with the references to the original works can be found in Michael Hahn, "Prakrit Stanzas in an Early Anthology of Sanskrit Verses," *Bulletin d'Études Indiennes*, 11–12 (1993–94): 355–68.

Stanza 68 Now Candragomin begins to describe the place most suitable for those who seriously enter the path to enlightenment and thus make best use of the human state. In the fourth line the order of words in the Sanskrit is very deliberately chosen: "In a blissful manner they spend their lives, that are (by nature) as mobile as the wind."

Stanza 69 Nandana is the name of Indra's celestial grove. This stanza occurs again in *Joy for the World* (Act II, 15; p. 33 of the English translation). The stanza is concatenated with the previous one not only by the word vanasthalīṣu, but also by the chain of attributes in the locative plural. It is concatenated with the following stanza by the repetition of the question kiṁ sā ratir (bhavati), "Could that same joy then rule," and by repetition of the word divyāṅganā, "celestial women, goddesses."

Stanza 71 Like stanza 64, this stanza is not available in the Sanskrit manuscript. It is commented upon in the Vṛtti, but not in the Ṭippaṇa. As in the case of stanza 64, it is not possible to give an objective criterion to prove or disprove its authenticity, other than the weight of the age of the Tibetan source material, which is older than the Sanskrit manuscript by almost three centuries. The mention of the hells does tend to break the flow of the description of the beautiful scenery of forest life and makes the stanza look a little like a later insertion.

The expression dmyal stong, "one thousand hells," is not certain because different spellings occur in the blockprints, e.g. dmyal sdong or even dmyal 'dong. There is also a rather puzzling explanation in the Vṛtti which runs: dmyal sdong ('dong D) ni khyim gyi grong 'dab bam chung ma ste | 'bras bu'i ming la rgyu btags pa'o | "As for dmyal sdong, it means the life (?) of a householder or [his] wife; the name of the fruit being attached to the cause." This seems to mean that the hells are (or at least can be) the fruit of life as a householder.

Stanza 72 This stanza, extraordinary in its poetic beauty, also occurs in *Joy for the World* (Act II, 19; p. 33 of the English translation).

Stanza 73 "If one wishes to remove the obstacles [that obstruct] the attainment [of enlightenment], one has to visualize the dangers of desire." (Vṛtti) Despite their illusory character, desire, wealth, and women have the power to drag the fools who take them for real to lower forms of existence.

Stanza 74 In a set of three stanzas (74–76), Candragomin points to the similarities as well as the differences between the pleasures of the senses (viṣaya) and poison (viṣa), taking as a starting point the phonetic similarity of these two terms in Sanskrit. In the first of these stanzas he uses a figure of speech called śleṣa or double entendre. Four sets of attributes are chosen in such a manner that they apply both to the pleasures of the senses and to poison. The punning can be retained almost completely in the English translation.

The two stanzas 74 and 75 occur again in *Joy for the World* (Act II, 19 and 20; pp. 34–35 of the English translation).

Stanza 75 In the second line the word viṣama, "dangerous," again enhances the linguistic pun.

After stanza 75 the Sanskrit manuscript inserts a stanza in the so-called śloka meter (the more scientific name is anuṣṭubh or vaktra) that repeats the main idea of the preceding stanza in very simple words:

viṣasya viṣayāṇāṁ ca dūram atyantagocaram |
upayuktaṁ viṣaṁ hanti viṣayāḥ smaraṇād api ||

A great and endless difference exists between poison and the pleasures of the senses—poison kills only when swallowed, the pleasures of the senses even when one merely thinks of them.

The same stanza, with some slightly better readings (upabhuktaṁ and atyantam antaram), can also be found in a medieval anthology of Sanskrit verses, Vallabhadeva's Subhāṣitāvali, where it is ascribed to a certain Candragopin, no doubt a distortion of the name Candragomin. Nevertheless, there can be little doubt that the stanza is out of place in the Śiṣyalekha: It is only a poor repetition of what has already been stated in a much more elegant way; the rather simple meter is used nowhere else in this poem; and neither the Tibetan translation nor the two commentaries show any trace of it. One can speculate that a well-read scribe remembered the śloka when he copied the Śiṣyalekha and added it to the text.

The stanza is nevertheless quite old and was associated with the name of Candragomin as early as the seventh century C.E. This is evidenced by the record of I-Tsing. In the first passage where he speaks about Candragomin, he says:

"In the East of India there was a great scholar named Yüe-kuan ('moon-official'). He was indeed a greatly talented bodhisattva, and existed still at the time when (I, I-)Ching reached (there)." (Taishō Tripiṭaka, vol. LIV, p. 229c4–5.)

Then he quotes a stanza spoken by this man:

"The difference between poisonous herbs and poisonous sense-objects is indeed very great. Poisonous herbs harm only when they are swallowed but poisonous sense-objects burn (as soon as you) think of them." (Ibid., 229c7–8.)

This is a very faithful rendering of the inserted stanza. It is nevertheless an open question whether Candragomin himself composed this abridgment or whether someone else wrote it and attached Candragomin's name to it.

Stanza 77 By the words vṛṣo and viṣama-, this stanza is phonetically concatenated with the three preceding ones.

Stanza 78 Candragomin combines the description of the celestial women bathing in the heavenly Ganges (whose other name is Mandākinī), which he introduced in stanza 70, with that of the hell-river Vaitaraṇī (see stanza 41), thereby creating a sharp contrast. His model was stanza 73 of the "Letter to a Friend:"

Having sat together with the goddesses of heaven
On a cushion of golden lotus petals, in a
Gently flowing stream [i.e., the heavenly Ganges], again
one falls into the
Intolerably hot salt river, the Vaitaraṇī, in hell."

—*Golden Zephyr*, p. 62

Stanza 79 As in the preceding stanza, Candragomin creates sharp contrast, this time between the bed of tender buds on which one has dallied with lovely companions, and the Asipattravana, the forest whose leaves are as sharp as swords, already mentioned in stanza 42. While both verses share the word saṁstareṣu, "on beds," the context is quite different. A second connection is established by vicchinnamūrtir and vicchinnagātram, this time used with the same meaning. Verses 78 and 79 are concatenated by the two words bhūyo bhramanti. Candragomin's model was stanza 72 of the "Letter to a Friend:"

Having enjoyed the pleasures of chasing daughters
Of heaven and of a life in a beautiful garden, again,
One gets one's legs, hands, ears, and nose slashed off
By branches of garden trees similar to sticks and swords.
—*Golden Zephyr*, p. 62

Stanza 80 The third consecutive contrast is created by the description of Mount Meru, whose surface is so soft that it sinks down and rises again under the feet, and the hot sands of the hell described in stanza 50. The two expressions uttaptavāluka and uttaptasaikata have exactly the same meaning. The influence of stanza 71 of the "Letter to a Friend" can be felt:

Even after having remained for a long time
on the summit of Mt. Meru,
Where one enjoyed one's strolls,
Again, one experiences the intolerable pains of walking in
The Hell of Fire Pit and the Hell of Dirty Swamp."
—*Golden Zephyr*, p. 61

Stanza 81 This stanza points back to stanza 13. The Vṛtti explains anantapāram, "boundless," as thar thabs med pa, "without a means to attain liberation."

Stanza 82 This stanza is modeled on stanza 69 of the "Letter to a Friend:"

Even after having become the praiseworthy Indra,
By the power of one's karma, one falls to earth again.
Even after having become a universal monarch,
One becomes a servant in the flow of saṁsāra.
—*Golden Zephyr*, p. 60

The first two lines are quoted in the Vṛtti. Note the nice alliterations in lines two (prabhāprakarapiñjarapādapīṭhaḥ) and three (ākulagatiḥ kugatīḥ).

Stanza 83 According to Hindu mythology, gods are distinguished from human beings by the following five external marks: The color of their bodies remains fresh, they do not touch the earth or the cushions they sit upon, the flower wreaths they wear do not wither, they do not sweat, and their garments always look fresh. Twelve years before their death, these marks begin to fade, causing great agony to the afflicted gods. Again, Candragomin's model can be found in the "Letter to a Friend," stanzas 98–100:

The pleasures of heaven may be great,
But the pain of their extinction will be even greater.
Therefore, supreme beings understand this and
Do not desire a heaven which comes to an end.

The color of the body turns ugly, one's cushion becomes
Unbearable, the wreath of flowers decays, clothing
Becomes soiled, and perspiration which was not
There previously appears on the body.

These five signs, which signify death in heaven,
Appear to the gods residing in heaven and
Are the same signs which signify
Death to men who live on earth.

—*Golden Zephyr*, p. 75

Stanza 85 Here Candragomin compares the Lord of Death to a fisherman fishing human beings from the ocean of existence. In referring to the fisherman, the two past participles, paryasta and praṇihita, are used in their very elementary meaning of "swung around (one's head)" and "cast forward (and down)." Thus they describe exactly the movements of an angler when he casts the line with the hook and bait attached to it into the water.

In referring to the Lord of Death, the two participles allow for another interpretation. Now one has to take the figurative meaning of paryasta, which is "turned around, perverted, perverse" and take praṇihita as noun, a synonym of praṇidhāna or praṇidhi, in accordance with the rule of the grammarians bhāve kta: "the perfect participle is also used to express the state of being (of the verb)." Thus it was understood by the Tibetan translators, who rendered paryastapraṇihita as log par smon pa, "perverse, perverted desire." The Vṛtti explains this expression as "the desire to attain being and the paraphernalia of being."

The wording of the Tibetan translation is slightly different:

| de ni gshin rjes srid mtshor rgyu ba'i sems can la |
| log par smon pas 'jigs pa dbyug pa nag po'i rtser |
| sred pa'i thi gu ring pos dam bzhag btags pa yi |
| mchil pa[s] nya la bya ba bzhin du btab pa yin | 85 |

It is the hook,
firmly attached with the long cord of greed
to the tip of his black club
that is dreadful with perverted aspirations,
which the Lord of Death has thrown out to the beings
wandering around in the ocean of existence
as if he were fishing.

The Tibetan translator added "at the tip" (rtser), which improves upon the image, and "deed" (bya ba), which makes the sentence clearer for a Tibetan reader.

Stanza 86 "This stanza gives an example of the wrong notion ('arrogance') of happiness with regard to suffering." (Vṛtti)

Stanza 87 "And then, for just a short time" is explained by the Vṛtti as "when being reborn as god or human being" and "somehow" as "having accumulated merit."

Stanzas 88–89 "When meditating on what counteracts the attainment of the path (leading to liberation), one has to visualize the suffering of samsara (88) . . . and what is unpleasant (89)." (Vṛtti)

The Sanskrit manuscript has only a mutilated text. Two lines are missing (3 and 8) and the order of the lines is apparently disturbed. Since the text of the Tibetan translation makes perfect sense, I have rearranged the lines of the Sanskrit text and restored the two missing lines from the Tibetan translation. Because of the strict parallelism of the construction, this was not difficult to do. Below I give the text of the Sanskrit manuscript, the figures at the right indicating the line number of the Tibetan translation:

yāvad yāvaj jagati sakale jāyate saukhyasaṁjñā [1]
tāvat tāvat¬ bahutaraśikho jāyate rāgavaṁhniḥ | [6]
yāva(6)d yāvad visarati śubhā bhāvanā bhāvyamānā [5]
tāvat tāvad bahalataratām eti mohāndhakāraṁ | | [2]
yāvad yāvan niyatam aśubhā bhāvanā yāti vṛddhiṁ [7]
tāvat tāvat taralataratām eti mohāndhakāraḥ | [4]

Stanza 90 In *Joy for the World* Candragomin himself repeatedly (1.14, 3.2+, 3.5, 3.6) makes this kind of comparison when describing the heroine Padmāvatī!

Stanza 91 This stanza occurs again in *Joy for the World* (Act II, 6; p. 27 of the English translation). It is modeled upon stanza 56 of the "Letter to the Great King Kaniṣka:"

While revolving in the circle of existence
again and again, like a rosary,
what have you not already done in the world
a hundred times, or even thousands?

Skt. śriyaḥ in line 3 can mean "good fortune, wealth, happiness" and "goddess(es) of happiness." Because of the "sweet smile," it is clear that Candragomin had the personified notion of the goddess of happiness (Śrī) in mind. The idea is further elaborated in the next three stanzas.

Stanzas 93–94 In stanza 66 of the "Letter to a Friend," a similar idea is expressed:

A father is a son, a mother is a wife,
A man becomes an enemy and then a friend,
Or vice-versa: therefore, there is
No certainty whatsoever in Saṁsāra.
—*Golden Zephyr*, p. 58

Stanza 95 In *Joy for the World* we find a similar stanza:

From time immemorial, the band of family members
consists of her in whose womb one was first caught,
and her upon whose bosom the husband
took his playful and ardent pleasure,
and finally of all those whose absence
causes deep and lasting grief."
—(Act II, 25; p. 38 of the English translation).

Stanza 96 The word ājavaṁjava (wrongly spelled ārjavaṁjava in the Sanskrit manuscript), belongs to the specific vocabulary of the Buddhists; see the entry in Edgerton's *Buddhist Hybrid Sanskrit Dictionary.* In Tibetan, it is traditionally rendered as "coming and going" (see the old Sanskrit-Tibetan dictionary Mahāvyutpatti, No. 5393: ājavaṁjavasamāpannaḥ = 'ong ba dang 'gro bar gyur pa) or, as in the Tibetan Śiṣyalekha, the Vṛtti and the Ṭippaṇa, as skye shi, "birth and death." Johnston translates the expression ājavaṁjavatā in Buddhacarita xii.41 as "the rushing torrent of birth and death." Interestingly, the oldest manuscript of the Buddhacarita has the same spelling mistake ārjavaṁ(javatā) that we find in the Śiṣyalekha manuscript. See E. H. Johnston, *The Buddhacarita; or, Acts of the Buddha*, Part 1, p. 133, for the text of xii.41, and Part 2, p. 174 for the translation (and the accompanying note).

In *Joy for the World* we find a loosely related stanza:

How could even an ego-centered person be happy
when his heart is consumed by grief

because his kin dwell in this world
in the midst of sorrow?
How then could a noble man, who bears upon his body
the suffering of all mankind,
ever be joyous, even if he lives
free from the burden of oppression?"
—Act II, 24; p. 37 of the English translation

Stanza 97 The Sanskrit manuscript has an unintelligible reading in line 3: tannisphalaḥ, "bearing no fruit with regard to that." Very tentatively I restore this as tā vatsalāh. See the discussion in "Restorations and Emendations," p. 279.

Stanza 99 "Having thus taught a means to meditate on love and compassion, (Candragomin now) shows the use of this practice and (specifically) points to the benefit of compassion." (Vṛtti)

Stanza 101 "Having thus illustrated the benefit (for oneself), (Candragomin now) describes, as an illustration of the proper conduct, the striving for loving conduct that brings about happiness for others." (Vṛtti). This stanza occurs again in *Joy for the World* (Act II, 22; p. 36 of the English translation).

Stanza 102 This stanza occurs again in *Joy for the World* (Act II, 23; p. 37 of the English translation). Note the fine assonance in the beginning of the first two lines.

Stanza 103 For the headbands of the Bodhisattvas and their being set on fire, see stanza 21 of the *Bodhisaṁbhāra ascribed to Nāgārjuna as translated in *Master of Wisdom* (p. 127) and the parallels quoted by Christian Lindtner. Although there are several canonical parallels, Candragomin most likely took the image from the "Letter to a Friend," stanza 104:

If one's hair or clothing suddenly caught on fire,
One would throw everything away to extinguish it.

Similarly, one must strive to avoid worldly concerns,
Because there is nothing more important."
—*Golden Zephyr*, p. 77

Stanza 104 The Avīci hell is one of the eight hot hells. Descriptions of some of these hells are given in *Path of Heroes*, pp. 151–52. The Buddhist poet Gopadatta, who flourished between the sixth and eighth centuries C.E. and wrote a collection of Buddhist birth stories (Jātakamālā) along the lines of his predecessors Āryaśūra and Haribhaṭṭa, mentions this hell repeatedly, and in one of his stanzas gives one of the popular etymologies of avīci:

vīciṁ vadanti vivaraṁ na ca tatra kā cid
duḥkhasya vīcir api tiryag upary adho vā |
yasmād avīcir iti tena ca saṁprasiddhaḥ
śīrṇas ta(no)(ti) (bha)vano narakāntareṣu || 29 ||

They say, vīci means interval or break,
and since there cannot be found
the minutest interval of suffering,
neither upwards, nor downwards, nor to the sides,
(this hell) is well-known under the name Avīci; . . .

(from: Michael Hahn, "Ajātaśatravadāna—A Gopadatta Story from Tibet," in *K. P. Jayaswal Commemoration Volume* (Patna 1981): 242–76.)

Stanza 105 In order to show the greatness of the Bodhisattvas, Candragomin again mentions the Asipattravana, the forest whose leaves are as sharp as sword-blades, and Indra's heavenly grove Nandana.

Stanza 106 Candragomin embellishes this last stanza of the main part of the "Letter to a Disciple" with a special figure of speech consisting of different forms derived from the same verb root. The root is tṝ, "to cross," and the four derivations are: tāraṇāya, "to make cross, to protect;" tīrṇāḥ, "have crossed;" vaitaraṇīṁ, "Vaitaraṇī, that is, the river which is hard to cross;" and taranti, "will cross."

Two similar instances can be found in two of the ten extant legends from Haribhaṭṭa's Jātakamālā or "Garland of Birth-Stories." The edition of the Sanskrit text appeared in the series *Publications of the Nepal Research Centre* (Kathmandu, Wiesbaden) in 1998.

Stanza 107 The long concluding portion of the "Letter to a Disciple," which begins with this stanza, consists of a series of exhortations and benedictions enhanced by various forms of linguistic repetition. In this stanza there are four instances of a noun repeated sequentially in two forms, accusative singular and genitive plural: bhūṣaṇaṁ bhūṣaṇānāṁ, bhāsuraṁ bhāsurāṇām, nandanaṁ nandanānāṁ, and maṅgalaṁ maṅgalānām. In stanza 108, double repetitions occur in sugata-vacanapuṣpa, sevanīyaṁ and niṣevyo, phalati phalam and madhuni madhu. In stanzas 110 through 112, the last line is the same, except for the final variation in the key term.

After having been quite brief for the last seventy to eighty stanzas, Prajñākaramati here begins again to give detailed explanations and to cite quotations—as if a bad conscience were urging him to try to make up for his previous brevity! According to him, this stanza alludes to the three trainings: bhūṣaṇa referring to morality, bhāsura referring to wisdom, and nandana referring to meditation. He tries to prove this by two quotations: "He who is endowed with morality is the best of all ornaments" and "O Muni, in dispelling the darkness of ignorance by the splendor of your knowledge, not even the sun, filled with fire, is able to match you." Maṅgala, "auspicious," in the last line then points to nirvana as the fruit of the three trainings.

Stanza 110 In this stanza nine central Buddhist terms are taught in the form of an elaborate simile.

Stanzas 111–12 The order of these two stanzas is reversed in the Tibetan translation, the Vṛtti, and the Ṭippaṇa.

Stanza 113 In the first line the text as transmitted in the Ms. is metrically incorrect: iti nigadatā yad upārjitaṁ puṇyaṁ mayā kiyat. After iti nigadatā we should have four long syllables followed by a caesura and then the sequence ∪ – ∪ ∪ – ∪ – . The Tibetan has | bdag gis de skad brjod pas bsod nams cung zad bsgrubs pa gang |. All we have to do is to replace kiyat, the equivalent of cung zad, by svalpaṁ and rearrange the words: punyaṁ svalpaṁ mayā yad upārjitaṁ.

Stanzas 113–15 Candragomin makes a triple dedication of merit: to the welfare and prosperity of all beings living in this world, to the unlucky beings suffering in the hells, and to the appearance of Buddhas in all world regions.

Stanza 116 The concluding stanza is identical to that of the bharatavākya or final blessing of the play *Joy for the World* (Act V, stanza 48; p. 134 of the English translation). Here Candragomin combines another blessing and dedication of merit with a pun on his own name in its abbreviated form, candra, "moon." While Prajñākaramati does not mention the pun, Vairocanarakṣita explains candrālokaḥ as tsandra go mi'i snang ba, "the splendor of Candragomin."

Part Two

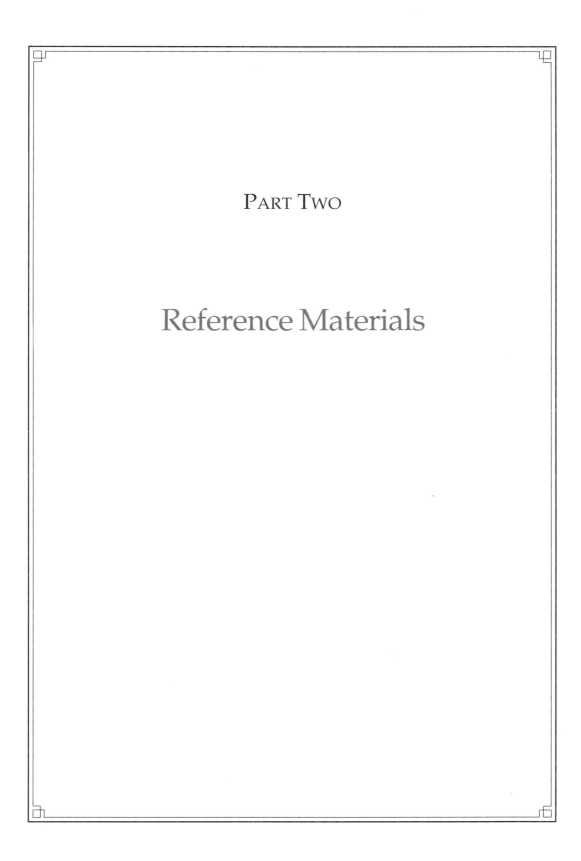

Reference Materials

About the Texts and Translations

"Letter to the Great King Kaniṣka"

The Sanskrit original of Mātṛceṭa's letter is lost. According to the colophon, the "Letter to the Great King Kaniṣka" was translated into Tibetan by the Indian abbot Vidyākaraprabha and the Tibetan translator Rin-chen-mchog; it was then corrected and edited by the teacher dPal-brtsegs.

In my opinion the Tibetan translation is an excellent piece of work, both lucid and pithy. As the Tibetan language of the early ninth century contains several archaic words and expressions, a few passages have remained unclear. It is also possible that some faulty readings have crept into the text in the course of transmission. One has always to bear in mind that five centuries elapsed between the original translation and its inclusion in the Tanjur, and another four centuries between the first handwritten copy of the Tanjur and the printed editions on which we rely today.

The Tibetan text presented here is based on my own critical edition of the Tibetan text, for which the four known xylographic editions of the Tanjur, those of Chone, Derge, Narthang, and Peking, were used.[1] For this publication it was also possible to use the manuscript Tanjur from Ganden, the so-called "Golden Tanjur."[2]

As far as the English translation is concerned, its first draft was written down in the summer of 1986, and precedes my

German translation published six years later. In the course of the revision of the English text done together with Zara Wallace in Berkeley in 1996 and 1997, every single line was reconsidered and in a number of places the interpretation could be slightly improved. The few unclear places the English translation still contains have to be credited to the transmission of the Tibetan text[3] and the limited abilities of the present translator.

"Letter to a Disciple"

My interest in this work goes back to 1972. While working on my German book on Candragomin's play *Joy for the World* in 1971 and 1972, I had briefly perused the "Letter to a Disciple" in the edition and (incomplete) Russian translation by the Russian scholar I. Minaev.[4] After the completion of my book in February 1972,[5] I wished to study the "Letter to a Disciple" more thoroughly and to compare it with its Tibetan translation, which had been published simultaneously with the Sanskrit text by another Russian scholar, Ivanovskij.[6] I had noticed that Minaev's edition contains quite a few gaps and unclear passages, several of which seemed to be emendable with the help of the Tibetan translation and other materials that will be described below.

The Sanskrit Sources

A: The Nepalese Manuscript from Cambridge

The most important source for the Sanskrit text of the Śiṣyalekha is an old palmleaf manuscript from Nepal that now belongs to the collections of the University Library, Cambridge. Its brief description in Cecil Bendall's catalogue[7] runs as follows: "Palm-leaf; 8 leaves, 8 lines, 12x2 in.; dated N. S. 204 (A.D. 1084)." It bears the library mark: Add. 1161. The manuscript is written in very neat characters in that older variety of the Newārī scripts that the Newārs of Nepal call Bhujimola or Bhoji(ṁ)mola. Its colophon is quite brief and matter-of-fact:

iti śiṣyalekhadharmakāvyaṁ samāptam || || kṛtir ācārya-candragomipādasya || samvat ā pka (?) 204 vaiśākhaṣukla aṣṭimyā somadine likhitam iti ||

"Herewith the Dharma poem Śiṣyalekha is completed. It is a work of the master Candragomin. It was copied on Monday in the (first) bright half of the month Vaiśākha of the year 204 [of the Nepalese era]."[8]

For my work I was able to use photostat copies that the late Prof. Frank-Richard Hamm, then director of the Indological Institute of the University of Bonn, Germany, had ordered from Cambridge at the end of the sixties. In 1976 I had a chance to go to Cambridge and see the original, which is still in good condition, although a little fragile and brittle. Only in the original can one see that some of the letters that had faded out in the course of time were redrawn by a later scribe, thereby overwriting what was still left of the old letter. As in the case of the oldest manuscript of the Buddhacarita, occasionally a presumably correct reading was thus replaced by a faulty emendation.

In a few places the manuscript is damaged. The first leaf has suffered most, so that parts of lines 4b, 5b, 6b, 7cd, 8cd, and 9d are lost. The right part of folio 2 is broken off; this affects, however, only the text on the reverse side. Thus one or two letters are missing in stanzas 20b, 21b, 22b, 23d, 25a, 26c, 28a, and 29c.

On the upper side of folio 3, the ends of lines 1 and 2 are broken off, which caused the loss of two syllables in stanza 28a and one syllable in 29c. On the reverse side of folio 3, the last two syllables are lost; they belong to stanza 47c.

The last minor mechanical damage occurs in the beginning of folio 7a, where five syllables in line 100a are completely or partially lost. There are a few other places where the scribe has inadvertently omitted a few syllables: 102c, 104c, 109b, and 110d. The manuscript is reproduced at the end of this book.

B: The Nepalese Manuscript from St. Petersburg

This is a manuscript now belonging to the Saltykov-Shchedrin Library in St. Petersburg, Russia. It was used by Minaev for his edition of the Śiṣyalekha. The manuscript consists of seven leaves and is written in Devanāgarī. Its colophon runs as follows:

ā pka nāma caturuttaradviśatamitanepālavarṣe tālapattre bhojiṁmolākṣaralikhitaṁ jīrṇībhūtaṁ dṛṣṭvā abhisāritam Amṛtānandācāryeṇa dvāsaptativārṣikenādrivedāṅka 947 varṣe vaiśākhe 'kṣayatṛtīyām iti | | śubham | |

"Having seen that [the text] written in Bhojimola characters on palmleaves in the year 204 of the Nepalese era was worn out, the teacher Amṛtānanda, at that time 72 years old, copied it[9] in the year 947 [of the Nepalese] era, on the third day of the bright half of the month Vaiśakha, the day of the Akṣayatṛtīya festival."

From this description it is quite clear that Amṛtānanda copied manuscript A. He indicates gaps in manuscript A with dashes and from them one can see that the latter was almost in the same condition it was 140 years later. Apart from a few obvious corrections, the manuscript contains several new mistakes and represents no independent testimony. For this reason we decided not to include its secondary variant readings.

C: The Nepalese Manuscript from Tokyo

Now kept in the University Library, Tokyo,[10] this manuscript is undated, and is, according to my impression, younger than B. It is written in Devanāgarī, and shows the same gaps as A and B. Therefore it must go back—either directly or indirectly—to A. It abounds in scribal errors and because of its secondary character, can be entirely neglected.

The Tibetan Sources

Much more important than the young manuscripts B and C are three Tibetan sources (D, E, F) preserved in the Tanjur:

D: The Tibetan translation of the Śiṣyalekha

This translation was done by Sarvajñādeva and dPal-brtsegs Rakṣi-ta at the beginning of the ninth century. Its numbers in the catalogues of the Derge and Peking canons are 4183 and 5683 respectively, and it can be found in the following places:

Chone	sPrin yig, vol. Nge, fols. 46b1–53a5	[C]
Derge	sPrin yig, vol. Nge, fols. 46b3–53a6	[D_1]
	Jo bo'i chos chung, fols. 65b6–72a6	[D_2]
Narthang	mDo 'grel, vol. Nge, fols. 286b3–294b7	[N_1]
	mDo 'grel, vol. Gi, fols. 70b6–78b1	[N_2]
Peking	mDo 'grel, vol. Nge, fols. 290a4–298b1	[Q_1]
	mDo 'grel, vol. Gi, fols. 81b4–89a3	[Q_2]

E: The Tibetan translation of Vairocanarakṣita's Śiṣyalekhaṭippa a

This text was translated by Sugataśrīmitra and Tshul-khrims rGyal-mtshan. Its numbers in the catalogues of the Derge and Peking canons are 4191 and 5691 respectively, and it can be found in the following places:

Chone	sPrin yig, vol. Nge, fols. 112a7–121b7
Derge	sPrin yig, vol. Nge, fols. 112a7–121b7
Narthang	mDo 'grel, vol. Gi, fols. 364b1–374a6
Peking	mDo 'grel, vol. Gi, fols. 376b2–389a5

F: The Tibetan translation of Prajñakaramati's Śiṣyalekhavṛtti

The translators were Vinayacandra and Chos-kyi Shes-rab. The text numbers in the catalogues of the Derge and the Peking canons are 4192 and 5692 respectively, and it can be found in the following places:

Chone	sPrin yig, vol. Nge, fols. 121b7–133a5
Derge	sPrin yig, vol. Nge, fols. 121b7–133a7
Narthang	mDo 'grel, vol. Gi, fols. 374b6–387a6
Peking	mDo 'grel, vol. Gi, fols. 389a5–404b3

Assessment of the Nepalese Manuscript

A careful comparison of the Nepalese manuscript A with the established text shows that it is marred by a great number of mistakes. They can be divided into two categories. The first and less important category consists of minor scribal errors. These minor mistakes can be classified under the following headings:

a. Careless use of vowel signs (either entirely omitted or a wrong sign is used; 25 cases)

b. Careless use of the visarga (omitted or wrongly added; 17 cases)

c. Careless use of the anusvāra (omitted or wrongly added; 17 cases)

d. Letter omitted or wrongly added (26 cases)

e. Confusion of the three sibilants (85 cases; predominantly sa for śa)

f. Confusion of the retroflex and dental nasals (12 cases)

g. Confusion of single or conjunct letters (18 cases)

h. Peculiar spelling (5 cases)

i. Wrong sandhi (3 cases)

j. Juxtaposition (2 cases)

This amounts to about 210 errors. In more than fifty percent of the cases (a, e and f), the correction was self-evident, since generally only spelling was affected. Even in the few cases where the misspelling yielded another correct word (sama for śama or sita for śita), the context and/or the Tibetan translation made immediately clear what was meant. In most of the other cases, the correct solution could be arrived at in a similar manner, very often by applying the basic rules of orthography and grammar. The few really difficult or ambiguous cases are discussed in the chapter entitled "Restorations and Emendations in the Śiṣyalekha."

The second category of mistakes consists of the following types:

a. Loss of text through mechanical damage to the manuscript

b. Text omitted (or added) by the scribe

c. Major corruptions (with both meaningful and nonsensical results)

d. Variant readings

The fifty or so cases belonging to this category are discussed in detail in the "Restorations and Emendations."

Assessment of the Tibetan Translation of the Śiṣyalekha

The Tibetan translation of the Śiṣyalekha was based on a Sanskrit manuscript that was much better than our manuscript A, and older by at least 270 years. There are four major discrepancies between these two manuscripts:

1. The older manuscript contained two additional stanzas, 64 and 71, whose authenticity is not quite clear.

2. The order of verses is reversed in stanzas 111 and 112.

3. The later manuscript contains an additional stanza which is obviously spurious.

4. The Tibetan translation of stanzas 88 and 89 was apparently based on a meaningful and correct text, whereas the Nepalese text has only six out of eight lines, and these are in disorder. Moreover, there are a few genuine variant readings like *kuliśaiḥ vs. kukṛtaiḥ (31b), *daṁṣṭrāṅkuśa vs damstrāṅkura (41b), and *meṣayugma vs. meṣayūtha (45a). I believe there is at least one common mistake in both manuscripts: kalike 'pi for *kati ke 'pi (95c).

The Tibetan translation in its original form was clearly an excellent piece of work, almost free of mistakes, written in a very good Tibetan style with a rich and expressive vocabulary, and remarkably free of "syntactical Sanskritisms," the unsuccessful imitation of the Sanskrit word order. The main problem connected with it is that it has suffered considerably in the course of the transmission in Tibet. The result is that the 18th-century editions of the Tanjur of the text are marred by a great number of mistakes and the variation among these editions is much greater than that among other comparable texts.

For the Śiṣyalekha we now have nine editions of the translation (the Ganden manuscript included), and five each for the two commentaries. That means that we have up to nineteen testimonies for a single word if that word is commented upon in the two commentaries. There are several cases where a word is corrupted not only in the Tibetan Śiṣyalekha but also in the commentaries (see the note on stanza 27, pp. 158–59), and it requires very time-consuming comparison and analysis to solve such cases. The restoration of the original Tibetan Śiṣyalekha as it was written down at the beginning of the ninth century, as far as is still possible, is a task that can be embarked upon only now, when the underlying Sanskrit text has been made available in an edited and fully documented form.

For the present edition of the Sanskrit text, all three Tibetan texts have been compared on the basis of my provisional editions. I have tried to include everything that has a bearing on the Sanskrit text.

About the Tibetan Commentaries

A word should be said about the two commentaries. Prajñākaramati's Vṛtti tries to explain both the surface structure and the deeper meaning of the Śiṣyalekha. Its general approach is very much like that of his huge commentary on Śāntideva's Bodhicaryāvatāra. However, after the first ten stanzas he confines himself to condensing the main idea of the stanza into a short sentence and to commenting on a few selected words. Only near the end, beginning with stanza 107, does he have a little more to say.

Vairocanarakṣita's Ṭippaṇa is meant to be a study-aid for the ordinary reader who has little more than a basic knowledge of the Sanskrit language. Because of its many detailed explanations of words and compounds, the Ṭippaṇa is very helpful in understanding the Tibetan Śiṣyalekha, and occasionally it gives a clue that leads to the solution of a textual problem in the Sanskrit text. I refer to the difficult *śā⟨ntye⟩kāntaṁ in line 109b where only the Ṭippaṇa contains a trace of both śānti and ekānta.

Footnotes

1 "Mātṛcetas Brief an den König Kaniṣka," *Études bouddhiques offertes à Jacques May, Asiatische Studien/ Études asiatiques* XLVI (1992), 147–79. It is preceded by the edition and translation into English by Frederick William Thomas, "Mātṛceṭa and the Mahārājakaniṣkalekha," in *Indian Antiquary* 32 (1903): 345–60. This was done when Indo-Tibetan studies in the West were still in their infancy.

2 I am grateful to Dr. Günter Grönbold, Oriental Section of the Bavarian State Library in Munich, Germany, for procuring me copies of the text, and to my colleague Dr. Roland Steiner, Marburg, for checking the variant readings on very short notice.

3 It is a great pity that among the Tibetan manuscripts found in the caves of Dunhuang there is not a single one of the Kaniṣkalekha.

4 "Poslanie k učeniku" [Letter to a Disciple], in *Zapiski vostočnago otdelenija imperatorskago russkago archelogičeskago obščestva* [Memoirs of the Oriental Section of the Imperial Russian Archeological Society] 4 (1889): 29–52.

5 It was published two years later under the title: *Candragomins Lokānandanāṭaka. Nach dem tibetischen Tanjur herausgegeben und übersetzt. Ein Beitrag zur klassischen indischen Schauspieldichtung.* Asiatische Forschungen 39. (Wiesbaden, 1974).

6 Tibetskij perevod "Poslanija k učeniku" [The Tibetan translation of the "Letter to a Disciple"], in *Zapiski vostočnago otdelenija imperatorskago russkago archelogičeskago obščestva* [Memoirs of the Oriental Section of the Imperial Russian Archeological Society] 4 (1889): 53–82. This is not a critical edition, since it is based on only one edition of the Tanjur and did not make use either of the Sanskrit text as edited by Minaev or the ancillary material described below.

7 See Cecil Bendall, *Catalogue of the Buddhist Sanskrit Manuscripts in the University Library, Cambridge* (Cambridge, 1883), pp. 31–32.

8 Vaiśākha is the name of the second lunar month, corresponding to the middle of April until the middle of May. The year 204 of the Nepalese era corresponds to the year 1084 C.E.

9 This is just a guess for abhisāritam, "made to meet."

10 For a detailed description, see Seiren Matsunami, *Catalogue of the Sanskrit Manuscripts in the Tokyo University Library* (Tokyo, 1965) no. 389, p. 140.

Other Examples of the Epistolary Genre

Siglinde Dietz's monograph on the epistolary literature of the Indian Buddhists presents nine of the thirteen letters in critical editions and annotated German translations. The long introduction informs the reader about the particulars of the thirteen epistles and also offers a literary study of the lekha genre. The following descriptions of ten epistles are primarily based on this publication.[1]

Letters of the Early Period 2nd–5th centuries C.E.

Nāgārjuna's "Letter to a Friend"

The famous "Letter to a Friend" or Suhṛllekha by Nāgārjuna is the oldest of the Buddhist epistles, and like Matṛceṭa's and Candragomin's letters, belongs to the early period of the second through the fifth centuries. The "friend" mentioned in the title of the work is most probably a South Indian ruler of the Sātavāhana dynasty, either Vasiṣṭhīputra Puḷumāyi II or Gautamīputra Śatakarṇī. The content of the epistle is basically an instruction in the principal tenets of Buddhism for a layman.

The structure of the Suhṛllekha is quite clear. After a brief introduction (stanzas 1–3), the most important constituents of the Buddha's teaching are put forward in an easy, almost narrative manner, frequently illustrated by well-chosen similes from common human experience (stanzas 4–64). The "positive" instructions are followed by a set of warnings that describe the seven evils of the circle of rebirth (stanzas 65–103). The various forms of suffering in the different spheres of rebirth, including god and demi-god, are depicted with particular vividness. The letter concludes with five exhortatory stanzas (119–23).

Despite the popularity of this work, not a single line of its 123 stanzas seems to have survived in any Sanskrit manuscript or quotation. The letter survives in one Tibetan[2] and three Chinese[3] translations. A commentary by a certain Mahāmati is also preserved in Tibetan translation.

The "Letter to a Friend" has been translated into modern languages several times. Siglinde Dietz lists nine translations, into English, German, Japanese, and Danish. One of the English translations, accompanied by Lama Mi-pham's commentary, "The Garland of White Flowers," translated by Leslie Kawamura, has been published as *Golden Zephyr* by Dharma Publishing in the Tibetan Translation Series. For valuable notes on the meaning of difficult words and terms in the "Letter to a Friend," the reader is referred to *Master of Wisdom, Writings of the Buddhist Master Nāgārjuna,* translated by Chr. Lindtner, also published in the Tibetan Translation Series. Because of the availability of these two books, we refrain from giving more details of the content of Nāgārjuna's epistle.

Letters of the Middle Period 8th–9th centuries C.E.

"Letter Sent to the Monk Rab-gsal gZhon-nu by the Noble Avalokiteśvara"

A brief prose portion introduces the letter, which is only eleven stanzas. In the letter, Avalokiteśvara informs his friend, the monk Rab-gsal gZhon-nu ("the prince or youth 'very brilliant'"), that he has attained enlightenment and then exhorts him to listen to religious instructions (stanzas 1–3). A prayer to Avalokiteśvara follows (stanzas 4–11). The letter is even less structured than most of the other letters in the Tanjur, and appears to be a remnant of a once longer epistle. The opening of the letter demonstrates its character:

Homage to all Buddhas and Bodhisattvas!

Once upon a time when the noble Avalokiteśvara and the monk Rab-gsal first developed the thought of enlightenment (bodhicitta), they became friends and promised one another that whoever first realized the way [to enlightenment] would help the other. When this way had first been realized by the noble Avalokiteśvara, he wrote a letter in order to assist the monk Rab-gsal gZhon-nu.

Friend, are you well?
Did you ever forget the promise?
How is it possible for someone to long for this desire
that is like a pit full of charcoal?
How is it possible that desire, the cause of being,
is still so strong
although the weary mind does not care for it at all ? [1]

Attain liberation by the best of the vehicles[4]
for the welfare of [all] beings!
If you do not immediately strive for the way
of liberation from being, untormented by
[thoughts of] guile, flattery, fame, or wealth,
you will be deprived of the profit
that is preserved with such difficulty
by the Victorious Ones of the three times. [2]

Please listen carefully
[to the following instruction]—
although it is subtle,
difficult to understand, and

beyond the realm of words,
and has been practiced
by all the seers of the three times,
who have abandoned concepts and
are free from conceptualization—
and keep (it) in your mind,
when (it) is explained to you
by the power of a Victorious One
[in such a way] that through conceptualization
only one level (of meaning) is attributed to it. [3] [5]

"Description of the [Eight] Kinds of Suffering" by Kamalaśīla

The Indian master Kamalaśīla, a disciple of Śāntarakṣita (740–795), was invited to Tibet during the rule of King Khri-srong lDe'u-btsan (742–797). There he took part in the famous debate at Samye (792–794), in which he successfully defended Indian Buddhism against the Chinese teacher Hva Shang, a follower of the Ch'an school. Shortly after his triumph, Kamalaśīla was murdered. Four of his works are preserved both in Sanskrit and Tibetan; sixteen more works dealing primarily with the "Perfection of Wisdom" literature and Madhyamaka philosophy are available only in Tibetan, among them this letter, which was originally composed in Tibetan.

The addressee of the letter is given both in the heading and in the colophon as lHo-za-mo Tshangs-pa'i dByangs. Since the letter was not translated from Sanskrit, it is clear that this must have been a Tibetan name. Tshangs-pa'i dByangs, meaning the "voice of Brahma," offers no difficulties, but lHo-za-mo, which is attested to nowhere else, remains unclear in both meaning and gender. From the gender suffix 'mo' we would expect it to refer to a woman. In any case, it is obviously a personal name and for that reason the work was included in the letter section of the Tibetan Tanjur, although it is termed "instruction" (nirdeśa) rather than "letter." While "instructions" are related to the "letters" in content, they are not usually addressed to an individual.

The letter must have been composed sometime between 788 and 795, and was written at the request of lHo-za-mo Tshangs-pa'i dByangs. It consists of a short prose passage followed by thirty stanzas of varying length: Stanzas 1 through 6 form a kind of introduction, stanzas 7 through 26 the central section, and stanzas 27 through 30 the conclusion. Here is a brief extract describing the suffering of death:

When his words have become confused
and his eyes have sunken in,
it is of no use to kiss the face of the dying one,
who wavers between hope and fear,
or to touch his breast;
it is of no use to weep or wail
or to hold and embrace him. [14]

It is impossible to resist
the suffering caused by the hangman "Death,"
who cuts life and tears the heart apart;
it is impossible to resist illness and death.
No man escapes death. [15][6]

"Letter to the Ruler, Nobility, and Subjects of Tibet" by Buddhaguhya

The author of this letter was the Indian Tantric teacher Buddhaguhya. In the Tibetan Tanjur we find, besides the letter, twenty-two more works attributed to Buddhaguhya, all of which belong to the Tantra class. According to Tibetan sources, Padmasambhava and Vimalamitra were among his disciples. Tāranātha relates that Buddhaguhya was a devotee of Mañjuśrī. He taught for some years in Vārāṇasī and then settled near Mount Kailāsa in order to attain spiritual perfection. There he received an invitation from King Khri-srong lDe'u-btsan to come to Tibet. He declined the invitation, like Mātṛceṭa sending a letter instead. In the letter, which was composed in Tibetan, he explains why he is unable to accept the king's invitation:

Having been invited from a high place,
I tried [to come]
but lacked the power.
The noble Mañjuśrī also prophesied
that I would die if I went to Tibet.
Since I lack the power [to come],
I have sent to the king as a present
the instruction called 'Yogāvatāra'
or 'Introduction to Yoga'. [1.9] [7]

The long letter consists of five sections—an introduction and four instructions: for the king, the ministers, the higher clergy, and the lower clergy. There is no instruction for the subjects or common people ('bangs) mentioned in the title and colophon. Perhaps such instruction was omitted because of the illiteracy of the common people at that time, or perhaps it has been lost.

The letter is written in verse, in a very elegant style that, because of its antiquity and its many archaic words, is not easy to understand. The length of the individual sections is 10, 26, 14, 6, and 20 stanzas respectively. The first two sections of the letter contain many interesting historical details that enabled Siglinde Dietz to determine the time of composition as between 780 and 790. Because of its historical, linguistic, and literary importance, this letter should be made accessible to the English-speaking world as soon as possible.

In stanzas 2.11 and 12, Buddhaguhya exhorts the king:

Where merits are high,
the wish-granting tree stands in full blossom.
In the kingdom of Tibet,
which has so far had only limited merits,
the Tāla tree "Henceforth No Rebirth"

has started to grow.
See to it that no harm is done to this tree,
and that it is not cut down. [11]

Monasteries, stupas, and palaces
are opposed to bad deeds
and are the foundation of [good] deeds.
Have the holy Dharma translated
and [the translations constantly] improved!
At the proper time it (i.e. the Dharma)
should be made the [sole] authority. [12] [8]

"Letter that Summarizes the Essence (of the Doctrine)" by dPal-dbyangs

dPal-dbyangs or "Voice of Bliss," the author of this letter, was one of the first seven Tibetan monks, called sad mi or "awakened beings," who were ordained by Śāntarakṣita at Samye Monastery in 779. He succeeded Śāntarakṣita as abbot of Samye and took part in the famous debate there on the side of Kamalaśīla. Seven more of his works are preserved in the Tibetan Tanjur. Most of them deal with philosophy, both Buddhist and Hindu.

The "Letter that Summarizes the Essence" was composed in Tibetan and is addressed to the people of Tibet. The second verse of the introduction gives a classification of social strata that undoubtedly represents the actual divisions of society at that time. The letter is meant to help the people of Tibet on their way to liberation. dPal-dbyangs does not mention a specific reason or occasion for the letter. Its date has been determined by Siglinde Dietz as between 779 and 788. Like Buddhaguhya's "Letter to the Ruler, Nobility, and Subjects of Tibet," this letter contains several historical details that alone make it a valuable document.

This is the longest of all the letters in the Tanjur; it covers eleven folios or twenty-two pages in the Derge edition. Apart from a few prose portions, the letter is written entirely in verse. In her edition and translation Siglinde Dietz divides the letter into the following sections:

Chapter 1 Introduction (6 stanzas)

Chapter 2 General instruction

2.1 The ten wholesome conditions (9 stanzas)

2.2 The 16 moral duties (3 stanzas)

2.3 The 10 things to be considered (3 stanzas)

2.4 The 10 kinds of religious conduct (5 stanzas)

2.5 The moral perfections (5 stanzas)

2.5 Conclusion (1 stanza)

Chapter 3 Instruction for the king

3.1 Extract from the "Letter to the Great King Kaniṣka" (21 stanzas)

3.2 Extract from the "Letter to a Friend" (11 stanzas)

3.3 Extract from Nāgārjuna's "Necklace of Jewels" (9 stanzas)

Chapter 4 General instruction

4.1 Instruction for the subjects (20 stanzas)

4.2 Instruction for the ministers (10 stanzas)

4.3 Instruction for the monastic Sangha (40 stanzas)

Chapter 5 Extract from "Entering the Bodhisattva Path" (84 stanzas)

Chapter 6 Conclusion
(22 stanzas, mainly from the "Necklace of Jewels")

For the most part this letter is a compilation of quotations from Buddhavacana or from the writings of famous Indian masters like Nāgārjuna, Mātṛceṭa, and Śāntideva. The introduction and chapters 4.2 and 4.3 seem not to be based on other works. The quotations are handled in a rather free manner, sometimes exactly reproduced from their source, sometimes interwoven with additional explanations and clarifications by dPal-dbyangs.

Letters of the Third Period 10th–12th Centuries C.E.

"Graded Course of the Purification of the 'Mind-Jewel'" by Jitāri

Jitāri was a famous Buddhist philosopher who lived in the second half of the tenth century. He is said to have been a professor at the Buddhist university of Nālandā and a teacher of Atiśa. Tāranātha gives a brief description of his life in his *History of Buddhism in India.* Twelve of Jitāri's philosophical works—most of them quite short—are preserved in Sanskrit. In the Tibetan Tanjur we find twenty-four more works: eight of them philosophical, thirteen relating to Tantra, and the one letter.

The addressee of the letter is not expressly mentioned, although invocations such as "ruler of the earth" and "lord of men" suggest that he was a king. The letter describes the five steps of the purification of mind, which is said to be "radiant by nature." Written in both prose and verse, the letter makes use of a great number of quotations from canonical and postcanonical works. Dietz divides the letter into eight chapters as follows:

Chapter 1 Introduction

Chapter 2 Purification from wrong notions through breathing techniques

Chapter 3 Purification from passion through visualizing the impure

Chapter 4 Purification from anger through the Four Immeasurables

Chapter 5 Purification from ignorance by understanding dependent arising

Chapter 6 Presentation of harmful wrong views

Chapter 7 Purification by means of constructing a mandala[9]

Chapter 8 Conclusion

The mature treatment of the subject matter, the purification of the mind, makes Jitāri's letter another valuable document within the genre.

"Letter to the Spiritual Teacher" by the Monk Āraṇyaka

The name of the author is reconstructed from the colophon of the Tibetan translation, where he is called dGon-pa-pa, "the one who lives in the solitude (of a forest)." It is uncertain whether he is identical with the Kālacakra teacher mentioned in the *Blue Annals,* and it is not known to whom this letter was written. From the date of the Tibetan translation (second half of the eleventh century), it is clear that the letter must have been composed before that date. The author himself divides the letter into four chapters:

Introduction (8 stanzas)

Chapter 1 Removal of passion (18 stanzas)

Chapter 2 Removal of craving (18 stanzas)

Chapter 3 Removal of carelessness (13 stanzas)

Chapter 4 Removal of the defilements (10 stanzas)

Although the title of the letter—its Sanskrit is Gurulekha—sounds like an allusion to the famous "Letter to a Disciple" by Candragomin, it cannot compete with the older work because it completely lacks originality. Chapters 1 through 3 quote verbatim chapters 2 through 4 of the Udānavarga, "Solemn Utterings (of the Buddha)," the enlarged Sanskrit counterpart of the Pāli Dhammapada, and the introduction and chapter 4 also make use of ideas expressed elsewhere. Dietz characterized the letter as "a student's exercise."

"Letter to the Son" by Sajjana

Sajjana, the author of this letter, lived in the eleventh century. No other of his works are preserved, either in Sanskrit or in Tibetan translation. Together with his Tibetan disciple Blo-ldan Shes-rab, he translated two important works by Maitreya and Asaṅga into Tibetan.[10] The name of the addressee, his own son, is mentioned in stanza 4.18 as skye bo chen po, "great (human) being." This corresponds to Skt. Mahājana, which occurs in the introduction of the letter (stanza 0.1) in Tibetan transliteration. The occasion for the letter is also mentioned in the letter itself:

The intelligent son may be enlightened
by the lamp of wisdom,
when he is wandering alone in the darkness
at the border of a barbarian country
after having recklessly abandoned like a blob of mucus
his loving parents and the host of his relatives. [0.2][11]

And in stanza 1.2cd he says:

How can it be right
to abandon one's own parents
for the sake of the pleasures of the senses,
and roam about in a despicable country?[12]

The purpose of the letter is to warn his son of the typical dangers to which a young man is subjected: sense pleasures, money, passion for women, and alcohol. Accordingly the letter can be structured into the following five sections:

Introduction (3 stanzas)

Chapter 1 Removal of the longing for pleasures of the senses (6 stanzas)

Chapter 2 Removal of the longing for possessions (6 stanzas)

Chapter 3 Removal of the longing for women (18 stanzas)

Chapter 4 Removal of the longing for alcohol (19 stanzas)

Conclusion (1 stanza)

The letter draws amply from canonical sources, Buddhist birth stories, and gnomic sayings, which are combined more skillfully than in the "Letter to the Spiritual Teacher," and has a warm personal tone.

"Letter Consisting of Flawless Jewels" by Atiśa

This letter was composed by the renowned Indian master Atiśa[13] (982–1054), the teacher of 'Brom-ston. A great number of his works are included in the Tibetan Tanjur. There are several detailed Tibetan biographies of Atiśa that have been analyzed by Indian and Western scholars.[14]

The "Letter Consisting of Flawless Jewels" is one of Atiśa's minor works. According to the biographical work rNam-thar-rgyas-pa, it was written in the year 1040 when Atiśa left for Tibet, and was sent to the Indian king Niryapāla or Nayapāla. This is, by the way, the only letter whose exact date of composition is known. In stanza 39cd Atiśa explains why he wrote this letter:

Although [this] has indeed been said
by many wise people,
I wrote (it) down, O king,
to end your suffering.[15]

The letter consists of forty stanzas, most in four lines, giving moral instructions of the most elementary kind. There is no discernible structural principle. The letter shares most of its stanzas with another work by Atiśa, the "Jewel Necklace for the Bodhisattva" (Bodhisattvamaṇyāvalī).

"Letter to King Candra" by Mitrayogin

The name of the author is given in stanza 2 of the letter as "a yogi by the name of Mitra," Grogs-po'i Ming-can rNal-'byor-(gyis). In the colophon, however, he is called Jaganmitrānanda, which according to Bu-ston's *History of Buddhism,* is another name of Mitrayogin, who was perhaps also called Ajitamitragupta. Ajitamitra, Ajitagupta, and Śrīmitra may have been other alternative names.

The *Blue Annals* contains a detailed biography of Mitrayogin, who must have lived in the second half of the twelfth century. In the Tibetan Tanjur there are four more works attributed to Mitrayogin that have not yet been analyzed. Twelve additional works, mostly belonging to the Tantra section, are attributed to Jaganmitrānanda, Ajitamitragupta, Ajitamitra, Ajitagupta, and Śrīmitra.

According to Dietz, the name Candra might refer to the Gāhaḍavāla ruler Jayacandra, who fell in a battle against the Muslims in the year 1193 C.E. If this is correct, then the letter must have been composed before that date. The letter consists of fifty stanzas, most with four lines per verse. Dietz proposes the following structure:

Introduction (stanzas (1–2)

General instruction about the common vices (stanzas 3–10)

Warning not to be enticed by the pleasantness of being (stanzas 11–25)

The circle of birth and rebirth (stanzas 26–36)

Teachings of the heretics (stanzas 37–45)

Conclusion (stanzas 46–50)

The letter is written in a simple and mellifluous style, obviously with the recipient in mind. It does not contain any quotations. Here is an example of its style:

O Lord, however rich you may be in this world,
the moment you proceed to the other world
after your death,
you are without your sons and without your wife,
as lonely as an ascetic in the solitude of a forest. [32][16]

Footnotes

1 Like Siglinde Dietz, we exclude from our survey the "Letter about Wisdom" (Prajñālekha) of Padmavajra (D 2455, P 3283) because it has been placed in the Tantra section of the Tibetan Tanjur by the editors of the Tibetan Buddhist Canon and is of a different character.

2 Translated in the beginning of the ninth century C.E. by Sarvajñādeva and sKa-ba dPal-brtsegs.

3 By Guṇavarman (431 C.E.), Saṅghavarman (434 C.E.), and I-Tsing (673 C.E.).

4 i.e. the Great Vehicle, the Mahāyāna.

5 | sngon 'phags pa spyan ras gzigs dbang phyug dang dge slong rab gsal gzhon nu gnyis dang por byang chub kyi mchog tu sems bskyed de grogs por 'thams nas | gang gis lam sngon du grub pa des cig shos la bstang bar dam bcas pa las | 'phags pa spyan ras gzigs dbang phyug gis lam sngon du grub ste dge slong rab gsal gzhon nu la bstang ba'i phyir phrin yig gis bzlugs pa |

| grogs khyod ci bde'am dam bcas brjed dam ci |
| 'dod pa me mdag dong 'dra 'di la ci zhig chags |
| shin tu skyo ba'i yid kyis rab tu mi 'bad par |
| srid rgyu 'dod pa da dung gang ba ga la srid | [1]

| theg pa mchog gis nges 'byung 'gro ba'i don byos la |
| sgyu dang kha gsag grags pa rnyed la mi gdung zhing |
| 'gro las rnam grol lam la myur du ma 'bad na |
| dus gsum rgyal bas bskyab dka' phan thag chad du 'ong | [2]

| rtog med rtog bral dus gsum thub pa kun gshegs shul |
| phra zhing shes dka' thsig gi spyod yul ma yin yang |
| phyogs tsam rtog pas sgro btags rgyal ba'i mthus brjod na |
| shin tu legs par rab nyon yid la gzung nus sam | [3]

From Dietz, *op. cit.*, pp. 132, 134.

6 | tshig kyang 'chol nas mig kyang khur bur bros |
| re gdung bred ngo 'o byas snying gtugs nas |
| ngus shing gdungs nas smre sngags mang po bton |
| 'jus shing 'phyangs kyang phan pa ci yang med | [14]

| gshed ma 'chi bdag srog gcod snying *gcu ba'i |
| sdug bsngal nad na shi ba mi phod de |
| shi las thar ba'i sems can gcig kyang med | [15]

From Dietz, *op. cit.*, p. 348.

7 | yas kyi sa nas bdag 'dra spyan 'dren pa |
| sku gnyer lags te bdag la dbang ma mchis |
| 'phags pa 'jam dpal zhal nas bod yul du |
| khyod kyis phyin na srog dang 'bral bar gsungs |
| bdag la dbang med khri *ldan skyes lan du |
| man ngag yo ga a ba ta ra brdzangs | [1.9]

From Dietz, *op. cit.*, pp. 362, 364.

8 | bsod nams che bar dpag bsam shing bu 'khrungs |
| bsod nams chung ba'i bod kyi rgyal khams su |
| shing bu ta la phyis mi skye ba 'khrungs |
| shing la gnod kyis 'chad pa shol cig mchi'o | [2.11]

| gtsug lag khang dang mchod rten khang bzangs rnams |
| sdig pa kun la gnod de las rmang yin |
| dam chos bsgyur ba zhu thug dag tu mdzod |
| lan cig dus su tshad mar byed par mchi'o | [2.12]

From Dietz, *op. cit.*, pp. 370, 372.

9 This chapter is also transmitted separately in the Tibetan Tanjur: D 3763, Q 4582.

10 The Mahāyānottaratantraśāstra by Maitreya (D 4024, Q 5525) and the Mahāyānottaratantraśāstravyākhyā by Asaṅga (D 4025, Q 5526).

11 | mchog tu brtse ba'i pha ma mdza' bshes gnyen 'dun tshogs |
| mchil ma'i thal ba bzhin du ltos med yal dor nas |
| mtha' khob kla klo mun pa'i nang na gcig 'khyam pa |
| blo ldan bu de shes rab sgron mes snang gyur cig | [0.2]

From Dietz, *op. cit.*, p. 272.

12 | 'dod pa'i don du pha ma yal dor nas |
| smad pa'i yul du rgyu ba ga la rigs |

From Dietz, *op. cit.*, p. 274.

13 Atiśa is an honorific title that he received during his stay in Tibet. His original (ordination) name is Dīpaṁkaraśrījñāna.

14 Alaka Chattopadhya, *Atīśa and Tibet* (Calcutta, 1967). This book has now been superseded by Helmut Eimer, *Berichte über das Leben des Atiśa (Dīpaṁkaraśrījñāna)* [Records of the life of Atiśa]. Asiatische Forschungen 51 (Wiesbaden, 1977) and *Rnam thar rgyas pa. Materialien zu einer Biographie des Atiśa (Dīpaṁkaraśrījñāna)* [rNam thar rgyas pa. Materials for a life of Atiśa], Pts. 1 and 2. Asiatische Forschungen 67 (Wiesbaden, 1979).

15 | mkhas pa mang pos gsungs pa yod mod kyi |
| rgyal po gdung ba gcad phyir bris pa yin | [39cd]

From Dietz, *op. cit.*, p. 316.

16 | lha cig ji ltar khyod 'byor kyang |
| gshegs nas 'jig rten gzhan bzhud tshe |
| mya ngan thang la dgra bcom ltar |
| gcig pu sras med btsun mo min | [32]

From Dietz, *op. cit.*, p. 332.

Variant Readings in the Tibetan Text of the Mahārājakaniṣkalekha

What follows is the critical apparatus to the Tibetan text of the Mahārājakaniṣkalekha, based on the Tanjur editions of Chone, Derge, Ganden, Narthang, and Peking. In the latter four editions the Mahārājakaniṣkalekha is contained twice. In agreement with the proposal by Helmut Eimer and Paul Harrison which was published in the proceedings of the 7th Seminar of the International Association for Tibetan Studies (Wien, 1997), we now use the abbreviations C, D, G, N and Q (from Qianlong) for the five editions just mentioned. The duplicate texts of the latter four editions are here distinguished by the index numbers 1 and 2: D_1, D_2, and so on.

For Chone I used the microfiche edition of the Institute for Advanced Studies of World Religions (Stony Brook, USA).

For Derge I used my own copy of the Derge Tanjur and the Jo bo'i chos chung.

For Ganden I used the Chinese reprint kept in the Bayrische Staatsbibliothek, München. I am obliged to Dr. Günter Grönbold, Director of the Oriental Section, for providing me with copies on very short notice and to my friend and colleague Dr. Roland Steiner for comparing its readings with my published edition of the Mahārājakaniṣkalekha (1992) while I was in Berkeley.

For Narthang I consulted the copy kept in the Staatsbibliothek zu Berlin, Preussischer Kulturbesitz, Orientabteilung. I am indebted to Dr. Hartmut-Ortwin Feistel, director of the Oriental section, for providing me with copies of the Narthang edition. Like almost all the Narthang editions known to the scholarly world (with the noteworthy exception of the copy belonging to the British Library), the one kept in Berlin is difficult to read or even illegible in many places and therefore the readings reported here are not always reliable.

For Peking I relied on the well-known Japanese reprint, Tokyo/Kyoto 1957.

The readings are presented in the following way: In the first section all the genuine variant readings are given, including all the many ambiguous readings that are due to the partly imperfect source material used for this edition. If I could have used clear prints of the original editions, their number would most probably be considerably less. I have also included the variant readings of the 21 stanzas quoted in the Sārasaṁgrahalekha or "Letter that Summarizes the Essence" by dPal-dbyangs (see "Other Examples of the Epistolary Genre," pp. 202–4 of this book); these readings are abbreviated by SSL.

The second section contains peculiarities of spelling, such as subscribed letters and contractions, as well as specific mistakes of individual editions that cannot be regarded as genuine variant readings. This was done in agreement with the principles of textual criticism and in order not to overburden the critical apparatus with unimportant scribal errors.

Because of the limitations mentioned above, the edition leaves much to be desired in terms of brevity and clarity, and it is certainly not wise to draw far-reaching conclusions from the readings of a relatively short text. I might come back to this point in connection with the proposed critical edition of the Tibetan Śiṣyalekha and its two commentaries. Nevertheless the tendency of the readings is clear and supports what we know from other Tanjur texts (except the stotra volume which shows a different picture): Chone (C) is clearly dependent on Derge (D_1) and deviates from it in only seven cases: 14c, 16c 20b, 28b, 62c, 69b, 83b. Five of these are definitely later deteriorations; only two (20b and 69b) are somewhat difficult to explain. Similarly Peking (Q_1) follows Narthang (N_1) almost slavishly. Only four out of twelve deviations (23c, 54b, 67c, 69d) cannot be explained graphically or phonetically.

As far as the other variant readings are concerned there are three greater groups which are clearly discernible:

1. $G_2N_2Q_2$ share 50 common readings against all the other testimonies. There are 3 more cases with the split G_2Q_2 - N_2 and N_2Q_2 - G_2 against the group $CD_1D_2G_1N_1Q_1$.

2. $G_1N_1Q_1$ share 44 common readings against the group $CD_1D_2G_2N_2Q_2$. In 5 more cases D_2 joins $G_1N_1Q_1$.

3. CD_1 share 23 readings against the group $D_2G_1G_2N_1N_2Q_1Q_2$.

Finally there are three subgroups CD_1D_2 (9 times against $G_1G_2N_1N_2Q_1Q_2$) and $CD_1G_1N_1Q_1$ (9 times against $D_2G_2N_2Q_2$) and D_2 (9 times against the rest of the readings). This shows the independent character of the Jo bo'i chos chung tradition in which D_2 again forms a separate branch and the close affinity of the member of the group $G_1N_1Q_1$ which has already earlier been observed. Likewise D_1 shows an independent stance that is certainly due to its well-known philological competence and carefulness.

"$G_2N_2Q_2$ rep." refers to the erroneous repetition of stanzas 11–13 after stanza 36 in these three editions, as mentioned in the critical apparatus.

The canonical editions contain the following editorial remarks in the beginning of the translation:

Pretitle: | | rgyal po chen po ka ni ka la springs pa'i 'phrin yig bzhugs so | | : Only in Q_1Q_2; 'phrin yig Q_1] spring yig Q_2

Transliterated Sanskrit title: | rgya gar skad du | ma hā rā dza ka ni ska le kha | ni ska $CD_1D_2N_2Q_2$] ni ka $G_1G_2N_1Q_1$

Tibetan Title: bod skad du | rgyal po chen po ka nis ka la springs pa'i 'phrin yig | : ni ska CD_1] ni ka $G_1G_2N_1N_2Q_1Q_2$, nis ka D_2; springs pa'i $G_1N_1Q_1$] spring ba'i $CD_1D_2G_2N_2Q_2$

1b de $CD_1D_2G_1N_1Q_1$] te $G_2N_2Q_2$

1d rga $CD_1G_1N_1Q_1$] rgas $D_2G_2N_2Q_2$; kyis D_2] kyi $CD_1G_1G_2N_1N_2Q_1Q_2$

2b kyi $D_2G_1G_2N_1N_2Q_1Q_2$] kyis CD_1

3a bgyi CD_1D_2] kyi $G_1N_1Q_1$, bgyis $G_2N_2Q_2$

3b sus $CD_1D_2G_2N_2Q_2$] su $G_1N_1Q_1$; thogs $CD_1D_2G_1N_1Q_1$] thog $G_2N_2Q_2$

3d brtol $CD_1D_2G_2N_2Q_2$] brdol $G_1N_1Q_1$; gyur $CD_1D_2G_2N_2Q_2$] 'gyur $G_1N_1Q_1$

4a bzlog CD_1] zlog D_2, zlogs $G_1G_2N_1N_2Q_1Q_2$

4b bsgos $CD_1D_2G_1Q_1$] bsgo-s N_1, bsgoms $G_2N_2Q_2$

4c thugs $CD_1G_1G_2N_1N_2Q_1Q_2$] thug D_2

5a gtod $D_2G_1G_2N_1Q_1$] gtong (?) N_2Q_2, bstod CD_1

5b gis $CD_1D_2G_2N_2Q_2$] gi G_1(bdagi)N_1Q_1; gsol ba $CD_1D_2G_1N_1Q_1$] gsol pa $G_2N_2Q_2$

5c ba'i phyogs $CD_1D_2G_2N_2Q_2$] ba yid $G_1N_1Q_1$

6c de $CD_1D_2G_2N_2Q_2$] dang $G_1N_1Q_1$

7a 'phung $G_2N_2Q_2$] phung $CD_1G_1D_2N_1Q_1$

7b bsten sten brten D_2

7c gdul $G_1G_2N_1N_2Q_1Q_2$] dul CD_1D_2

8a kyi CD_1D_2] kyis $G_1G_2N_1N_2Q_1Q_2$; nyes $D_2G_1G_2N_1N_2Q_1Q_2$] nyos CD_1; gyur pa'i $CD_1D_2G_1N_1Q_1$] 'gyur ba'i $G_2N_2Q_2$

9d kyis $CD_1D_2G_2N_2Q_2$] kyi $G_1N_1Q_1$

10a na $CD_1D_2G_1N_1Q_1$] ni $G_2N_2Q_2$; kyi $D_2G_1G_2N_1N_2Q_1Q_2$] kyis CD_1

10b nyam $CD_1D_2G_1N_1Q_1$] nyams $G_2N_2Q_2$

11a las $CD_1D_2G_2N_2Q_2$] la $G_1N_1Q_1$

11b brgal $CD_1D_2G_2N_2Q_2$] sgal $G_1N_1Q_1$

11c bskyed $CD_1D_2G_1N_1Q_1$] skyed $G_2N_2Q_2$

11d dgyes $CD_1D_2G_1N_1Q_1$] bgyis pa'i $G_2N_2Q_2$

12a bgyi $CD_1D_2G_1N_1Q_1$] gyi G_2Q_2, gyis N_2

13b pa yi $CD_1G_1N_1Q_1$] pa yis $G_2N_2Q_2$, spyod pa'i D_2

13c da ltar $CD_1G_1N_1Q_1$] de ltar $D_2G_2N_2Q_2$

13d between lines 36b and c stanzas 11–13 are repeated in $G_2N_2Q_2$ with several variant readings; see there.

14b nyung zad $D_1D_2G_1N_1Q_1$] nyung zod C; cung zad $G_2N_2Q_2$

15c 'gyur $CD_1D_2G_1G_2N_1Q_1$] 'gyu N_2Q_2

16a dpe $CD_1D_2G_1N_1Q_1$] de $G_2N_2Q_2$

16d dges $D_1G_1G_2N_1N_2Q_1Q_2$] dgos C, dgyes D_2, SSL 3.1.9d

17d kyi CD_1] kyis $D_2G_1G_2N_1N_2Q_1Q_2$

18a kyis $D_2G_1N_1N_2Q_1Q_2$] kyi CD_1G_2; phongs $CD_1G_2N_2Q_2$] 'phongs $D_2G_1N_1Q_1$

18b brkam $D_2G_1G_2N_1N_2Q_1$] brgam Q_2, skams CD_1; zhing $D_2G_1G_2N_1N_2Q_1Q_2$] shing CD_1

18c kha gsag $CD_1D_2G_1N_1Q_1$] kha ba $G_2N_2Q_2$; bzad pa CD_1D_2] bzang ba $G_1G_2N_1N_2Q_1Q_2$, SSL 3.1.14e

18d na'ang $D_2G_1N_1Q_1$] nang $G_2N_2Q_2$, na rang CD_1; bstsal

19a yi $CD_1D_2G_2N_2Q_2$] yis $G_1N_1Q_1$

20a dka' $CD_1D_2G_1N_1Q_1$] dga' $G_2N_2Q_2$

20b dor $CD_2G_1G_2N_1Q_1$] 'dor $D_1N_2Q_2$

22b 'dun $CD_1D_2G_1G_2N_1Q_1$] mdun N_2Q_2

22d phal par CD_1D_2] phal pa $G_2N_2Q_2$, phan pa $G_1N_1Q_1$

23c bden pa $D_2G_2N_2Q_1Q_2$] bde ba $CD_1G_1N_1$

24b yang $CD_1D_2G_2N_2Q_2$] dbyangs $G_1N_1Q_1$

24d zhig $D_2G_1N_1Q_1$] shig CD_1, cing G_2N_2(?)Q_2

25b gnang $CD_1D_2G_1N_1Q_1$] snang $G_2N_2Q_2$

25c bgyid $D_2G_1G_2N_1N_2Q_1Q_2$] bgyis CD_1; kyang $CD_1D_2G_1N_1Q_1N_2$] dang G_2Q_2

26a dang $D_2G_1N_1Q_1$] dangs $CD_1G_2N_2Q_2$

26b 'jig N_2Q_2] 'jigs $CD_1D_2G_1G_2N_1Q_1$

26c sla CD_1D_2] bla $G_1G_2N_1N_2Q_1Q_2$

26d min $CD_1D_2G_1N_1Q_1$] yin $G_2N_2Q_2$

27b bgyi $CD_1G_2N_2Q_2$] bgyid $G_1N_1Q_1$, bya D_2

28b pa'am $CD_1D_2G_1G_2N_2Q_1$] pa 'am N_1Q_2; spyod $CD_1D_2G_1N_1Q_1$] dpyod $G_2N_2Q_2$; pa'am $CD_2G_1G_2N_1N_2Q_1$] pa 'am D_1Q_2

29b par $CD_1D_2G_1N_1Q_1$] pas $G_2N_2Q_2$

29c sā $CD_1D_2G_1N_1Q_1$] sa $G_2N_2Q_2$; 'khri $CD_1D_2G_1N_1Q_1$] 'khril $G_2N_2Q_2$

30a bzham $D_2G_2N_2Q_2$] gzhom CD_1, bzhom $G_1N_1Q_1$

30d gcad $CD_1D_2G_1$] bcad $G_2N_1N_2Q_1Q_2$; bgyi $D_2G_1N_1N_2Q_1Q_2$] bgyid CD_1

31a gcugs $CD_1D_2G_2N_2Q_2$] bcugs $G_1N_1Q_1$

31b dman $CD_1D_2G_1N_1Q_1$] sman $G_2N_2Q_2$

33a pas $CD_1D_2G_2N_2Q_2$] pa $G_1N_1Q_1$

33d 'dris $D_2G_1N_1Q_1$] 'dis $G_2N_2Q_2$, 'drin CD_1

34a ba $G_1N_1Q_1$] la $CD_1D_2G_2N_2Q_2$

34b brnyas pa med par $CD_1G_1G_2N_1Q_1$] brnyas pa med pa N_2Q_2, ma brnyas par ni D_2

34d 'dra $CD_1D_2G_2N_2Q_2$] 'dri $G_1N_1Q_1$; bar $CD_1D_2G_1N_1Q_1$] ba $G_2N_2Q_2$

36a yis $CD_1D_2G_2N_2$] yi $G_1N_1Q_1Q_2$

36bc Between these two lines stanzas 11–13 are repeated in $G_2N_2Q_2$ with the following variants:

11c mthun skyed (for mthu bskyed) $G_2N_2Q_2$

12d pas (for par) $G_2N_2Q_2$

13b yis (for yi) $G_2N_2Q_2$

13c da (for de) $G_2N_2Q_2$

36d la $D_2G_1G_2N_1N_2Q_1Q_2$] kyis CD_1; zhabs CD_1D_2] zha $G_1G_2N_1N_2Q_1Q_2$; bgyid $CD_1D_2G_2N_2Q_2$] bgyi $G_1N_1Q_1$

37b kyis $D_2G_1N_1Q_1$] kyi $CD_1G_2N_2Q_2$

37d kyis $D_2G_1N_1Q_1$] kyi $CD_1G_2N_2Q_2$

38a bzhes $CD_1D_2G_2N_2Q_2$] zhe na $G_1N_1Q_1$

38b 'phang $CD_1G_1G_2N_1N_2Q_1Q_2$] 'phel D_2

38c pa'i $CD_1D_2G_2N_2Q_2$] pas $G_1N_1Q_1$, pa SSL 3.1.15c

39a na $CD_1D_2G_2N_2Q_2$] nas $G_1N_1Q_1$

39b lta bur $CD_1D_2G_1$] lta bu $G_2N_1N_2Q_1Q_2$, 'gro bzhin SSL 3.1.16b

39c skye bo'i $CD_1D_2G_2N_2Q_2$] skyes bu'i $G_1N_1Q_1$

40a ni $CD_1D_2G_2$] kyi $G_1N_1N_2Q_1Q_2$; zhugs $CD_1D_2G_1N_1Q_1$] bzhugs $G_2N_2Q_2$

40d 'di $D_2G_2N_2Q_2$] de $CD_1G_1N_1Q_1$

42a gna' $CD_1D_2G_1N_1Q_1$] mna' $G_2N_2Q_2$

42b bzang ba $D_2G_1G_2N_1N_2Q_1Q_2$] bzang po CD_1

42c pa ni $CD_1D_2G_1N_1Q_1$] byed pa $G_2N_2Q_2$

42d smad $CD_1D_2G_1N_1Q_1$] slad $G_2N_2Q_2$

43b gna' $CD_1D_2G_1N_1Q_1$] mna' $G_2N_2Q_2$

43c skas CD_1D_2] kas $G_1G_2N_1N_2Q_1Q_2$

43d pa $CD_1D_2G_1N_1Q_1Q_2$] par G_2N_2

44b lha $CD_1D_2G_1G_2N_1Q_1$] lta N_2Q_2

45b 'grib par mdzod (for 'grib pa dang) SSL 3.1.18b

46a mes $CD_1D_2G_2N_2Q_2$] sems $G_1N_1Q_1$

46b steng CD_1D_2] stengs $G_1G_2N_1N_2Q_1Q_2$

46c khang $D_2G_2N_1N_2Q_1Q_2$] gang gi CD_1G_1

47a gyi CD_1D_2] gyis $G_1G_2N_1N_2Q_1Q_2$

47b skas $CD_1D_2G_1N_1Q_1$, skal N_2Q_2, skyal G_2; mi $D_2G_1G_2N_1N_2Q_1Q_2$] ma CD_1

47c rig $CD_1D_2G_1N_1Q_1$] rigs $G_2N_2Q_2$

48b spyad $CD_1D_2G_2N_2Q_2$] dpyad $G_1N_1Q_1$

48d bstan $CD_1D_2G_2$] ston $G_1N_1Q_1$, bsten N_2Q_2; pas $CD_1G_2N_2Q_2$] pa'i $D_2G_1N_1Q_1$

49a rjes $CD_1D_2G_1G_2N_2Q_2$] rjesu N_1, rjes su Q_1; bslabs $CD_1D_2Q_2$] bslab $G_1N_1Q_1$, brlabs G_2N_2; pa $D_2G_2N_1N_2Q_1Q_2$] pas CD_1, om. G_1

49b ku $CD_1D_2G_1N_1Q_1$] kun $G_2N_2Q_2$

50b rgas $D_2G_1G_2N_1N_2Q_1Q_2$] rga CD_1

50c grongs $D_2G_1N_1Q_1$] 'grongs $CD_1G_2N_2Q_2$

51c 'gyur $D_2G_2N_2Q_2$] bsgyur $CD_1G_1N_1Q_1$

51d 'jig $CD_1D_2N_2Q_2$] 'jigs $G_1G_2N_1Q_1$; yin D_2] yi $CD_1G_1G_2N_1N_2Q_1Q_2$

52a ma 'chi $CD_1D_2G_2N_2Q_2$] mi 'chi $G_1N_1Q_1$

53d mi $CD_1D_2G_2N_2Q_2$] med $G_1N_1Q_1$

54b 'byung $CD_1D_2G_2N_2Q_1Q_2$] 'gyur G_1N_1; cir $G_1G_2N_1N_2Q_1Q_2$] cis D_2, phyir CD_1; mkho $CD_1G_1N_1Q_1$] 'kho $G_2N_2Q_2$, khums D_2

54c des pa $CD_1D_2G_1N_1Q_1$] des pas $G_2N_2Q_2$

55a 'dir $CD_1D_2G_1N_1Q_1$] 'di $G_2N_2Q_2$

55b pa D_2] pa'i $CD_1G_1G_2N_1N_2Q_1Q_2$

56c brgya'am C] brgya 'am $D_1D_2G_1G_2N_1N_2Q_1Q_2$

57a slad $CD_1D_2G_2N_2Q_2$] smas $G_1N_1Q_1$; yis $D_2G_1G_2N_1N_2Q_1Q_2$] yi CD_1

57c 'di $CD_1D_2G_2N_2Q_2$] 'dis $G_1N_1Q_1$

57d log go $CD_1D_2G_1N_1Q_1$] log<o> G_2N_2, lo[ ]go Q_2

58a bshes $CD_1D_2G_2N_2Q_2$] shes pa $G_1N_1Q_1$

58b glo $D_1D_2G_1N_1Q_1$] blo $CG_2N_2Q_2$

58c zhes $CD_1G_1G_2N_1N_2Q_1Q_2$] gzhes D_2, SSL 3.1.20c

58d bsnyur $CD_1G_2N_2Q_1Q_2$] snyur G_1, myur D_2, smyur N_1Q_1, SSL 3.1.20d

59a deng $D_1D_2G_1G_2N_2Q_1Q_2$] dang CN_1

60c mngon $D_2G_1G_2N_1N_2Q_2$] sngon CD_1

60d rkyong CD_1D_2] skyong $G_1G_2N_1N_2Q_1Q_2$

61a de slad $D_2G_1G_2N_1N_2Q_1Q_2$] de las CD_1

61b 'chor $CD_1D_2G_2Q_1$] 'tshor $G_1N_1N_2Q_2$; med pa $D_2G_1G_2N_1N_2Q_1Q_2$] med par CD_1

62b ni $CD_1D_2G_1N_1Q_1$] kyis $G_2N_2Q_2$; gyur pa $CD_1D_2G_1N_1Q_1$] 'gyur ba $G_2N_2Q_2$

62c gsar D_1D_2] sar $G_1G_2N_1N_2Q_1Q_2$, gsal C; zhing CD_1D_2] cing G_1G_2 $N_1N_2Q_1Q_2$

64a non $D_2G_1G_2N_1N_2Q_1Q_2$] gnon CD_1

64b mi $CD_1G_1N_1Q_1$] ni $D_2G_2N_2Q_2$

65a dman $CD_1D_2G_2N_2Q_2$] sman $G_1N_1Q_1$

65d sgrub $CD_1D_2G_1$] bsgrub $G_2N_1N_2Q_1Q_2$

66d bden $D_2G_2N_2Q_1Q_2$] bde $CD_1G_1N_1$

67b la'ang $CD_1D_2G_2N_2Q_2$] pa'ang $G_1N_1Q_1$

67c rje $CD_1D_2N_2Q_1Q_2$] rjes $G_1G_2N_1$; la $CD_1D_2G_1G_2N_2Q_2$] ba N_1Q_1

67d yis $CD_1D_2N_2Q_2$] zhig $G_1N_1Q_1$; bgyis $CD_1D_2N_2Q_2$] bgyi $G_1N_1Q_1$

68a mdzad cing $CD_1G_2N_2Q_2$] mdzad pa $D_2G_1N_1Q_1$

68c brtse ba'i $CD_1D_2G_2N_2Q_2$] brtse bas $G_1N_1Q_1$

69a kyis $CD_1D_2G_1N_1Q_1$] kyi $G_2N_2Q_2$

69b 'ben $D_1G_1N_1Q_1$] gnyen $CD_2G_2N_2Q_2$; la $CD_1D_2G_1N_1Q_1$] las $G_2N_2Q_2$

69d mchi ba $CD_1N_2Q_2$] mchi bar D_2, 'gro ba G_1N_1, 'gro na Q_1

70b kyi $CD_1D_2G_2N_2Q_2$] kyis $G_1N_1Q_1$; bshugs $G_1G_2N_1N_2Q_2$] bshug CD_1, shugs D_2

70c bzhengs D_2 mngon $CD_1D_2G_1N_1Q_1$] sngon $G_2N_2Q_2$; gnod CD_1 $D_2G_2N_2Q_2$] mnod $G_1N_1Q_1$

71d gdungs $CD_1D_2G_2N_2Q_2$] gdung $G_1N_1Q_1$

72b de ñyid kyis $CD_1D_2G_1N_1Q_1$] 'di nyid kyi $G_2N_2Q_2$

72c mgar $CD_1D_2G_2N_2Q_2$] dga' $G_1N_1Q_1$

72d sreg $CD_1D_2G_1N_1Q_1$] bsreg $G_2N_2Q_2$

73a dgyes $D_2G_1G_2N_1N_2Q_1Q_2$] bgyis C, dgyis D_1

73b log $CD_1D_2G_1N_1Q_1$] ldog $G_2N_2Q_2$

73d pa $CD_1D_2G_1N_1Q_1$] par $G_2N_2Q_2$

74a khyod $CD_1D_2G_1N_1Q_1$] spyod $G_2N_2Q_2$

74c khyod ni D_2] khyod la $CD_1G_1G_2N_1N_2Q_1Q_2$ (one actually expects khyod *kyis)

75a mnga' $CD_1D_2G_2N_2Q_2$] lam $G_1N_1Q_1$

75c rtabs $CD_1D_2G_1N_1Q_1$] stabs $G_2N_2Q_2$; ba la $D_2G_1G_2N_1N_2Q_1Q_2$] ba las CD_1

76b de D_1D_2] te $CG_1G_2N_1N_2Q_1Q_2$

77a ltung $CD_1D_2G_2N_2Q_2$] lhung $G_1N_1Q_1$

77d 'gums $CD_1D_2G_1N_1Q_1$] 'gug N_2, 'gum G_2Q_2

78b yi $CD_1D_2G_1N_1Q_1$] yis $G_2N_2Q_2$

78d kyis $D_2G_1N_1Q_1$] kyi $CD_1G_2N_2Q_2$; rje $D_2G_2N_2Q_2$] rjes $CD_1G_1N_1Q_1$

79a bsrung $CD_1D_2G_1G_2N_2Q_2$] srung N_1Q_1

79b gis $CD_1D_2G_1N_1Q_1$] gi $G_2N_2Q_2$

79c gsol $D_2G_1G_2N_1N_2Q_1Q_2$] gsal CD_1

79d mnga' $CD_1D_2N_2Q_2$] lags $G_1N_1Q_1$

80a bzung $CD_1D_2G_1N_1Q_1$] gzung $G_2N_2Q_2$

80b kyi $CD_1D_2G_1N_1$] kyis $G_2N_2Q_1Q_2$

81b khum $CD_1D_2G_1N_1Q_1$] zhum $G_2N_2Q_2$

82b bar $CD_1D_2G_1N_1Q_1$] ba $G_2N_2Q_2$

82d gtang $D_2G_1N_1Q_1Q_2$] btang $CD_1G_2N_2$; ba $CD_1D_2G_1G_2N_1Q_1$] N_2Q_2; bgyi $CD_1D_2G_1N_1Q_1$] bgyid $G_2N_2Q_2$

83a slar rjes $CD_1D_2G_2N_2Q_2$] slar dgyes $G_1N_1Q_1$

83b dogs pa Q_1] dogs (without pa) $CG_1G_2N_1N_2Q_2$, dog sa D_1, dog pa D_2; gzung $CD_1D_2G_1Q_1$] bzung $G_2N_1N_2Q_2$

83c mi $CD_1D_2G_1N_1Q_1$] ma $G_2N_2Q_2$; thogs N_2 thog Q_2

83d zla ba zla ba N_1Q_1] zla ba nya pa $CD_1G_2N_2Q_2$, zla ba zla dbang D_2; mdzod $CD_1D_2G_1G_2N_1Q_1$] bzod N_2Q_2

84a las $CD_1D_2N_2Q_2$] la $G_1N_1Q_1$; ltar $CD_1D_2G_1N_1Q_1$] dang $G_2N_2Q_2$

84c las $D_2G_1G_2N_1N_2Q_1Q_2$] la CD_1

85c bgyis $D_2G_1G_2N_1N_2Q_1Q_2$] bgyid CD_1

85d brtan $D_2G_1G_2N_1N_2Q_1Q_2$] brten CD_1; med par $CD_1D_2G_1N_1Q_1$] med pa $G_2N_2Q_2$; ring $CD_1D_2G_1N_1Q_1$] rings $G_2N_2Q_2$

colophon: ma ti $CD_1D_2G_2N_2Q_2$] mā tri $G_1N_1Q_1$; ka nis ka $CD_1D_2G_2Q_2$] ka ni ka $G_1N_1N_2Q_1$; 'phrin yig $D_2G_1N_1Q_1$] spring yig $CD_1G_2N_2Q_2$;

bha D_2] bhā $CD_1G_1G_2N_1N_2Q_1Q_2$; zhu chen gyi om. $D_2G_2N_2Q_2$; lo tsa C; bande $D_2G_1G_2N_2Q_2$] ban de $CD_1N_1Q_1$; ā $CD_1D_2G_2N_2Q_2$] a $G_1N_1Q_1$; tsārya $CD_1N_1Q_1$] tsarya $D_2G_1G_2N_2Q_2$; brtsegs $CD_1D_2G_2N_2Q_2$] rtsegs $G_1N_1Q_1$; phab pa'o $CD_1D_2G_2N_2Q_2$] phab pa $G_1N_1Q_1$

Peculiar Spellings and Individual Mistakes

Subscribed final -s and 'a chung:

2c gyis̲ G_2 (at the end of line 2)

3c lags̲ N_2

7d nyams̲ Q_2

11c [$G_2N_2Q_2$ rep.] mkhas̲ Q_2

13d nus̲ Q_2

22a mdza'̲ G_1

32b lags̲ G_1

44c yis̲ Q_2

47c nams̲ N_2

49a rnams̲ Q_2

49c rigs̲ N_1

52d las̲ N_2

60b brtsams̲ (for rtsal) D_2

75c nas̲ G_2

Contractions:

5d nyamsu G_1G_2

20d nyamsu G_2

21b gnasu G_2

39c rjesu $G_1G_2N_1$

41d bcosu G_2

43d khrimsu N_1

48c gshegsu G_2

49a rjesu (for rjes) N_1

49b rigsu G_1G_2

51c yongsu $G_1G_2N_1$

62b yongsu G_1G_2;

69d skyabsu $G_1G_2N_1$

75a gzhonu'i G_2

80b lugsu G_2N_1

84d 'tshalo G_2

Du for tu:

4b kun tu $G_1G_2N_1N_2Q_1Q_2$] kun du CD_1D_2

6d kun tu $D_2G_1G_2N_1N_2Q_1Q_2$] kun du CD_1

25d dag tu $CD_1D_2G_1N_1Q_1N_2$] dag du G_2Q_2

28c kun tu $G_1G_2N_1N_2Q_1Q_2$] kun du CD_1D_2

64c shin du (for shin tu) D_2

Individual mistakes or variants:

3a mang por (for phal cher) SSL 3.1.1a

4d mdzem (for 'dzem) Q_1

5a ltar (for ltas) D_2, SSL 3.1.2a

5b gsan (for gson) D_2

5c sgrub (for bsgrub) N_2; gtang (for btang) SSL 3.1.2c

7b pa (for pas) D_2

8c rang ddu . . . yis (for dang 'dul ba yis) N_2

9b dkyil (for dkyel) N_2

9d ba (for bar) Q_1

11d [$G_2N_2Q_2$ rep.] bgyis (for dgyes) G_2; mdzad (for mdzod) Q_2

12a [$G_2N_2Q_2$ rep.] stan (for bstan) N_2; 'don (for gdon G_2)

12c [$G_2N_2Q_2$ rep.] dpyad te (for dpyad de) Q_2

12d nas las ni (for pa la ni) D_2

13c yis (for yi) G_2

14c nyung ngu (for nyung du) G_2; nyung du'ang bstsags na (for nyung du bsags na'ang) SSL 3.1.8a; des (for nges) Q_2

14d thogs G_2

15b bab (for 'bab) SSL 3.1.8d

16a ji ltar (for de ltar) D_2, SSL 3.1.9a

16b pos (for po) SSL 3.1.9b

16d mdzad (for mdzod) SSL 3.1.9d

17a nor gyi (for nor ni) SSL 3.1.10a

17c bzo 'phongs (for gzo phongs) D_2

18c kha gcam (for kha gsag) SSL 3.1.14d

18d gnas . . . ma (for gnas su ma) C

20a skyod (for spyod) Q_2

21c yis (for yi) C

21d spyod (for 'dod) D_2

22a da (for de) D_1

23c legs (for lags) D_2

24d gzung (for bzung) D_2

25d mdzod (for mdzad) C

26c kyi (for kyis) G_2

27a bgyid las (for bgyis pas) D_2

28d brten (for bsten) D_2

29a ni (for na) D_2

32c brtso n G_1 (gap of one letter)

33d gyis (for kyis) C

35b kyi (for kyis) N_1

36c yi (for yi) C

38a dgyes (for bzhes) SSL 3.1.15a

38b 'bar (for 'phang) SSL 3.1.15b

39a lam (for las) Q_1

40b 'drangs (for 'brangs) D_1

40c skyes (for skye) D_1; khyod kyi rjes 'brangs pas (for khyod mdzad rjes 'brang ba'i) SSL 3.1.17c; line c in smaller script in G_2 (obviously first overlooked and then added to later)

41b bsgrim (for bsgrims) Q_1

41d gsar (for sar) D_2; pas (for par) C

46a kyi (for kyis) D_2

47b pa'i twice C

48a bsnyangs (for bsnyengs) C; mdzad (for mdzod) D_2

48c khar (for kar) D_2

49d brgyud (for rgyud) D_2

50d smos (for smon) D_2

51d pa (for pas) D_1

52b ba yis (for ba na) D_2

54a nas om. Q_2

55b ma (for mi) N_2

56a 'phreng (for phreng) G_1

56c lan om. D_2

59a sang{s} G_1 (mark of deletion above the -s)

60b brtsams (for rtsal) D_2

60c 'ong{s} G_1 (mark of deletion above the -s)

61a med de (for med des) Q_2

61b bzang (for bzad) C

63a gtogs pa (for gtogs par) D_2, SSL 3.1.21b

63b logs na (for log nas) Q_2

64a zhing (for cing) D_2

64b slan (for rlan) Q_2

65d bgyis (for bgyid) G_1

66a dwags (for dags) D_2

66b dang (for dam) G_2; 'jug par (for 'jug pa) N_1

67b dga' (for gda') Q_1

67d skye ba (for kye ma) D_2

68b bgyid la (for bgyid pa) D_2; mdzad pa (for mdzad pas) D_2

68d ga (for ka) G_2

69a bgyid (for bgyis) Q_1

69c khyod ni (for khyod nyid) D_2

70d phan par (for mun par) C; gtam (for tam) G_1

71c mchi ba'i (for 'chi ba'i) N_1

73b bcod (for gcod) Q_1; dgyes pas (for dgyes las) C;

73d lag (for lags) C

74b mthong{s} G_1 (mark of deletion above the -s)

74c dwags (for dags) D_2

75a dwags (for dags) D_2

75b dwags (for dags) D_2

79c bgyid (for bgyis) D_2

81a pham (for phan) Q_1

81d bsol (for gsol) G_1

84b zung (for gzung) D_2

84d 'tshal te SSL 3.1.3d

85a legs N_2 bsgrub (for legs) Q_2

85b yont<an> N_1

85+ spring ba'i (for springs pa'i) D_2; bidy(ā) N_1; ka om. N_2; shad (after bsgyur) om. Q_2; kyi (for kyis) Q_2

The Tibetan Vocabulary of the Mahārājakaniṣkalekha

Note: The abbreviations P, F, and I are used to indicate the past, future, and imperative tenses. Portions of the Tibetan vocabulary in parentheses can be (or are) omitted in verse for metrical reasons.

ka ni ka	(also spelled ka nis ka or ka niska) (the king) Kaniṣka 0, 43c (ka ni skas)
ku śa'i rigs	the Kuṣāṇa dynasty 49b
kun	all, everybody 34d, 35a, 39d, 52c
kun tu	everywhere 4b, 6d, 70d, 71a, 71b
kun tu bsgo ba	to permeate, pervade 4b
kun tu spyod pa	to practice, to behave, to conduct (one's life) 28c
kun nas nyon mongs	complete defilement 54a [Skt. saṁkleśa]
kyang	(concessive particle) although, even 1b, 4c, 25c, 34a, 35c, 43b, 84b
kye ma	alas! 67d
dka' thub (can)	ascetic 31d
dka' ba	(to be) difficult; a difficult matter 20a, 20b, 20c, 20d, 26d *see* bkur dka', bsnyen dka', dor bar bya dka', bya dka', bzod par dka' ba

dkyel che	of great extension, vast 9b
bka' khrims	command, law 43a
bka' mchid	(eleg.) (my) word, speech, message 82d
bkug	*see* 'gug pa
bkur (bar) dka' (ba)	(to be) difficult to carry, accept 20d
bkren (pa)	(to be) poor, indigent, hungry 31b
skad cig	moment; happening in a moment 51d
skor ba PF bskor	to encircle, surround 29a (bskor ba na)
skyabs	protection 69d
skyabs su 'gro ba, mchi ba	to take refuge 69d
skye dgu	human being, living being 40c, 40d
skye ba PI skyes	to be born; to become 3d (skyes par gyur)
skye ba can	'one who has been born', a living being 50a
skye bo	man, human being, people 19a, 22d, 39c, 84d
skyed PF bskyes	to cause to be born, create, produce 11c
skyes (bu)	man, human being, people 14a, 60b
skyong ba P bskyangs F bskyang I skyongs	to protect 46b (bskyang)
skyon	fault 43a, 44c
brkam pa	(to be) greedy; greediness 18b
kha gsag (pa)	(to be) talkative, garrulous 18c
khum	*see* 'gums pa
kho na	only, sole 40b, 44b, 44d

khyad du 'gums (pa)	(eleg. for khyad du gsod pa) to despise, scorn 82c
khyad par	specialty, distinction; special 19b, 19c, 30b
khyad par (du)	(adv.) especially, particularly 2d
khyu	flock, herd 39b
khyu mchog	leader (of a flock) 39b
khyod	you 1a, 2b, 2c (twice), 3c, 8a, 17d, 18a, 24d, 25b, 27a, 27c, 28d, 30a, 32c, 34b, 36b, 36d, 37b, 37d, 40a, 40c, 44a, 44c, 47a, 49b, 59c, 62b, 63c, 66d, 67a, 67c, 68c, 69c, 70c, 73a, 74a, 74c, 75a, 76a, 76b, 76d, 78d, 79a, 85d
khrims	*see* bka' khrims
khrims su bca' ba	the act of establishing as law 43d
khrims su 'cha' ba	to establish as law 43d
khro ba	to be angry 25a, 67a
mkho (ba)	(to be) necessary, desirable 54b
mkhan po	abbot; master 85+
mkhas pa	(to be) skilled, wise; 12d (mkhas par mdzod), 17b, 74a; a skilled, wise person 7b, 11d, 27a, 60d, 72c *see* thabs la mkhas pa
mkhyen pa	(resp. for shes pa) to know 19b, 19c, 44c, 63d
'khor	attendance, retinue 36b
'khor ba	wheel of existence, samsara 56a *see* yongs su 'khor ba
'khyud pa	to embrace 29d
'khri shing	creeper 29c
'khrung ba P khrungs	(resp. for skye ba) to be born 49b
'khrul (ba)	to err, go astray 31d ('khrul byed pa)

gang	who; who? what; what? 5d, 20a, 34a, 42b, 53a, 53b, 53c, 53d
gang ba	to be full 15c
gang zhig	whosoever 15c, 72a
gang yang	whosoever 30d (gang du'ang)
gang yang rung (ba)	whosoever it may be 34a, 51a
gang lags (pa)	(resp. for gang yin pa) he who (often followed by de) 1b, 3c, 42c, 76
gal te	if 38a, 81a, 81b, 85a
gus (pa)	(to be) respectful, respect, devotion 1c, 21c, 79c
go	(emphatic particle, used after pronouns and case particles) 69c (mdzad na go)
gong nas gong du	upper and upper, higher and higher 38b
gya gyu	cunning, cheating, duplicity 40a, 40b
grang	(auxiliary verb expressing a polite wish) should 79d
grogs (po)	friend 22b, 23a, 29a
glo bur	all of a sudden, unexpectedly 58b
dga' ba	to rejoice, take pleasure in, be happy 6a, 31c, 36d, 76b, 76c *see* yid mi dga' ba, rang dgar spyod pa
dge ba	(to be) good, wholesome; good, virtuous action 63a
dges pa	(resp. for dga' ba) to rejoice, take pleasure in, delight in 16d
dgongs pa	(resp. for sems pa) to think, wish, intend 37b, 37d
dgon pa	hermitage 48c

dgyes pa	(resp. for dga' ba) to rejoice, take pleasure in 11d, 25d, 27c, 73a, 73b, 76d, 82a, 83a, 83b
dgra bo	enemy 84b
bgyi ba	to be done, deed 55a, 55c
bgyid pa P bgyis F bgyi I gyis	(elegant) to do, to cause; ; auxiliary verb 1d, 2d, 3a, 6a, 6b, 6c, 12a, 17c, 25c, 27a, 27b, 30d, 32b, 36b, 36d, 55b, 55c, 56d, 57a, 57b, 65d, 67b, 67d, 68a, 68b, 69a, 70a, 76c, 79c, 82d, 83c, 85c
bgrang phreng	rosary 56a
bgre ba PI bgres	(resp. for rga ba) to become old 50c (ma bgres)
bgres	*see* bgre ba
bgres ka	(resp. for rgas ka) old age 48c
bgrod par bgyi (bar) 'os (pa)	worthy to be approached 1a
mgar ba	blacksmith 72c
mgon (po)	protector 10c, 65b, 77b
mgon med pa	(to be) without a protector 10b, 65b, 77b
'ga' yang	whosoever; (with negation) nobody 63b
'gug pa PF bkug I khug	to summon, to invite 1b (bkug)
'gum(s) pa P bkums F bkum I khum(s)	(resp. for gsod pa) to kill, slaughter 68a, 77d, 81b (khum), 83a *see* khyad du 'gums pa
'gegs pa P bkag F dgag I khog	to obstruct, hinder 67d (dgag par bgyis)
'gyur ba PI gyur	to turn into; to become; auxiliary verb 3d, 8a, 10b, 10d, 14d, 15c, 29b, 29d, 37b, 37d, 38b, 38d, 39d, 40d, 53b, 53d, 58b, 59c, 60b,

	62b, 69b, 70d, 73c, 82a, 83a, 83b, 85a *see* yongs su 'gyur ba
'grag pa P grags	to be known 80b (grags)
'grib pa P grib	to become covered, dark 45b
'gro ba PI song	to go, depart 53d living being; world 63b, 65a
'grong ba PI grongs	(resp. for 'chi ba) to die (ma grongs)
rga (ba)	(to be) old; old age 1d, 48a
rgal ba PF brgal	(with abl.) to cross over 11b (ma brgal bar du)
rgas (ka)	old age 50b, 51b, 51c, 52a
rgya gar	India; Indian 85+
rgyags pa	pride 6b
rgyan	ornament 85b
rgyal po	king 9a, 16b, 26b, 41c, 42a, 43c, 66b, 80c
rgyal po chen po	a great king 0
rgyal po chen po ka nis ka la springs pa'i 'phrin yig	Tibetan translation of the Sanskrit title mahārājakaniṣkalekha 0a, 85+
rgyal srid	kingdom, rule, sway, sovereignty 9d, 48b, 73c
rgyas par	extensively 54d
rgyu	reason, cause 77d
rgyu mthun pa	common basis, basis, foundation 68d
rgyud	family; category (of beings) 79c
rgyun	stream 15a, 84c
rgyun gcod pa	to cut, interrupt 43b (rgyun chod la)
sgo	door, gate 6d

sgom pa P bsgoms F bsgom I sgoms	to meditate 54d
sgyur ba PF bsgyur	to translate 85+
sgrim pa	*see* rab tu bsgrims nas
sgrub pa P bsgrubs, F bsgrub, I sgrubs	to accomplish 5c, 65d, 85a
bsgo ba P bsgos I sgos	to permeate, pervade 4b (kun tu bsgos pas)
bsgom pa	meditation 54d
brgya	one hundred 56c *see* lan brgya
brgya la	at some time, occasionally; somehow 85c
brgyan pa	to adorn, decorate 45d
bsgyur	*see* sgyur ba
bsgrub (bya)	what is to be accomplished 5c (short for bsgrub par bya)
ngang pa	goose 26a
ngang pa'i rgyal po	king of the geese (haṁsarāja) 26ab
ngan pa	(to be) bad, wicked 37c, 38c, 84d
nges par	certainly, necessarily 14c, 50a, 82d
ngo	side, half *see* mar gyi ngo, yar gyi ngo, g.yul ngo
ngoms pa	*see* mi ngoms pa
dngos po	state 13c
mnga' ba	(resp. for yod pa) 75a, 79d
mngon du gnod (pa)	to kill openly 70c [Skt. abhi-han]
mngon du 'ong (ba)	to appear visibly, in person 60c [Skt. abhi-gam]

rngo thogs (pa)	to be able 3b
rngo mi thogs pa	to be unable 83c
sngon	earlier, of earlier times 43a, 62a
sngon chad	formerly 69a
can	(possessive particle) endowed with 17b, 18a, 50a, 57c, 60a, 71c
ci	what? 52d, 56d, 73c
ci ga	(emphasized) what? 66c
ci ste	is it perhaps . . . ? 9a, 38c, 81c, 82c
ci la	wherefore? for what? 50d
ci zhig	what kind? 73d
ci (yi) slad (du)	wherefore? what for? 74d, 75d
cir	wherefore? what for? 54b
ces	(after direct speech) thus 50c, 52a, 58c, 59a, 67b
ces bya ba	thus to be said, to be called (title), 59ab
co	the head; the central, main points 80a (co nas bzung ste)
gcig tu	alone, only, exclusively 53c, 81b
gcugs pa	planted, cultivated 31a *see* 'thab gcugs pa
gcod pa P bcad F gcad I chod	to cut 30d (gcad), 73a, 73b *see* rgyun gcod pa, chad pas gcod pa, srog gcod pa
bca'	*see* 'cha' ba
bcos	*see* 'chos pa, bstan bcos
cha	part 8b *see* mtshon cha

chags pa	to arise 43a, 85c
chags pa	to long for; longing, passion 43a, 85d
chad pa	punishment 30d, 81b
chad pas gcod pa	to punish 30d
chu	water 65c
chu (yi) thigs (pa)	water droplets 15a
chung (ba)	(to be) small, weak *see* stobs chung ba
chus 'jig pa	destruction by water, flood 26b
che (ba)	(to be) great 47b *see* dkyel che
ched du	for the sake of, in order to 5a
chen po	(adj.) great 67a *see* zhu chen
ches	(adv.) to a great extent 78c
chod	*see* gcod pa
chos	law, the laws 12c, 46b, 48b, 71c; one's own dharma 35a, 35b; the Dharma 16c *see* phongs chos, dam pa'i chos
chos kyi bstan bcos	dharmaśāstra, law book 12a
chos lugs	lawful behavior 8c; religious system 49d
mchi ba	(eleg. for 'gro ba and smra ba) to go; to speak 69d
mchid	(eleg.) saying, speech *see* bka' mchid
mchis (pa)	(eleg.) to be 1b, 3a, 15d, 32d, 43b, 48d, 50b *see* 'bras (bu) mchis (pa)
mchog	excellent 4b *see* khyu mchog, mi mchog
mchod pa	to honor 33c

mchod (par) 'os (pa)	(to be) worthy to be honored 33c
'cha' ba P bcas F bca' I cho	to prepare, to establish *see* khrims su 'cha' ba
'chi bdag	the Lord of Death 58a, 60a, 62d
'chi ba P shi	to die; death 48a, 50b, 51b, 51d, 52a, 53d, 71c
'chor ba P shor	to escape 61b
'chor med pa	'which cannot be escaped' 61b
'chos pa P bcos	to mend, repair, remedy 8d, 41d

ji lta bu zhig	what kind of? 15d
ji lta bar	in the manner of, like 36a, 36c
ji ltar	= ji lta bar 76d
ji bzhin du	in the same manner as (introducing a relative clause) 84c
ji srid	as long as (followed by de srid) 11a, 61c
'jam (pa)	mild, tender, well-meant 23c, 24b
'jig rten	world; people 10a, 52c, 56d
'jig pa	to destroy; to be destroyed 26b, 51d, 53b *see* chus 'jig pa
'jug pa P zhugs	to enter; to become involved 10d 40a
'jug pa P bcug F gzhug I chug	to cause to enter; to cause 66b (gsod jug)
'jog pa P bzhag F gzhag I zhog	to put, place, assign, appoint 17d, 21b, 23d (thugs la bzhag par mdzad du gsol)
'joms pa P bcom D gzhom I choms	to destroy 32b
rjes su 'tsho ba	to live depending on somebody 39c [Skt. anu-jīv]

rjes (su) 'brang ba	to follow after 39d, 40b, 40c, 63c [Skt anu-gam, anu-vṛt]
rjes (su) 'brel (ba)	to be connected with, bound to 62c [Skt. anu-bandh]
rjes (su) bslabs pa	instructed, taught in accordance with 49a [Skt. anu-śiks, anu-śās]
nyam(s)	strength
nyam chung (ba)	(to be) of little strength, weak 10b
nyams pa	to decay, become polluted; to perish 40d, 41d, 49d, 73c
nyams smad (pa)	to weaken 7d
nyams su bzhes (pa)	(resp. for nyams su len pa) to take to heart, accept readily 5d
nyams su len pa	to take to heart, accept readily 20d
nyi ma	the sun; solar 49c, 83c
nyid	(a particle emphasizing the preceding word) just, very 5a, 8d, 16d, 66d, 69c, 79a; (after a pronoun) same 51b, 55a, 72b; (as an independent word) own 70b; (after a noun) the fact that 77b (gnas pa nyid)
nyung du	(adv.) in small quantities 14c
nyung zad	just a little bit 14b
nye mgon	intimate (?) 2d
nyes pa	failing, fault, evil 8a, 35c, 45
nyes (pa) med (pa)	(to be) faultless 44d, 65b
nyon mongs med pa	(to be) undefiled, unstained, free of emotional taint 9c
gnyis	two 5c
gnyis ka	the two, couple 68d

gnyen	'a near person', friend, assistant 17a
gnyen 'dun	relatives 22a
gnyer (ba)	to care for, seek for 17a *see* don du gnyer ba
mnyam pa	(to be) equal to 47b *see* mi mnyam (pa)
snyan	(resp. for rna) ear 5a (snyan gtod pa, to lend one's ears)
snyan (pa)	agreeable, pleasant 24a *see* mi snyan pa
snying rje	compassion 9b, 17b, 64a
snying (po)	essence 85c
snyung ba PI bsnyungs	(resp. for na ba) to fall ill, become sick 50c (ma bsnyungs)
snyur ba PF bsnyur	to make effort 58d (bsnyur te)
snyeng ba P bsnyengs F bsnyeng I (b)snyengs	(resp. for 'jigs pa) to fear, be afraid of 48a
brnyas (pa)	contempt 1c, 34
bsnyur te	(used adverbially) with great effort 58d
bsnyen pa	to worship 26c, 26d
bsnyen (par) dka' (ba)	difficult to worship 26c
bsnyen (par) sla' (ba)	easy to worship 26b
gtang (bya)	what is to be given up 5c (short for gtang bar bya ba)
gtan (pa)	(to be) lasting 32d

gtan la phab pa	codified, edited 85+
gtum po	fierce, cruel 18c
gtogs pa	to belong to 63a
gtong ba P btang F gtang I thongs	to give up, abandon 5c, 62b, 82d *see* yongs su gtong ba
gtod (pa)	to bestow, grant 5a (snyan gtod)
btang	here secondary form of gtang 5c
btod	*see* srol btod
rtag tu	always 9c, 15a, 16d, 19a, 45d, 47d
rtab pa P rtabs	(to be) confused, in a hurry, frightened 75c (rtabs nas)
lta ba P bltas F blta I ltos	to look, look at 31b, 75c
lta bur	in the manner of, like 39b
ltar	in the manner of, like 72c, 83c, 84a
ltung ba PFI lhung	to fall 38d
sten pa PF bsten	to adhere to 7b, 28d
stong	one thousand *see* lan stong
stod pa PF bstod	to praise 25c
stobs	strength, power
stobs chung (ba)	of little strength, weak 33a
stobs mthu	power 7d
stobs dang ldan pa	(to be) endowed with strength, strong 33a
brtags pa	(to be) fickle; (to be) afflicted with 78b
bstan pa	teaching(s) 48d
bsten	*see* sten pa
bsten pa	adherence to 48d (variant reading)

bstod pa	praise 25c
tha snyad	business, transaction 34c
thabs	means 74a
thabs la mkhas pa	'(to be) skilled in means', skilled (in the use of), expert 74a
thams cad	all 0, 2a, 3b, 35b, 35d, 63b, 71c, 71d
thal mo	the palms of the hands 79b
thigs (pa)	drop, droplet *see* chu (yi) thigs (pa)
thugs	(resp. for yid, sems) mind; heart 23d, 24d, 41b
thugs rje	pity, compassion 67c, 78d
thugs thub pa	to work with self-reliance, being confident in one's own abilities 4c
thugs mi rje (ba)	(to be) without compassion, heartless 75d
thugs tshod	consideration 79d
them skas	ladder, staircase 47b
thog ma med pa	(to be) without a beginning, beginningless 57c
thogs pa	*see* ring por mi thogs pa
thob pa	to attain 35a
mthu	might, power, strength 11c *see* stobs mthu, blo mthu
mthun pa	(to) match, (to be) in harmony (with) 21c *see* rgyu mthun pa, mi mthun pa
mtho ris	heaven 47
mthong ba	to see 74b
'thab gcugs (pa)	to sow strife 31a ('thab gcugs byed pa)

da ltar byung ba	present 13c
da dung	now 57b
dag pa	(to be) pure; purity 34
dang ba	(to be) clear 26a (rab dang)
dam pa	(to be) good, noble 7b, 14a, 16c, 26c, 28c, 39a, 80b
dam pa ma yin (pa), min pa	not good, bad; a bad, ignoble person 24c, 26c
dam (pa'i) chos	the good, the noble doctrine, the Buddhist doctrine 6c, 48d, 58d
dug	poison 84c
dud 'gro	animal 67c, 78c
dul ba	(to be) tamed, disciplined 7c
dus	time 57c
dus ston	festivity, ceremony 46d
dus dus su yang	'at any time whatsoever', always 14b
de	this, that 1b, 3c, 5d, 6c, 7a, 8b, 11a, 12b, 15d, 19c, 21c, 22a, 22b, 32d, 42b, 42c, 51b, 55b, 55c, 59d, 61a, 61c, 72b, 76b
de nyid	that very, the same *see* nyid
de lta bu	of such a kind, such 16a
de ltar	in such a manner, thus 16a, 52c, 80c
de ltas	(older form of de ltar) in such a manner, thus 5a
de bas	therefore 11a, 41a
de bzhin gshegs pa	Tathāgata 0
de srid	(corresp. with srid) so long 61d
de slad	therefore 54c, 61a
deng	today 59a

des pa	fine, brave, noble, good 54c
dogs pa	fear, misgivings 83b
don	interest, advantage 22c, 61d, 79a *see* rang (gi) don
don gyi tshul	'way of meaning', way of interpretation (of the law books) 12b
don (du)	(postposition) for the sake of, for the purpose of 79a
don (du) gnyer (ba)	to care for, seek, strive for 27b, 44a
don med (pa)	(to be) useless 6d
don med (par)	(adv.) uselessly 60b
dor ba	to give up, abandon 20b
dor bar bya (bar) dka' (ba)	(to be) difficult to abandon 20b
drang srong	seer 41c
dran pa	to remember; (to be) mindful; mindfulness 29a, 30c
gdams pa	to teach 3b
gdams (par) bgyi (ba)	what is to be taught 3a
gda' ba	(eleg. for mchi ba and 'dug pa) to say; to stay 67b, 68d
gdung rgyud	family, lineage 49d
gdung ba P gdungs	to torment 13a, 71d
gdon mi za bar	(adv.) inevitably 10d, 59d
bdag	I 2a, 3d, 5c, 41a, 64a, 79b, 81a, 81b, 81d, 82b, 82c
bdag nyid	self, nature 6c, 9b, 17b, 46a
bde ba	(to be) happy, comfortable; happiness 21d, 28a, 35, 53c

bden pa	(to be) true, truthful 23c, 24b, 30a, 66d
mda'	arrow 61b
'di	this (here), that (here) 5b, 10a, 32a, 39d, 40d, 55a, 57a, 57c, 59a (twice), 64c, 73d, 79a, 82d, 85b
'di ltar	in such a manner, thus 69b, 72a
'dir	here, in this place 14a, 55a
'du byed	composite things 53b
'dul ba	discipline 8c
'dod pa	to wish, long, desire; desire, passion 21d, 23a, 30c, 32a
'don pa P bton, F gdon I thon	to recite 12a (gdon bgyi zhing)
'dra ba	to be similar, to resemble 2b, 34d, 75b, 76a, 77a
'dren pa P drangs P drang I dron(s)	to draw, pull, drag 62d
ldan pa	(to be) endowed with *see* stobs dang ldan pa
ldog pa P log	(intr.) to return, turn back, revert 57d (log go), 63b (phyir log nas), 73b (phyir log na)
sdig pa	(to be) bad, evil, unwholesome; evil deed 63a
sdud pa P bsdus F bsdu I sdus	to collect, gather 11d
sdug pa	(to be) dear 71b, 80d *see* mi sdug pa
sdug bsngal	sorrow, suffering 28b, 54a, 71d, 72b, 78b
sdom pa	vow 31d

na (ba)	to fall ill, to become sick 52a
na gzhon	'tender age', youth 13b
nad	illness 1d
nad med (pa)	absence of illness, health 13b
nan tan	zeal, persistence 11d
nam zhig	when 59c
ni	(isolation particle; emphasizing the preceding word) as for . . . 2a, 3d, 4b, 5d, 7d, 8b, 9b, 11b, 12d, 13a, 13d, 14a, 14c, 16b, 16c, 17a, 21a, 22a, 23b, 25a, 26b, 27c, 29b, 32c, 33b, 33d, 34c, 35c, 37a, 37c, 39a, 39b, 40a, 40d, 41b, 42c, 50a, 51a, 52b, 55a, 55c, 56b, 59c, 61b, 61c, 62b, 62d, 64a, 64b, 65b, 65c, 67a, 68d, 71a, 72b, 72d, 73a, 74c, 76d, 77c, 78a, 82d
nus (pa) med (pa)	impossible 13d
nor	possessions, wealth 17a
gnang (ba)	to grant, grant permission, consent
gnang chen	one who generously consents 25b, 33b
gna'	antiquity, past 41c, 42a, 43b
gna' (yi) rgyal (po)	'the kings of old', the ancient kings 41c, 42a
gnas	place; the right place, what is appropriate 21b
gnas (pa)	to live, stay, abide, abide by 18d, 29b, 39a, 53c, 66d, 77b
gnas min (pa)	'what is not a right place', inappropriate 21a
gnod pa	to harm 67b, 68a, 68b, 69c, 70a, 70c, 74d, 83c, 85b *see* mngon du gnod pa

rnam (par) dpyod (pa)	to consider thoroughly 12c (rnam dpyad de) [Skt. vi-car]
rnam (par) smin (pa)	(to become) ripe, bring fruit; ripening 62a [Skt. vi-pac]
snod	vessel 15d
d**p**ag chen	of great size, extent 61a
dpal	glory, good fortune 30d, 48b, 85b
dpal brtsegs	name of the reviser of the Tibetan translation 85+
dpe	example 16a
dpyod pa PF dpyad	to consider, scrutinize 12d
spang	*see* spong ba
spong ba P spangs F spang I spongs	to give up, abandon 7a, 42d, 84d
spyan	(resp. for mig) 75a, 75b, 76a, 77a
spyi brtol	impudent; talkative 3d
spyod pa PF spyad	to live, to practice 7d, 20a, 38c, 48b, 60d, 63d, conduct 40a; (ordinary) life (?) 28b *see* kun tu spyod pa, rang dgar spyod pa
spyod lam	sphere of activities; higher pursuits (?) 28c
spring ba P springs	to send a message or letter 0 (springs pa)
pha	father 36a, 36c
pha rol	opponent, adversary 85b
phangs pa	lifted up, high, important 71a
phan pa	(to be) useful 23a, 23b, 24a, 25a, 81c *see* mi phan pa
phal cher	mostly, for the greater part 3a, 65b
phal pa	(to be) ordinary, plain 22c, 37a, 37c, 65d

phung	*see* 'phung ba
phun sum tshogs pa	welfare, prosperity 19d
phongs chos	'the dharma of the thrifty', stinginess 17c, 18a
phyag	(resp. for lag pa) hand; arm 70b
phyag 'tshal (ba)	to worship, pay homage to 0
phyin pa	*see* tshar phyin pa
phyir	(postposition) in order to 11c, 22c, 27c, 47b, 76a, 85c
phyir	(adv.) back 63b, 73b
phyir ldog pa	to return 63b (phyir log nas), 73b (phyir log na)
phyug pa	(to be or become) rich, enriched 85c (phyug par bgyis na)
phyugs	cattle 66a
phyogs	direction 4b, 5c, 70d
'phags rigs	a noble family 49c
'phang ba P phangs	to be lifted 38b
'phangs	*see* 'phen pa
'phung ba P phung	to degenerate, to decay 7a (phung bar byed pa)
'phen P 'phangs F 'phang I phongs	to cast, fling, throw 61c
'phel ba P phel	to increase 46d
'phrad pa P phrad	to meet with 28b
'phrin yig	written message, letter 0
bag rkyong (ba)	(to be) comfortable, at ease 60d
bag yod pa	(to be) watchful; watchfulness 29b

bande	(fr. Skt. vandya, venerable) a title of monks 85+
bar chad	obstacle 1d
bar chad med pa	having no obstacle, uninterrupted 15b
bar du	(postposition) until 57d
bas (pa)	(= zad) to be sufficient; only 22d
bi dyā ka ra pra bha	the Indian translator Vidyākaraprabha
bu	son 36a, 36c, 80d
bod skad du	in Tibetan 0
bya	bird 65d
bya	*see* byed pa
bya ba	*see* ces (or zhes) bya ba
bya ba ma yin (pa)	what should not be done, a bad deed 9c
byang grol	liberation 47a
byams pa	to love; love 36b
byas (pa) mi gzo (ba)	not to acknowledge what has been done (for oneself), (to be) ungrateful 18b
byas (pa) gzo (ba)	to acknowledge what has been done (for oneself), (to be) grateful 17c
byis pa	(to be) a child, childish, foolish 57a
byung	*see* 'byung ba, rang byung
byed pa P byas F bya, I byos	to do, to commit, practice 9d, 10c, 28c, 58c, 59a, (auxiliary) 7a, 20a, 20c, 21a, 31a, 31d; to say; *see* ces bya ba 59ab *see* 'du byed
blun (po)	(adj.) foolish, stupid 18a
blo	mind 11c
blo gros	mind 10a, 13d
blo mthu	strength of mind 11c

blon po	minister 9a
dbang po	sense organ 7c
'bad pa I 'bod	to endeavor, make effort 61d
'bab pa P babs	to fall down 15b; (with glo bur) to drop in 58b
'bar ba	to burn 52c
'ben	target 69b
'bod	*see* 'bad pa
'byin pa P phyung F dbyung I phyungs	(causative of 'byung ba) to bring forth, make appear 62a
'byung ba PI byung	to arise, come into being 47c, 54b
'byed pa P phye, phyed, phyes F dbye	to open, to separate 30c
'byor pa	riches, wealth 27b
'brang ba P 'brangs	to follow 22c *see* rjes su 'brang ba
'bral P bral	(to be) separated from, free from 30c
'bras (bu)	fruit 48d, 65c
'bras (bu) mchis (pa)	bearing fruit, fruitful 48d
'brel ba	to be connected with *see* rjes su 'brel ba
sbyar	*see* sbyor ba
sbyin pa PI byin	to give; giving 30b
sbyong ba P sbyangs F sbyang I sbyongs	to clean, remove by cleaning; to practice, exercise, train 80a
sbyor ba PF sbyar	to join, unite, lay together
sbyor bas	(postposition) 'through the connection of', by 85a
sbrang rtsi	honey 84a

ma	(negation, with perfect and prohibitive) not 1b, 1c (thrice), 11b, 13a, 18d, 24d, 25d, 32d, 49d, 50c (thrice), 52a (thrice) *see* bya ba ma yin pa
ma ti tsi tra	the Indian poet Mātṛceṭa 85+
ma gtogs par	(postposition) not belonging to, save, except 63a
ma yin pa	not being . . ., the opposite of . . . 24c, 53a, 56d, 57a, 57d, 58c, 61c, 63a, 70d, 82a
ma lags (pa)	not being . . ., the opposite of . . . 24a, 24b
ma hā rā dza ka ni ska le kha	transliteration of the Sanskrit title mahārājakaniṣkalekha
mang po	(adj.) much 14d
mang ba	(to be) much, numerous, frequent *see* lan mang
mar gyi ngo	the lower, the decreasing half (of the moon) 45a
mi	man, human being 4c, 20a, 22c, 59b, 78a
mi	(negation) not 13d, 14d, 15c, 17c, 18b, 27b, 30d, 31c, 33b, 33c, 33d, 37d, 53b, 53d, 54b, 55b, 58a, 59a, 63c, 64b, 67a, 68b, 68c, 72a, 73a, 75d, 76d, 77d, 79b, 82a, 83a, 83b, 83c, 85d *see* thugs mi rje ba, gdon mi za ba, yid mi dga' ba
mi bgyi ba	not to be done 55d
mi ngoms (pa)	(to be) insatiable 27d
mi mchog	an excellent human being 4b, 85a
mi mnyam (pa)	(to be) unequaled, matchless 47b
mi mnyam (pa dang) mnyam (pa)	(to be) equal to the unparalleled, matchless 47b
mi snyan (pa)	(to be) unpleasant 23b

mi brtan pa	(to be) unstable 85d
mi mthun (pa)	(to be) disagreeable, disharmonious, unpleasant 53a
mi sdug (pa)	(to be) disagreeable 35c
mi phan (pa)	(to be) not useful, harmful 25c, 81a
mi bzad pa	(to be) fierce, harsh, wild, unbearable 18c, 61b
mi rigs pa	(to be) inappropriate 42c, 66c
mi *bshes pa [xyl. shes]	not acquainted with 33d
mig	eye 76a
min pa	(ant. of yin pa) not to be 32a, 59c
mun pa	(to be) dark, darkness 70d
med pa	not to be available, to be absent, to be without 4a, 4d, 34b, 35c, 52d, 54d, 59c, 61b *see* mgon med pa, nyes (pa) med (pa), nyon mongs med pa, thog ma med pa, don med pa, nus pa med pa, bar chad med pa, brtse ba med pa, bzod pa med pa, bzlog pa med pa, rang dbang med pa
mod (pa)	(emphatic verb) to be indeed (generally followed by kyi) 2b, 3a
mya ngan	sorrow 13a
myur du	quickly, rapidly 11b
dman pa	(adj.) low, base 31b, 65a
smad pa	to blame, revile 42d *see* nyams smad pa
sman pa	(= phan pa) to be useful 50d
smon pa	to wish, to pray *see* legs par smon pa
smos 'dris (pa)	(to be) closely acquainted with 34d

smra ba P smras I smros	to speak, say; one who speaks 25a, 25c, 52b (twice), 84b
smre sngags	wailing, lament, lamentation 64c
tsam	only 19c, 22c
rtswa	grass 65c
rtsa ba	root 32b
rtsal	skill 60b
stsal ba	(resp. for gtong ba, sbyin pa) to give, grant, permit 18d
brtse (ba)	to love; love 2b, 60a, 68c (twice)
brtse ba med pa	(to be) without love, pity; heartless 60a
brtson pa	to strive for 21b, 32c (rab brtson)
tshad ma	authority, valid means of cognition 16b
tshar phyin pa	to have done a thing thoroughly, to go to the furthest limit to avoid 55d
tshig	word 23a, 24a, 24c, 82c, 84d
tshim (pa)	to be(come) satisfied 27a
tshul khrims	morality
tshul khrims (dang) ldan pa	(to be) endowed with morality, a moral being 31c
tsher ma	thorn; enemy 84a
tshogs	heap, multitude, flock 39c, 45b
tshod	*see* thugs tshod
mtsho	lake 26a
mtshon cha	weapon 74a
mtshon pa P mtshan	to mark 43c

’tshal ba	to beg, desire, ask 55b, 57b, 72a, 79b, 82b, 83b, 84d; to offer 70b
’tshig pa P tshig	to be burnt 72d (tshig pa)
’tsho ba	to live, to be alive 35b, 39c, 65d *see* rjes su ’tsho ba
m**dz**ad pa	(resp. for byed pa) to do, act, perform, accomplish; (auxiliary) 8d, 11d, 12, 16b (mdzad nas), 16d, 19b (mkhyen par mdzod), 23d (mdzad du gsol), 25b, 25d (mdzad cig), 26d, 27d (mi ngoms mdzod), 32d, 34b, 35b (’tsho bar mdzod), 35d (mdzad du gsol), 38c (mdzad na), 42b, 42d (smad par mdzod), 43c, 43d, 44b, 44d, 45d (brgyan mdzod), 46d (mdzad du gsol), 48b (bsnyengs mdzod de), 48d, 49d (ma nyams mdzod), 54d (rgyas par mdzod), 58d, 63d (mkhyen par mdzod la), 64d (mdzad du gsol), 68a, 68b (’gums mdzad pas), 69c (mdzad na go), 70c, 74d, 76d (dgyes mdzad), 78a (mdzad pa bas), 78d (mdzad du gsol), 81d, 82a (dgyes mdzad par), 82c, 83d, 85a
mdza’ bshes	friend 4d, 22a
mdzod	*see* mdzad pa
’dzin pa P bzung F gzung I zungs	to grasp 24d, 80a, 83b, 84b
’dzem pa	to be ashamed; to shun 4d
rdzogs (pa)	(to be) completed 85+
zhabs ’bring	attendance, service; worship 36d
zhing	field; (suitable) receptacle 30b
zhu chen	’great reviser’, a title of translators 85+

zhu ba P zhus	to correct 85+ (zhus te)
zhus	*see* zhu ba
zhes	*see* ces
zhog	*see* 'jog pa
gzhan (pa)	other 22d, 41a, 52d, 55b, 70a, 73c, 79c
gzhi	basis, foundation 8a
gzhung lugs	view, world view, conviction 38a
gzhon nu	young, a young person 75a
bzham pa	mild 30a
bzhi po	the four, a group of four 32a
bzhin (du)	in the manner of, like 4d, 26b, 29c, 37b, 37d, 44b, 44d, 45a, 45c, 46a, 46c, 48b, 56a, 60c, 72d, 80d, 81d, 83c *see* ji bzhin du
bzhugs pa	to be contained in 0
bzheng P bzhengs	(resp. for slong ba) to raise 70c
bzhes pa	(resp. for len pa) to take, accept, adopt 38a (for bzhed pa) to say 58c *see* nyams su bzhes pa
za ba	gdon mi za bar
zil gyis (g)non pa	to overcome, overwhelm 64a (zil gyis non cing)
zla ba	moon 45a, 45c, 83d (twice)
zlog P bzlogs, F bzlog I zlog	to make return; to ward off, to hinder 4a (bzlog), 21a
gzigs pa	(resp. for lta ba) to see 34d
gzo (ba)	*see* byas pa mi gzo ba
bzo rig	craft, art 47c
bzang po	(adj.) good 17d, 29d, 38a, 42b, 59b

bzang (ba)	(to be) good 37a
bzung ste	starting from (with abl.) 80a (co nas bzung ste)
bzod pa	to bear, tolerate 20c, 67b, 68a
bzod (pa) med (pa)	(to be) unbearable, intolerable; irresistible; impatient 61a
bzod par dka' ba	(to be) difficult to bear 20c
bzlog pa med pa	not to be returned, irresistible 4a
'ang	*see* yang
'am (and its variants)	or 28a (dam), 28b ('am, twice), 56c ('am), 66b (dam), 66c (sam), 70d (tam), 73c (ram)
'o byams pa	to regard with affection 21d
'og nas 'og tu	lower and lower 38d
'ong ba P 'ongs	to come 59d, 60c *see* mngon du 'ong ba, yid (du) 'ong (ba)
'os pa	to be worthy 33c *see* mchod par 'os pa
yang	again, once more 72d *see* yang srid
yang	even 22c, 23b, 24b, 25a, 50d, 67b, 70a, 76c, 85d *see* 'ga' yang, re re yang
yang dang yang du	again and again 57b, 82b
yang na	or 56c
yang srid	rebirth, reincarnation 52d
yab mes	forefather, ancestor 46a, 46c, 49c
yar gyi ngo	the upper, the increasing half (of the moon) 45a

yid	mind, heart
yid (du) 'ong (ba)	pleasant, agreeable, congenial 84d
yid mi dga' ba	(to be) melancholic 64b
yin pa	to be 51d
yun ring	(lasting for) a long time 85a
yul	land, territory, realm 18d, 32c, 77b; sense objects 6a
yongs su 'khor ba	to whirl around (in the wheel of existence) 56b
yongs su 'gyur ba	to change, to be transformed 51c
yongs su gtong ba	to give up completely 62b
yod pa	to exist, be available 52d, 53a
yon tan	quality, virtue 2c, 3c, 4a, 8d, 17a, 27c, 27d, 44a, 44b, 45d, 85b
g.yul ngo	battle 74b
g.yo ba	(to be) immobile, fickle, unsteady 85c
rag las (pa)	to depend on 19d
rang	own 35a, 61d
rang dgar spyod pa	to act acording to one's own pleasure 6c
rang (gi) don	one's own interest, advantage 22c, 61d
rang byung	'self-born', epithet of the Buddha 49a
rang dbang med pa	(to be) helpless (to determine one's own fate), dependent 85d
rang bzhin	character, nature 37a, 37c
rab (tu) dang (ba)	(to be) very clear 26a
rab tu sgrim pa	to be very attentive, diligent
rab tu bsgrims nas	very diligently 41b
rab (tu) brtson (pa)	to take great care 32c

ri dags	deer, game 66a, 74c, 75a, 75b, 76c, 77c
rig rig (pa)	very anxious, timid 75b
rigs	family; lineage 49b *see* ku a'i rigs, 'phags rigs
rigs (pa)	(to be) appropriate 5d, 66c *see* mi rigs pa
ring por mi thogs (pa)	not taking long, within a short time 14d
rin chen mchog	name of a Tibetan translator 85+
rung ba	to be suitable for 77d
re zhig	now 64d
re re	single, each individual 15a
re re yang	each single, each individual 77c
rung (ba)	(to be) appropriate 9d, ought, should 77d
rlan	moisture 64b
rlon pa PF brlan	to make moist, make wet, soak 64c
brlan	*see* rlon pa
lags pa	(resp. for yin pa) to be 1a, 1c (twice), 22b, 23c, 24a, 24b, 32b, 51b, 71b, 73d, 80c, (auxiliary) 74b (mthong lags na), 79d (mnga' lags grang), 80d (gsol ba lags) *see* gang lags (pa)
lang tsho	youth 6b
lan	turns, times
lan brgya	a hundred times 56c
lan stong	a thousand times 56c
lan mang	many times 56b
las	deed; karma 9d, 39a, 62a, 62c, 74d *see* rag pas pa, sug las

lugs	manner, way 41c, 73d, 80b
legs pa	(to be) good
legs par	well 63d, 79d, 84b, 85a
legs (par) spyad (pa)	virtuous conduct 85c
legs par spyod pa	to act well, behave well 63d
legs (par) smon (pa)	well-wishing; prayer (for someone's well-being) 50d
legs par smras pa	well said 84b
legs par mdzad pa	virtuous behavior 85a
lo tsā ba	lotsawa, translator (from Sanskrit into Tibetan) 85+
log pa	perverted, perverse 31a
log (par) ltung (ba)	to fall back 65a, 77a
log pas	in a perverted manner 31a
longs pa	pride, self-confidence 13b
longs spyod	enjoyments 28a
longs spyod byed pa	to enjoy oneself 28a
shing	wood, tree 84a *see* 'khri shing, sā la'i shing
shin tu	very, very much 64c
shes rab	wisdom 7c
gshegs pa	(resp. for 'gro ba, 'ong ba) to go; to come 48c
bshugs pa	(resp. for gso ba?) 'to strengthen', to raise, to feed 70b
*bshes pa [xyl. shes pa]	(to be) acquainted with, intimate with *see* mi bshes pa
sa	earth; stage 11a

sa steng	(the surface of) the earth 46b
sa bdag	'ruler of the earth', king 83d, 84a
sā la'i shing	the sal tree 29c
sang	tomorrow 59a, 59d
sang dag	(= sang) tomorrow 58c
sar pa	new 41d
su	who? 3b, 58a, 67d, 69d
su zhig	whosoever 60d, 72c
sug las	(eleg. for phrin las?) deed 69a
sems can	living being, sentient being 2a
sel ba	to remove, ward off 85b
so so	individual 19a
sog(s) pa P bsags F bsag I sog(s)	to heap up, accumulate 14c, 47d (sogs)
srid pa	what has come into being; being; existence 51a, 54a, 54c
srung ba P bsrungs F bsrung I srung(s)	to protect 41a, 79a
sreg pa P bsregs F bsreg I sregs	to burn 72d
srog	life 71a, 73a, 73b
srog gcod pa	'to cut life', to kill 73a, 73b
srol	custom, usage, practice
srol btod	application, use, practice 74b
sla (ba)	(to be) easy 26c
slad (du)	for the sake of 17d, 41a, 57a *see* ci (yi) slad (du), de (yi) slad (du)
slar rjes	(adv.) henceforth 83a
slob dpon	teacher 85+

slob pa P bslabs F bslab I slobs	to teach, instruct; to learn *see* rjes su bslabs pa
gsag pa	*see* kha gsag pa
gsan pa I gson	(resp. for thos pa) to listen, to hear 5c, 12b, 12c, 14b, 16c, 64d
gsar pa	new 43d, 62c
gsal (ba)	(to be) clear 16a
gsung ba PI gsungs	(resp. for smra ba) to say, speak 66d, 69d, 73d
gsum	three 7a
gsum po	the three, triple 8b
gser gyi ri	'the golden mountain', Mount Meru 84c
gsod (du) 'jug pa	to cause someone to kill 66b
gsod pa	to kill 60b, 60c, 66b
gson	*see* gsan pa
gson pa	to live, be alive 71b
gsol ba	to make a request, request 5b, 50d, 79c, 80d, 81b, 81c, 81d, 82b, (auxiliary, with terminative of the verb) please do . . . 23d (mdzad du gsol) 34d (gzigs su gsol), 35d (mdzad du gsol), 41d (bcos su gsol), 42d (spang du gsol), 46d (mdzad du gsoł), 48d (gshegs su gsol), 64d (mdzad du gsol), 78d (mdzad du gsol)
bsags	*see* sog pa
bsam pa	thought 21c
bsod nams	(religious) merit 47c
bslab (pa)	'what is to be studied', the subject of studies 80a
bslabs	*see* slob pa

lha	lord, ruler; god 44a, 44b, 44c, 44d
lha khang	'house of god', temple 46c, 47d
lhag par	(adv.) exceedingly 2d, 78b, 78c
ā tsārya	transliteration of the Skt. title ācārya, teacher (≈ doctor or professor) 85+

Restorations and Emendations in the Śiṣyalekha

Each instance where the edited text deviates from the palm-leaf manuscript is discussed below. The majority of cases are textual corruptions or lost portions of the Sanskrit manuscript; only rarely are there genuine new or variant readings. In a few cases—whenever the result was another correct Sanskrit word or compound—I have also included what is most likely only a scribal error. All other scribal peculiarities are listed in the chart on pp. 286–92.

In many cases the Tibetan translation of the Śiṣyalekha and those of Prajñākaramati's Vṛtti and Vairocanarakṣita's Ṭippaṇa were of invaluable help. Once these three texts are available in critical editions, we may have a better picture of how the Śiṣyalekha was understood in the eighth and ninth centuries in India and Tibet.

4a vicchidyamānam api: The manuscript reads vicchidyasāvayami, which is unintelligible. The Tibetan has (dbu) rnam[s] gcod byed kyang, "even if he cuts (his own head) off completely," which is the active counterpart of vicchidyamānam api, "even if being cut off completely."

4b ⟨unmīla⟩yan: The first three syllables are lost in the manuscript; the fourth syllable clearly reads: sa(n). The Tibetan has 'byed, "to open" (trans.). I could find only the present participle unmīlayan as a word that suits both the required meaning and the metrical structure. Other suggestions are most welcome.

4d kṛpāṇadhārā: Here the manuscript reads kumāridhārā, which is meaningless. One can still see, however, that this was written by a later hand over an original reading that most likely read kṛpāṇadhārā. The Tibetan confirms this: ral gri so, "the edge of a sword."

5b The two letters after **śuklaika** (the manuscript reads śukleka instead) are hardly legible, and the next three syllables are completely lost. In the last line two letters are worn away: **ja(ga?)t (p)⟨r⟩ākāsam**. This is what the Tibetan translation has:

| zla ba yar gyi ngo ltar yon tan gsal ba rdzogs |
| nyes pa'i mun pa sel mdzad gcig pu yid du 'ong |
| 'jig rten phan pa brtson pa rab tu gsal ba byung |
| de shar zla ba bzhin du 'gro ba bsil [v.l. *gsal] bar mdzad | 5 |

When he has appeared, like the waxing moon
endowed with radiant and perfect virtues,
a unique remover of the darkness of moral faults,
pleasing, devoted to the benefit of the world,
brilliant in his presence,
then he cools (or: *illuminates) the world like the moon.

The Tibetan translation of Vairocanarakṣita's Ṭippaṇa offers the best help for the restoration of the five missing syllables because it quotes all five words of the compound in line b:

| **gsal 'byung** ni gang zhig shar bas so |
| de'i **phyogs gcig** ni *yar zla ba phyed do |
| **dkar po** yang yin la **phyogs gcig** kyang de yin pas so |
| de la **yongs su rdzogs pa** yang yin la **yon tan** yang de yin pas des **gsal ba'o** |

"As for 'brilliant presence', (it refers to) 'when he appeared (on earth)'. His 'one side' refers to the waxing half of the moon. Since he is both 'white' (Skt. śukla) and '(belonging to) the one side' (Skt. ekapakṣa), he is that (i.e. śuklaikapakṣa). In addition to that he is 'completely perfect' (paripūrṇa) and has 'virtues' (guṇa), and through them he is 'radiant' (Skt. ujjvala)."

Thus pakṣa and paripūrṇa are the two missing words. As for the predicate of the sentence, bsil bar mdzad, "cools," this form can also be found in Prajñākaramati's Vṛtti; hence it must be based on a Sanskrit reading that I am unable to determine. Vairocanarakṣita, however, explains prakāśam:

| rab tu gsal ba ni gsal bar skyed par byed pa zhes brjod do |
"(He) is very illuminating means 'he is one who illuminates'."

6b phaṇinām (va)⟨rāṇām⟩: My tentative reconstruction is based on the Tibetan, which translates this passage as klu mchog gdengs ka can, "the excellent Nāgas with their hoods." I think that "Nāga," which would be understood from the Sanskrit wording, was added by Sarvajñadeva and dPal brtsegs for the sake of clarification. Neither of the commentaries refers to this expression.

7cd The greater part of line c and the first two letters of line d are lost in the manuscript. The last three letters of line d are there but are almost illegible. My restoration is therefore based on the Tibetan translation:

| chos kyi sprin de phan pa mdzad pa'i don du g.yos |
| chos kyi bdud rtsi mya ngan 'das pa mchog gi rgyu |
| ro gcig gdung ba sel ba char chu bzhin du bab |
| de ni snod la brten nas ro rnams du mar gyur | 7 |

That cloud of the holy Dharma
that had come forth[a] for the welfare (of the world)
poured down like rain the nectar of the Dharma,
the cause of the highest form of complete liberation,
which has a unique flavor and clears away pain and sorrow;
depending on the (condition of the vessel in which
it was collected) it took on various tastes.

[a]In the interpretation of the word g.yos in line a, I follow Vairocanarakṣita's gloss, which agrees with the extant Sanskrit text (abhyudito): | g.yos pa ni skyed [*skyes] pa'o |.

The first incomplete word in line c is easy to restore. Tāpā(pa), rendered by gdung ba, is there, and for the second part I suggest hāri. Apahāri occurs again in line 9a, and there it is rendered by the same sel ba that we find here after gdung ba. It is followed by mya ngan das pa mchog gi rgyu. Mya ngan 'das pa renders nirvāṇa or its more general synonym nirvṛti; mchog stands for para, and rgyu for the (unmetrical) hetu or kāraṇa. Kāraṇa is almost confirmed by the Vṛtti: | de'i rgyu ni des de ma thob pa thob par byed pa'o | "Its 'cause'—it lets one attain what one has not yet attained." The causative formation thob par byed pa points to the causative formation of kāraṇam.

This leads to the compound paranirvṛtikāraṇaṁ ca for the third line. The letters ni⟨r⟩v⟨ṛt⟩i are preserved. The first two syllables in line d have to be pātrā because brten nas, rendering āśrayeṇa (the manuscript still has ś⟨r⟩ayena), is preceded by snod, the standard translation of pātra, as in the following stanza. With the help of ro rnams du ma (gyur), one can decipher anekarasa(ṁ). The predicate, however, remains unclear and what is still visible does not support the tentative reconstruction babhūva. Other perfect forms also seem possible, such as jagāma, babhāra, avāpa (?) etc.

8a As stated in the Notes on stanza 8 (pp. 144–47), according to Prajñākaramati it illustrates the "perfect disposition of mind" (bsam pa phun sum tshogs pa, Skt. āśayasaṁpad) of the members of the Sangha. This remark makes it quite clear that Prajñākaramati read āśayeṣu, not āśrayeṣu, at the end of line a, as did also Vairocanarakṣita and the manuscript used by Sarvajñadeva and dPal brtsegs. The Tibetan translation has bsam pa dang ldan pa, which undoubtedly reflects āśaya, "disposition of mind." Vairocanarakṣita explains:

| **gnas** ni sems kyi gnas gang dag yin pa'am | **bzod pa** ni de gzhan gyis gnod pa byed pa bzod pa zhes bya'o | "As for 'place', [it means] the place (or condition) of mind, and 'able to bear' refers to the ability to bear the harm done by others."

The nature of the explanation as well as the order of the terms discussed in Vairocanarakṣita's notes—he strictly follows the order of words in the Sanskrit stanza—prove that gnas here renders āśayeṣu, not (tat)saṁsthitaṁ, which is (de) gnas pa in the other two translations. Prajñākaramati first translates āśaya by gnas su gyur pa, "having become a place," which reflects the meaning of āśaya when referring to the (great) lake. A little later he explains it when referring to the Sangha, and here it is rendered by bsam pa, not less than four times:

| de la dge 'dun ni rgyud yon tan gyi snod du gyur pa dang | **yangs pa'i bsam pa** ni (= vistīrṇāśaya) tshad med pa bzhi yid la byed pa ste | ⟨**zab pa'i bsam pa** ni⟩ (= nimnāśaya) gting dpag dka' ba'i phyir ro | | **dri ma med pa'i bsam pa** (= vimalāśaya) ni dri ma drug dang bral ba'i phyir ro | | **gsal ba'i bsam pa** ni (= prakaṭāśaya) ngon mongs pa'i mun pa sel ba'i phyir ro |. For the translation see the Notes.

The same mistake—āśraya for āśaya—occurs also in 57b and 112a. 8a and 112a are almost identical in their imagery, particularly in line a: for vistīrṇa in 8a we find vipula in 112a; for nimna, *prahvāgādha (which covers both meanings of nimna); for vimala, prasanna; and prakaṭa is repeated verbatim. Therefore the last word in both lines has to be the same and consequently both emendations support one another.

8cd The completion of line c as sarvajano⟨**pabhogyaṁ**⟩ offers no difficulties, since nye bar spyad bya is a frequently attested to Tibetan equivalent of Skt. upabhogya. Following the Tibetan translation,

| mtsho chen mi yi gzugs can de la phyag 'tshal lo |
Homage to that great lake which has the form of human beings!

and taking into account the metrical structure of the stanza, one arrives almost effortlessly at **tasmai namaḥ puruṣarūpamahā-hradāya**. In the note to the translation of this stanza I have given the arguments in favor of this reconstruction. The only flaw is the fact that the manuscript clearly has -(ā)ḥ at the end of this line instead of -a. For metrical reasons, namaḥ is not possible at the end of the line, and there is no dative (singular) ending in a Visarga. Do we have to read **tebhyo namaḥ puruṣarūpamahā-hradebhyaḥ**? In that case one would have to reconsider the interpretation of stanza 8 and its linkage with the preceding seven relative clauses.

9d The first eight letters of this line are almost completely lost. Most of the preceding line is also affected by the missing portion of the leaf, although the remnants of the letters can easily be completed. The first letter of line d seems to be followed by a long ī, and the second letter is perhaps preceded by an r. This speaks for dīrghā- as its beginning, since the Tibetan translation runs:

| yun ring nad kyis thebs pa sman chen mi bsten bzhin |
Like someone suffering from a protracted disease who
does not stick to an effective medicine.

The syllables ṣadham at the beginning of leaf 2 most likely were preceded by **mahau**, thus yielding the equivalent of Tibetan sman chen. This leaves us with the six syllables – – ∪ – ∪ ∪ to be filled with the Sanskrit equivalents of "suffering from a protracted disease," the negative particle na and a particle of comparison. A very tentative and clumsy reconstruction is **dīrghārtavan na ca**. In this case ca would connect the two incongruous predicates mohitā and ādriyante.

10b **sādharaṇas**: The manuscript has sādhāraṇa, which would then refer to the "triple world." This is, of course, possible, but it implies a certain repetition (which is not the case with jagato 'khilasya in the first line). The Tibetan translation certainly presupposes *sādhāraṇas:

| de ni sa rnams gsum po'i spyi mthun sgron ma ste |
He is the common light of the triple world.

Therefore I restore **sādhāraṇas**. Neither of the commentaries comments upon this attribute.

11c The Sanskrit Ms. reads anivartamānā, "not returning," while the Tibetan translation has rjes su sgrub pas, which rather points to *anuvartamānā, "following, going on and on." Vairocanarakṣita and Prajñākaramati do not comment upon the word. From the stylistic point of view the positive expression *anuvartamānā (when contrasted with the following vivartamānā-) seems to be preferable to the double negation a-nivartamānā, and therefore I readily follow the older textual tradition and emend accordingly.

20b ni⟨ṣpī⟩ḍyamāna: The syllable broken off in the manuscript was restored according to the Tibetan translation btsir ba, "squeezed." With the preceding syllable ni and the following syllable ḍya there is actually little choice.

21b ba⟨ha⟩logragandham: The syllable broken off in the manuscript was restored according to the Tibetan translation dri nga mi bzad ldang, "(from) which an unbearable stench rises." This is a rather free translation and unfortunately neither of the two commentaries comments upon this compound. However, with only one syllable missing, there is little choice and the adjective bahala-,"thick, intense," perfectly suits the context.

22b upajātakaṭhorabh⟨āvaḥ |⟩: The two syllables broken off in the manuscript were restored according to the Tibetan translation mkhrang ba'i dngos gyur nas |, "having changed into a hard, robust state." dNgos (po) is the standard translation of Skt. bhāva.

23d ⟨lali⟩taṁ: The two syllables broken off in the manuscript were restored according to the Tibetan translation sdug pa, "nice, pleasant." The Ṭippaṇa has rol pa, which is the standard translation of lalita.

25a balā⟨d a⟩nicchataḥ: The syllable broken off in the manuscript was restored according to the Tibetan translation mi 'dod bzhin . . . nan mnan nas, "unwilling . . . exercising pressure." This leaves no other choice for the Sanskrit.

26c akṛtāni ⟨karo⟩ti: The two syllables broken off in the manuscript were restored according to the Tibetan translation bya ba min byed, "does what is not to be done."

27d jarānujaḥ: The manuscript reads jarābhujaḥ, "(of) the devourer (of) Old Age." As a nominative, however, bhujaḥ can only mean "hand, arm," which is out of place here. The root noun bhuj, "one who eats, devours," is a consonantic stem that cannot be construed. The Tibetan translation has rgas pa'i nu bo (partly corrupted as ngo bo), "the younger brother of old age," which presupposes *jarānujaḥ. The Ṭippaṇa even gives an etymological explanation—"born after"—but interestingly also comments upon jarābhujaḥ as a variant reading. See the note on the translation.

28a ta⟨to⟩: The syllable broken off in the manuscript was restored according to the Tibetan translation de nas, "then."

28d jīvitā (?): The manuscript reads jīvitāsā, which is too long by one syllable. The problem is that *jīvitā, the shortened conjectural reading, is not easy to explain whereas the metrically wrong reading of the manuscript (if emended as jīvitāśā, "the hope to live") yields a meaning that perfectly suits the context. However, the Tibetan translation confirms neither jīvitā nor jīvitāśā; it has sdig pa, "bad deed." There is no Sanskrit word of this meaning that is graphically close to jīvitā(sā).

While the Vṛtti is silent about this word, the Ṭippaṇa has an interesting explanation: | **chags pa** ni re ba'o | "As for 'craving', it means hope." In re ba we have at least a trace of Skt. āśā, "hope, expectation, longing." Can it be that Vairocanarakṣita explains the word that originally stood in the place of sdig pa and was later replaced by an editor who regarded sdig pa, "bad deed," as a more appropriate expression? In the context of the stanza, however, chags pa, "longing, desire," the characteristic vice of youth, yields a much better contrast with the decaying body of an old man. See also lines 91d and 92d, containing the refrain vardhate eva rāgaḥ, "(and yet) human desire continues to grow." Since the meter permits neither jīvitāśā (the emended reading of the manuscript) nor rāgaḥ (the reading of the lines just quoted), we have basically two options: first, to stick to the manuscript as closely as possible, take jīvitā and interpret it as jīvi-tā, "the state of being alive," i.e. "(the desire to attain) the state in which one is alive;" or second, to make a bold emendation that is based on the Ṭippaṇa (and lines 91d and 92d) and read *rāgitā, "the state in which one is (still) filled with desire." For the time being I choose the more conservative option.

29c upa⟨ga⟩cchati: The syllable broken off in the manuscript was restored according to the Tibetan translation 'gro gyur pa "has gone to" (with the variant reading 'gro 'gyur ba "goes"). The Ṭippaṇa explains this as / **'gro bar gyur pa** ni thob pa zhes bya'o / "[He] 'has gone' [to the state] means he has attained [it]." The Vṛtti uses the present form 'gro bar 'gyur ba.

31a iti (ce)⟨ti ca⟩: The two syllables broken off in the manuscript were restored according to the Tibetan translation de lta de lta bur, which clearly shows the repetition. The reading is confirmed by the Ṭippaṇa.

31b kuliśaiḥ: The manuscript has kukṛtaiḥ, "by thoughts of regret, repentance," which yields perfect sense. However, both the Tibetan translation and the Vṛtti, which precede the Sanskrit manuscript by almost three centuries, obviously read *kuliśaiḥ, "by thunderbolts," because they translate rdo rje, "vajra; thunderbolt." Candragomin used this word also in lines 38b, 41b, and 48a. I find that kuliśaiḥ, "by thunderbolts," goes better with the verb math, "to crush" (in cittamāthibhiḥ), than does kukṛtaiḥ.

32c ⟨nijaṁ⟩ kaḍevaraṁ: The two syllables broken off in the manuscript were restored according to the Tibetan translation lus yid 'ong 'dris pa, "the pleasant and familiar body." 'Dris pa, "familiar," for *nijaṁ is not the standard translation (that would be either rang gi or gnyug ma); the Vṛtti, however, offers some further clarification: / **'dris pa** ni thog ma med pa nas nga'i lus snyam du zhen pa'o / "'Familiar' means: It is dear because one thinks 'From beginningless time this is my body'." Note that Skt. nija also means "peculiar; continual, perpetual." It is obviously this aspect of meaning that the translators wished to emphasize.

39a tuhinānilo: The manuscript reads tuhitānilo, which is certainly not a variant reading but only a graphical error. Nevertheless the result is a somewhat meaningful wording—"however (tu) a wholesome wind (hitānilo)"—that was adopted by the two previous editions (Minaev and Vaidya). The Tibetan correctly and very aptly translates bu yug, "snowstorm."

41a cañcajjaṭānikara: The manuscript reads cañcacchaṭānikam(pī). Chaṭā, "mass, assemblage; luster, splendor, light" does not suit the context and nikam is meaningless. The solution is given by the Tibetan, which has ral pa'i tshogs mang, "an ample mass (nikara) of locks (jaṭā)." This is confirmed by the Ṭippaṇa:

| **ral pa'i tshogs mang ba** ni skra'i tshogs bsgyings pa'o | "An 'ample mass of locks' means a fluttering mass of hairs."

41b daṁṣṭrāṅkuśāgra: The manuscript reads daṁṣṭrāṅkurāgra. The Tibetan translates the word in question by gzongs ring, "lengthy chisel." The Ṭippaṇa has lcags kyu. The latter word usually renders aṅkuśa, "goad." Both from the image—aṅkusa is generally used only with small and delicate things—and from the phonetic point of view, this reading is much better, so that I don't hesitate to follow the older textual tradition and emend accordingly.

42d nicitā: The manuscript reads nijitā, which is meaningless. The meaning required here is "full of," which is what the Tibetan has: gang ba'i. I emend accordingly.

45a meṣayugma: The manuscript has meṣayūtha, "flock of rams," which is also meaningful. However, I find the image of two rams attacking each other with the delinquent between them much more precise and cogent. And this is what the Tibetan has:

| ri dang mnyam du lug ru 'jigs su rung ba gnyis |
two frightening rams, (as massive) as a mountain.

This is confirmed by the Ṭippaṇa:

| **'dus pa'i phrag** ste lug de dag 'dus pa'i phrag tu ste | de dag gi zung des 'joms pa ni btag pa ste | des na **phye mar rlog cing 'joms** pa'o | "Their 'crashing together' means the crashing together of the two of them; he is smashed by the pair (consisting) of those two; therefore he is ground to pieces and shattered."

51c kartum: The manuscript has hartum, "in order to take away." This does not go with saṁcālamātram api, "even the smallest movement." The Tibetan has:

| bskyod pa tsam yang bya bar mi nus bzhin du gson |
They live as if they were incapable of performing even the smallest movement.

This presupposes kartum and I emend accordingly.

52a pralayatā: The manuscript has praṇayatā, "by him who is leading out, accomplishing, . . ." which is not meaningful in this context. The Tibetan has (rus pa la yang) thim pa yis, "seeping (even into their bones)," which is what we would expect. It presupposes pralayatā and I emend accordingly. The reason for this mistake is certainly the graphical similarity of the two letters la and ṇa.

54c śakalāvalī: The manuscript reads sakalāṭalī, which is completely meaningless here, although sakala and aṭala are Sanskrit words. The Tibetan has (dkar) dum phreng ba'i, "of a garland of tiny (white) pieces." This presupposes śakalāvalī and I emend accordingly.

54d sagajacarma: The manuscript has sa(mba)jacarma, which is unmetrical and meaningless. The Tibetan translates glang chen pags gyon, "clad in an elephant's hide." This presupposes sagajacarma and I emend accordingly.

57b mokṣāśayā: The manuscript has mokṣāśrayāḥ, "(who are) shelters of liberation," which is meaningful, but not in this context. The Tibetan translates thar par 'dod pas, "in (their) hope to escape)." This presupposes mokṣāśayā and I emend accordingly. Cf. also 8a and 112a.

57c ghāṭitaṁ: The manuscript has ghaṭitaṁ, "united; planned; made of," which is unmetrical. The Tibetan translates bcad gyur pa, "cut; closed," which is confirmed by the Ṭippaṇa, which has bcad pa. I emend ghāṭitaṁ, "joined, united," which describes the closing of the door-panels at the doorway to hell. Apparently it was thus understood by the Tibetan translators and by Vairocanarakṣita.

63b āropayanti: The manuscript has ācopayati, which is both meaningless and unmetrical, although there is a Sanskrit root cup, copayati, "to move slowly." The Tibetan has 'debs gyur pa, "cast, placed," which points to āropayanti as the original reading. The scribe of the Sanskrit text omitted the anusvāra above ya and mixed up the letters ra and ca, which are quite similar in the older scripts of eastern India. I emend according to the Tibetan.

63b śivam uttama°: The manuscript has śiva(nentasa), which is unintelligible. The Tibetan translates byang chub mchog gi sa bon dge ba'ang, "(and [planted] the) auspicious (seed of) supreme (enlightenment)." dGe ba, "auspicious," renders Skt. śivam and mchog, "supreme," Skt. uttama. Thus the writing error can easily be corrected.

75a kāmaṁ viṣaṁ ca: The manuscript has kāmā viṣañ=ca. From the two preceding stanzas it is clear that only two things are to be scrutinized, poison and the pleasures of the senses. Both occur in line 75a, each followed by ca, "and." Thus it is not possible to add kāmā, "(various) forms of lust" to them. Accordingly we do not find a trace of kāmā in the Tibetan translation. The reason is that the original reading was kāmam, an adverb used in the beginning of sentences to express a kind of assent followed by a partial reservation: "That may be true, it may be so that . . . (however) . . . ." In the Tibetan this is reflected in the conditional particle na at the end of the first line.

77c nāsthita eva lābhaṁ: The manuscript has nāstuta eva lābhaṁ, which is unintelligible in the context of the stanza. The Tibetan has rnyed pa grub pa med par, "without attainment (of one's desires) having been accomplished." Thus also the Vṛtti:

| **rnyed pa grub** (sgrub P) **pa med pa** ni rtswa lo ma zos pa'o | "'The attainment (of one's own desires) not having been accomplished' (in this case) means not having eaten the grass and the leaves."

The only word that comes to my mind that is both semantically and paleographially close to the meaning of the Tibetan translation is nāsthita, "not having attained or got."

81c nirāśrayam: The manuscript has sthirāsrayam, "having a firm support or foundation," which is somewhat strange as an attribute of "blinding darkness." The Tibetan translates skyabs med, "without protection." This is not the literal translation of the supposed nirāśrayam, which would be rten med pa. However, the Ṭippaṇa contains an etymological explanation of āśraya:

| **gnas pa** ni yun rings par gnas pa gang yin pa'o | "It is called '(resting) place' (āśraya) because one rests there (āśrayate) for a long time."

The negative verb med makes it clear that Sarvajñadeva and dPal brtsegs read nirāśrayam, and this is indeed a meaningful attribute of andhaṁ tamaḥ, "blinding darkness." Hence I emend accordingly. Note that in this context, "without protection" is a better interpretation than the literal "without support or foundation."

95c kati ke 'pi: The manuscript has kalike 'pi. This is a difficult passage. The first half of the stanza runs: "Of those with whom we used to laugh, to play, to sing, to drink, to eat, to converse in the same place." This is followed by "(those) who were dear to us have, over the (course of) time, been forced to depart, even if . . . (?) (kalike)." The Tibetan translates this line as follows:

| dus kyi rim pas me tog rna rgyan dengs byas dang |
and who in the course of time have made the ear ornaments
of flowers wither.

This is, I'm afraid, nonsensical; however, it indicates that the translators also read kalike 'pi, since kalikā means "a digit of the moon; a division of time; an unblown flower, a bud; a digit, streak." The grammatical problem is the form kalike 'pi, which does not go with the Tibetan translation; it presupposes kalikā api, which is unmetrical. The Ṭippaṇa seems to support the Tibetan translation. There we read:

| dus ni me tog dang ldan pa'o | "'Time' here means to be endowed with flowers."

Does this refer to kāla or to kalike? Then follows: | **dengs pa** ni khyer nas gzhung kha cig las ni **dus kyi rim pas** zhes pa brjod do | "'Withered' (gamitāḥ) here means having carried away; in another manuscript it is written 'in the course of time'."

All this is very confusing, especially the mention of the flowers. What I miss is the pronoun corresponding to yaiḥ in line a. That I see in ke 'pi, here enforced by kati: not just some few, but the majority of those mentioned in the first half of the stanza. Thus both the construction and the meaning become much smoother. The mistake can be explained graphically by the similarity of the letters la and ta in certain Indian scripts.

97c ***tā vatsalāḥ:** The manusript has tannisphalaḥ, "bearing no fruit with regard to that." This is completely unintelligible in the context of the stanza and not supported by the Tibetan, which presupposes a different text: byams pa bsten [ma rten D_2] pa de dag. De dag certainly renders *tāḥ, which is required as the correlative of yāsāṁ, as in 98c. Byams pa bsten pa (D_1), "relying on, adhering to, love," or byams ma rten pa (D_2), "not relying on, adhering to, love," is difficult. From the Vṛtti, which has:

bu'i ched du las kyi mtha' sna tshogs la 'bad pas **ngal ba mang** po **bsten** [ston P] kyang bu la **byams pa bsten** [la sten P] **pa de dag**, "these [mothers] who with effort did many deeds for their sons and who still keep their love towards them although (the sons) played many naughty pranks on them,"

it seems to be clear that the underlying Sanskrit compound referred to the object tāḥ, "those (beings)," not to the subject ko nāma, "who on earth." I translate according to the Tibetan version, although I am not able to offer a convincing Sanskrit term for byams pa bsten pa. Could it be *vatsalāḥ, "full of tender love"? See byams rendering vātsalya-, "affectionate, tender love (of a mother toward her child)" in the "Hymn in 150 Stanzas," 105 and 116.

100a ⟨na yānaiḥ⟩ (kṣemair) naiva ca: The first three letters of the line are completely lost. The following two letters are partly preserved, but the only thing one can say about them is that both were conjunct letters. The following three letters are clearly discernible as na, va, and ca. The very provisional reconstruction of the first five letters is based on the Tibetan, which has only gzhon bdes mi (thob), "not (to be attained) by comfortable vehicles." While na yānair seems to be clear, *kṣemair, "by comfortable (vehicles)," is only scarcely attested as a Sanskrit equivalent of bde ba, "comfortable." The caesura in the middle naiva is not fortunate, although similar cases in classical Sanskrit literature are discussed in Ronald Steiner's *Untersuchungen zu Harṣadevas Nāgānanda und zum indischen Schauspiel*, Swisttal-Odendorf 1997 (Indica et Tibetica, 32).

100c kathaṁ cit sā prāpyā viṣayasukha⟨sa⟩ṁbhogaparamair: The manuscript has kathaṁ cit saṁprāpya viṣayasukhaṁ bhogaparamair. That reading is unmetrical—the syllable pya has to be long and thereafter we have only four short syllables instead of five—and does not allow for a meaningful translation. This line is to be connected with line d, which runs: labhante ya⟨ṁ⟩ prīti⟨ṁ⟩ parahitasukhādhānaniratāḥ. The Tibetan translation of these two lines is:

| gzhan phan bde ba bskyed par brtson pas dga' ba rnyed pa gang | | de ni yul bde'i longs spyod lhur len rnams kyis ji ltar yang | "That attainment of pleasure which [one obtains] by the endeavor to create happiness [and] welfare of others [cannot be found] at all by those who yearn to enjoy the happiness created by sensual objects."

This interpretation is confirmed almost verbatim by the Vṛtti:

| **gzhan** la mya ngan las 'das pa'i **phan** yon ((131a)) dang | lha mi'i **bde ba bskyed par brtson pas dga'** [brtson pa pa bdag dga' D] **ba rnyed pa gang** yin pa **de ni** ste de [ste | de D] dang mnyam pa **yul** lnga'i **bde ba'i longs spyod lhur len** pa **rnams**

kyis ji ltar thob ces 'og ma [[401b]] dang sbyar ro | "The pleasure that one attains by the endeavor to create for others welfare, e.g. nirvana, and heavenly and worldly happiness—as far as that is concerned, how can [a pleasure] that matches it be attained by those (pa) for whom the enjoyment of the happiness of the five spheres of the senses is the greatest good?"

Since dga' ba is the object of rnyed pa, it is clear that yā prīti (unmetrical) of the manuscript has to be corrected as yāṁ prītiṁ. De (in line b) of the Tibetan translation points to a relative pronoun refering to yāṁ. That has to be sā, and the only way to insert it is to change saṁ into sā. From the Tibetan thob it becomes clear that prāpya has to refer to the subject of the sentence, sā; hence it is to be changed into prāpyā. Thereby the metrical problem is also solved. Since no particle like tu or hi can be inserted after the caesura, the missing short syllable has to be inserted elsewhere. The easiest solution is to expand bhoga to saṁbhoga, using the anusvāra that is already there and forming a single compound. This is absolutely necessary because after the inevitable change of saṁprāpya into sā prāpyā, there is no verb-form governing the remaining (unmetrical) accusative visayasukhaṁ. All these changes together produce a correct and meaningful Sanskrit sentence that is in perfect agreement with the Tibetan. Without the Tibetan translation the restoration of these two lines would have been almost impossible.

102c prakṛtir iyam eṣaiva: The manuscript has prakṛtir iyaṁ [sic] eva. One short syllable is lacking. The Tibetan has rang bzhin 'di 'dra ste, "the nature [of great men] is of this kind." The Ṭippaṇa offers the following interesting explanation:

| **rang bzhin de 'dra ba** ni rang gi ngo bo de'o | | **'di** ni 'di lta bur gyur pa'o | "'The nature like that' means that own nature. 'This' means it has become like this."

The use of de 'dra ba and 'di among the words to be explained indicates, in my opinion, that the Sanskrit text contained two pronouns, one followed by eva, which was here rendered by 'dra ba. This is the basis of my reconstruction iyam eṣaiva, which I regard as an emphasized expression for "of *exactly* this kind, of *exactly* such a kind." The Tibetan translation is therefore absolutely adequate.

104c parārthe svārthe tu: The manuscript has only parārthe, so that the third line is lacking three long syllables. This is most likely an inadvertent scribal error. The Tibetan has nyid kyi don du, "for their own sake," with *tu, "however," left untranslated, since the opposition between the two parts of the stanza is easily deducible from their content. The text to be added is therefore quite obvious.

109a nityākīrṇān: The manuscript has nītyākīrṇān, "full of (the right) conduct," which is a possible, but in this context, meaningless compound. Since the Tibetan has rtag tu 'khrugs pa'i, "always agitating," all we have to do is to shorten the first vowel in order to get the equivalent of rtag tu. 'Khrugs pa, "agitating," is a somewhat unusual, but not impossible translation of ākīrṇa. Its justification can be found in the Ṭippaṇa:

| **'khrugs pa** ni rnam par g.yengs pa ste dag pa nyams pa'i phyir ro | "'Agitating' means completely stirring up because [it] spoils what is pure." A similar paraphrase occurs in the Vṛtti:

| skad cig la lus 'jig longs spyod zad cing rtag tu ste | gnyen po skyes kyi bar du sems g.yeng zhing 'khrugs par byed pa'i yul lnga po rnams spongs | "Abandon the five spheres of the senses which always, i.e. until a remedy is found, stir up and agitate the mind, and whose enjoyment ends in a moment, when the body is destroyed."

109b śā⟨ntye⟩kāntaṁ: The manuscript has sākā(nt)aṁ with one long syllable missing. Here the restoration of the missing portion is not easy. The Tibetan translation has gcig pu dben pa, "single and solitary." The Vṛtti explains:

gcig pu grogs la mi bltos par **dben pa** ste 'du 'dzi med pa **bsten,** "yearn (for the bliss of tranquility) alone, that is, without looking for friends, and solitarily, that is, free from attachment."

This is not very clear. More help is offered by the Ṭippaṇa:

| **dben pa** ni mtha' gcig tu nges pa'i rang bzhin te | mtha' gcig tu zhi bas sam dben pas so | "As for 'solitude', having one's heart solely devoted to it; [this means one is] exclusively [absorbed] by peacefulness or solitude."

mTha' gcig tu clearly renders ekāntam, and the alternative zhi bas sam dben pas reveals that dben pa is the explanation and zhi ba the original word to be explained. Zhi ba, "peacefulness," renders both śama and śānti, with only the latter word suiting the meter. Therefore I restore the compound as *śā⟨ntye⟩kāntaṁ, "solely devoted to peacefulness." The proposed restoration produces a nice assonance with its three consonant clusters -nt-.

110d ⟨bhava⟩ bhavamarau: The manuscript has only bhavamarau. The two missing syllables can easily be restored from lines 111d and 112d, which have the same beginning.

112a *prahv**āgādhaḥ:** The manuscript quite clearly reads (prakaṭavipula)yakāgādhaḥ. Yakā has no meaning, and the first syllable has to be long, likewise the preceding la. The Tibetan has byin gzhol gting zab, "splendidly inclined, with a deep bottom." The Vṛtti gives the following explanation:

byin gyis gzhol ba ltar dge ba la gzhol ba dang | **gting zab pa** ltar chos zab mo rtogs pa dang | "As [the lake] is splendidly inclined, [the Buddha] is deep in his inclination toward what is wholesome; as the lake has a deep bottom, [the Buddha] has understood the deep Dharma."

The Ṭippaṇa has only a brief explanation of agādha:

| **mtsho zab pa** ni de'i gting du'o | "As for 'the lake [is] deep', this means 'with regard to its bottom'."

I suspect that the Sanskrit underlying byin gyis gzhol ba must have been prahva. Its basic meaning is "sloping, slanted, inclined." When referring to the lake, prahva would express that it is gently sloping and therefore not dangerous for beings who take a bath in it. The other, metaphorical meanings of prahva are: "stooping, bent down, bowing humbly down; submissive, humble, modestly submitting; devoted or attached to, engaged in, engrossed by." When referring to the Buddha, prahva could mean either "gently bowing down (to human beings)" or "devoted to (the well-being of all beings)" or "inclined to (what is) wholesome," as Prajñākaramati explains. Most probably the 'prefix' byin, "splendidly," was meant to characterize the quality of the Buddha, while the simple form gzhol ba referred to the lake. In the translation of the commentary, both terms became transposed because the term used in the translation of the Śiṣyalekha had to be quoted first. This transposition can be observed frequently in the translation of Indian commentaries into Tibetan.

The third compound in line a reads prasannatarāśrayaḥ in the Sanskrit manuscript. For āśrayaḥ, "resting place; receptacle; shelter," the Tibetan has bsam pa, "thought, reflection; will; soul, heart," which usually renders Skt. āśaya, "resting place; receptacle; mind, heart; disposition of mind."

The Vṛtti explains the compound in the following way:

rab tu dang ba ltar dang ba'i dad pa dang ldan pa, "As [the lake] is completely clear, so [the Buddha's] intentions are clear."

This also points to āśaya as the underlying Sanskrit. Since āśaya produces a better double meaning, I think it is the genuine meaning and emend accordingly. See also the commentary on 8a and 57b.

112b jālavyālapramāda: The manuscript has jalavyālanāda. The first syllable has to be long and between la and nā, one syllable is missing. The Tibetan translation has sbrul gdug rnyi yi[s] bag med 'jigs spangs pa, "having abandoned the danger of carelessness through the net [laid out] for poisonous snakes." The *Vṛtti* explains this as:

| **sbrul gdug pa'i rnyi yis bag *med med pa** ltar dug gsum med pa dang | "As the net for poisonous snakes frees [the lake] of danger, so [the Buddha] is free of the three poisons." The Ṭippaṇa has:

| **sbrul gdug** ni chu srin la sogs pa'o | | **rnyi** ni rtsa la sogs pa'o | | **bag med pa** ni mun pa'o | "'Poisonous snakes' refers to makaras and other (water animals). A 'net' [is made of] grass and other things. 'Carelessness' [here means] 'darkness'."

From the term "net," it is clear that the first word is to be restored as jāla; likewise, "carelessness" points to the emendation pramāda for the defective nāda. The interpretation of the Sanskrit text nevertheless remains somewhat difficult, since jāla-vyāla, "net-snake," can certainly not be translated as "'snake net', net for catching snakes." I propose to translate the compound as "free of the danger of poisonous water-snakes" when referring to the lake (with jāla- "relating to water, from jala-, water") and as "free of negligence with regard to the snake 'net', i.e. greed." I understand the snake 'net' as a circumlocution for jālinī, 'the ensnaring one', which is used quite often in Buddhist poetry as a synonym of tṛṣṇā, (sred pa) "greed." *See* Haribhaṭṭa's Jātakamālā, stanza 11.43 (= stanza 20.63) or Gopadatta's Jñanavatī 16, Matsarananda 77, and Puṇyarāśi 59.

116d śiśirasubhagaś candrā: The manuscript has satataśiśiraḥ subhagacandrā, which has three too many syllables. The Tibetan has rab bzang bsil bas, which renders subhaga- and śiśira-. There is no trace of satata- in any of the three Tibetan sources. The scribe of the manuscript inadvertently repeated the beginning from 112b: satataśiśiro. Because of the order of words in the manuscript, I restore śiśirasubhagaś and not subhagaśiśiraś, as the Tibetan would suggest. The Vṛtti and the Ṭippaṇa do not offer any clue as to the order of these attributes.

A Classified List of Scribal Errors in the Sanskrit Manuscript of the Śiṣyalekha

	MANUSCRIPT READING	RESTORED FORM
1.	**Vowel sign omitted**	
2b	sandarībhiḥ	sundarībhiḥ
44b	jvalata	jvalita
51b	jarjjaratasūna	jarjaritaśūna
77a	rūḍha	rūḍho
78c	vaitaraṇa	vaitaraṇī
79a	astīrṇṇa	āstīrṇa
83c	(varggaḥ)	vargāḥ
86b	kṛtvādgrīvaṁ	kṛtvodgrīvaṁ
99a	vikīrṇṇa	vikīrṇṇe
111a	mabhair	mābhair
112c	cchedā	cchedo
115a	vijita	vijitā
2.	**Wrong vowel sign**	
3c	tadaiva	tad eva
11b	saupāna	sopāna
14d	ter eva	tair eva
46b	punar aiva	punar eva
48c	lauho	loho
63c	ipi	api
65b	ābhavāñchitam	abhivāñchitam
76c	yuktā vā	yuktaṁ vā
84c	mṛtyo vādanam	mṛtyor vadanam
93c	satvau	sattvo
103c	śiraiveṣṭanā	śiroveṣṭana
115a	mārīnīkāḥ	mārānīkāḥ
115c	klaiśā	kleśā

3.	**Visarga omitted**	
15d	puna	punaḥ
17d	cetaspṛhā	cetaḥspṛhā
18d	gatī	gatīḥ
28b	gati	gatiḥ
34c	ghorai tānta	ghoraiḥ kṛtānta
56d	seṣakriyā	śeṣakriyāḥ ǀ ǀ
72b	parikarā	parikarāḥ ǀ
73d	bālā patanti	bālāḥ patanti
75Ad	viṣayā	viṣayāḥ
96d	eka prayāti	ekaḥ prayāti
97b	rasa	rasaḥ
112a	vipula	vipulaḥ
115b	ramyā	ramyāḥ
116b	manorathā	manorathāḥ
4.	**Visarga wrongly added**	
11c	mānāḥ	mānā
19c	yathaivaḥ	yathaiva
5.	**Anusvāra omitted**	
13c	mucanti	muñcanti
36b	taru	taruṁ
57a	apāvṛta	apāvṛtaṁ
58b	ayorasa	ayorasaṁ
66a	para muhūrttād	paraṁ muhūrtād
76a	śānti	śāntiṁ
76c	yuktā vā	yuktaṁ vā
92c	yāta	yātaṁ
99c	ruca	rucaṁ
6.	**Anusvāra wrongly added**	
41d	viṁṣama	viṣama
47c	prasahyaṁ	prasahya
48a	prasahyaṁ	prasahya

68b	vāriṁ guru	vāriguru
88b	mohāndhakāraṁ	mohāndhakāraḥ (for Visarga!)
89b	rāgavaṁhniḥ	rāgavahniḥ
101b	gāḍhaṁ tṛṣitaḥ	gāḍhatṛṣitaḥ
7.	**Omission of a letter (or part of a letter)**	
20c	sadya tathāpi	sadyas tathāpi
21c	smṛtti vraṇam	smṛtir vraṇam
34c	ghorai tānta	ghoraiḥ kṛtānta
35a	dūrā nirīkṣya	dūrān nirīkṣya
39a	tāpāditasya	tāpārditasya
55c	kaṭaṭkaṭiti	kaṭaṭkaṭaditi
57c	paṭṭai dṛ	paṭṭair dṛ
61d	dullabham	durlabham
63c	guṇaughai mā	guṇaughair mā
65a	dullabham	durlabham
69a	rati bhavati	ratir bhavati
72d	kleśāgne vayam	kleśāgner vayam
80b	mero ni	meror ni
84c	mṛtyo vādanam	mṛtyor vadanam
109c	pathāgala(ṁ)	pathārgalaṁ
8.	**Addition of a letter**	
8a	ṭāśrayeṣu	ṭāśayeṣu
20d	tad evat	tad eva
21c	smṛtti vraṇam	smṛtir vraṇam
41b	draṁṣṭrāṁkurā	daṁṣṭrāṅkurā
49b	aśaktnuvantaḥ	aśaknuvantaḥ
51d	pāsanibarddha	pāśanibaddha
57a	rnirīkṣya	nirīkṣya
70c	surassaritsu	surasaritsu
79d	grātram	gātram
83d	burdbuda	budbuda
84c	apāvṛttaṁ	apāvṛtaṁ

96a	ārjavaṁ	ājavaṁ
112a	rāśrayaḥ	rāśayaḥ
9.	**Confusion of sibilants**	
A	*śa for sa*	
2c	śaṁkucanti	saṁkucanti
52d	vaśālaśī	vasālasī
52d	śruta	sruta
55b	medaśi	medasi
73d	śaktāḥ	saktāḥ
93a	aśakṛn	asakṛn
101b	śalilaṁ	salilaṁ
105b	aśi	asi
114b	viśā	bisā
114d	śaśīkara	saśīkara
115b	gagaraśalila	gaganasalila
B	*śa for ṣa*	
61c	lokeśv	lokeṣv
C	*ṣa for śa*	
44d	karkkaṣa	karkaśa
50d	viṣanti	viśanti
53d	bhṛṣan	bhṛśaṁ
79c	niṣitākula(sastra)	niśitākula(śastra)
D	*sa for śa*	
12d	socati	śocati
18c	{sa}taśaḥ	śataśaḥ
27c	sirasi	śirasi
29a	kramasas=ca	kramaśaś ca
29b	saktir	śaktir
32b	visann	viśann
33b	pāsa	pāśa
34a	saila	śaila
34d	pāsaḥ	pāśaḥ
35c	kesaughasaivala	keśaughaśaivala

38a	saṁsino	śaṁsino
38b	kulisopala	kuliśopala
38c	pisaṅgam	piśaṅgam
40d	parisoṣam	pariśoṣam
42c	sitaśūlasakti-	śitaśūlaśakti-
43c	sata	śata
45a	sailā	śailā
45c	saitya	śaitya
45d	śatasas	śataśas
46a	sva	śva
47a	pāsair	pāśair
49a	sita	śita
49c	sastra	śastra
51b	jarjjaratasūna	jarjaritaśūna
51d	pāsanibarddha	pāśanibaddha
56d	seṣakriyā	śeṣakriyāḥ
58a	nisita	niśita
58b	rasmi	raśmi
59b	pisaṅga	piśaṅga
61a	vivasā	vivaśā
66a	svaḥ	śvaḥ
66c	pisaṅgita	piśaṅgita
66d	saṅke	śaṅke
67b	sasāṅka	śaśāṅka
70d	suci	śuci
72a	sailānāṁ	śailānāṁ
75a	viṣayās=ca	viṣayāś ca
76b	rais=ca	raiś ca
77c	svabhre	śvabhre
80d	saṁsīrya	saṁśīrya
86b	nisvāsa	niśvsa
87a	avaso	avaśo
90d	visanti	viśanti
94b	bahusaḥ	bahuśaḥ
95b	asitañ=ca kṛtas=ca	aśitaṁ ca kṛtāś=ca

95d	samās=ca viṣamās=ca	samāś ca viṣamāś ca
97a	vivasena	vivaśena
98a	kṛtāvakāso	kṛtāvakāśo
99a	vivase, asaraṇe	vivaśe; aśaraṇe
107d	sama	śama
106a	asaraṇa	aśaraṇa
109d	sadasva	sadaśva
110c	prasānti	praśānti
111b	yaso	yaśo
111c	prasamita	praśamita
114d	sobhāṁ	śobhāṁ
116c	samā	śamā
E	*sa for ṣa*	
18d	visamas=ca	viṣamaś ca
31c	sabāspa	sabāṣpa
59b	mastiska	mastiṣka
92d	duspūraṇas	duṣpūraṇas
97c	tannisphalaḥ	???
108c	rāgir nnisevyo	rāśir niṣevyo
10.	**Confusion of Nasals**	
A	*na for ṇa*	
7d	ś⟨⟨r⟩⟩ayena	śrayeṇa
37b	janitolbana	janitolbaṇa
40d	ās{y}oṣmanā	āsyoṣmaṇā
49d	ākṛṣyamāna	ākṛṣyamāṇa
70a	veni	veṇi
75a	nirūpyamānāḥ	nirūpyamāṇāḥ
95c	kramena	krameṇa
48b	nidrāryamānavapur	nirdāryamāṇavapur
B	*ṇa for na*	
72c	rair=ṇṇirjhana	rair nirjhana
82c	karmāṇilā	karmānilā
87a	aṇisam	aniśam
114a	kṛśāṇavaḥ	kṛśānavaḥ

114a	kṛśāṇavaḥ	kṛśānavaḥ
11.	**Confusion of letter (based on similarity of letters)**	
6a	ranna	ratna
19d	mahan=sa	mahat sa
24c	parāt¬ vicūrṇayan	parān vicūrṇayan
27a	prahasanv=ivā	prahasann ivā
28a	satvayo	saṁdhayo
29d	bhīmaṇava saḥ	bhīma eva saḥ
30c	mayāsnakaḥ	mayāntakaḥ
32d	yanna	yatna
34b	kaṇṭhaka	kaṇṭaka
56c	tiḥśṛta	niḥsṛta
56d	thanita	dhvanita
72c	rair=ṇṇirjjhana	rair nirjhara
79b	suravateṣu sakhaṁ	suravaneṣu sukhaṁ
86c	subahunir	subahubhir
108c	rāgir nnisevyo	rāśir niṣevyo
110c	cchāyaṣa	chāyaḥ
114d	dadhanu	dadhatu
115b	gagara	gagana
12.	**Peculiar spelling**	
20d	durlaḍitan	durlalitaṁ
70b	viḍaṇvinīṣu	viḍambinīṣu
73c	durlaḍita	durlalita
78a	mandāginī	mandākinī
13.	**Sandhi**	
61b	nirayāṁ	nirayāt
92c	ta(ṁ) na	tan na
94c	bandhuḥ	bandhur
14.	**Juxtaposition**	
48b	nidrāryamānavapur	nirdāryamāṇavapur

The Sanskrit Vocabulary of the Śiṣyalekha

The following abbreviations are used in this analysis :

abl.	ablative	n.	noun
adj.	adjective	nt.	neuter
adv.	adverb	num.	numeral
beg.	beginning	part.	particle
caus.	causative	postp.	postposition
cf.	confer, compare	ppp.	past participle passive
comp.	compound		
conj.	conjunction	prep.	preposition
denom.	denominative	pron.	pronoun
f.	feminine	v.	verb
fr.	from	*	reconstructed form
gen.	genitive	°	omission for brevity
ind.	indeclinable		
m.	masculine	+	(in 116+) colophon after stanza 116
Ms.	manuscript		

Nouns are given in their nominative singular form. Whenever the nominative form is ambiguous, the last part of the stem is given in parentheses. The gender of a noun is mentioned only when the nominative form is ambiguous.

In cases in which a noun is recorded in the dictionaries as having two (or more) genders, all the known genders of that noun are mentioned here, unless Candragomin's usage makes it clear which gender he assigns to a particular noun. This occurs only very rarely.

Adjectives (including past participles) are given in their stem forms.

A reconstructed word that occurs only once is marked by an asterisk in the left column. When there is more than one occurrence, the asterisk appears with the line numbers in the right column.

aṁśuḥ m.	n. ray 104b
akṛtajña-	adj. ungrateful 107c
akṛtam	n. an unperformed act; an unheard-of, outrageous deed 26c
akhaṇḍa-	adj. unbroken; untainted 6c
akhila-	adj. whole 10a, 113b
agaṇita-	adj. uncounted, not having counted 102b
agadadharaḥ	n. (holder of an) antidote 76b
agādha-	adj. not shallow, deep 112a
agniḥ m.	n. fire 59d, 60b, 72d, 84a, 103b
agraḥ	n. tip 41b
aṅkaḥ	n. lap 97a; *see also* śaśāṅkaḥ
aṅkita-	ppp. marked with, full of 35d (fr. √aṅk)
aṅkuraḥ	n. sprout 41b, 114b
aṅkuśaḥ	n. hook, goad 25c
aṅganā	n. woman 1d, 44c, 69b, 70a, 90b
aṅgam	n. limb; body 19d, 38c, 41b, 51b, 90b
aṅgāraḥ, °ram	n. charcoal 38b
acetana-	adj. unconscious, senseless; lacking understanding 23a

ajara-	adj. not aging, not becoming old 23c
atyanta-	adj. exceeding, excessive 15b, 19b, 65a
atyartham	adv. to the utmost degree 3c
atyāyata-	adj. extremely long, extremely extended 94a
atyugra-	adj. exceedingly horrible, extremely fierce 19a, 39c
atha	conj. then 25a, 27a; atha ca 77c
adaḥ (adas-)	pron. that one: asau 45d, 91a, 94c
adya	adv. now, today 66a; adyāpi 1c
adhaḥ	adv. down, downward 13d
adhaḥśirasā	adv. with the head pointing downward, headlong 81d
adhomukha-	adj. pointing down(ward) 46c
adbhuta-	adj. remarkable, wonderful 2a, 10d
ananta-	adj. endless 61c, 81c
anantara-	adj. having no interval, immediately before or after 58a
anabhijña-	adj. not knowing, ignorant of 12d
analaḥ	n. fire 55d (twice)
anāpnuvant-	adj. not attaining 50d (fr. √ āp)
anicchant-	adj. not desiring, not wishing 25a (fr. √ iṣ)
anilaḥ	n. wind 36a, 39a, 65c, 68d, 82c, 111b
anivartamāna-	adj. not turning back 11c (fr. ni-√ vṛt)
aniśam	adv. incessantly 18a, 87a
anīkaḥ	n. army 115a
anujaḥ	n. the younger brother 27d
anu-√ bhū	v. to experience, enjoy: anubhūya 78b

anubhūta-	ppp. enjoyed, experienced 91b, 93a (fr. anu-√ bhū)
anuyāta-	ppp. followed, accompanied 97b (fr. anu-√ yā)
anu-√ vṛt	v. to follow; pursue: anuvartamānāḥ 15b
anṛtam	n. untruth, lie 90c
*anekarasa-	adj. having various flavors 7d (Ms. ane⟨karasaṁ⟩)
antaḥ	n. end 47a, 73c, 77a
antakaḥ	n. 'he who ends', the Lord of Death 27a, 30c, 42d, 85d
antara-	adj. different from, other than 57d, 75d
antaram	n. the interior, inner part of 34a, 54a, 55c, 57a
antarita-	ppp. separated 3d (fr. antar-√ i)
antram	n. intestines 49d, 56c
antarālam	n. intermediate space or region or time, interval 13c
andha-	adj. blind, blinding, dark 81d, 103a
andhakāraḥ	n. darkness 5c, 13b, 19b, 74c, 88b, 88d
anya-	adj. other 50d
anvita-	ppp. (having) followed 77d (fr. anu-√ i)
apatyam	n. child 100b
apathaḥ, °tham	n. 'not a way', a wrong path 24b (apathena)
apara-	adj. other, else 16d
apavādaḥ	n. abuse, calumny, slander 16a
apa-√ hā	v. abandon, give up: apahāya 96c
apahārin-	adj. taking away 7c, 9a

apāvṛta-	ppp. wide-open 57a, 84c (fr. apa-ā-√ vṛ)
api	ind. 1c, 4a, 14a, 15c, 23a, 26b, 36c, 37c, 39ab, 40b, 51c, 52a, 57bcd, 63ac, 65d, 73d, 75d, 82a, 84d, 86b, 87c, 91d, 92cd, 93d, 94d, 95c, 97d, 98ad, 99d, 101a, 104a, 104c, 105d, 106b; *see also* katham api, ko 'pi
aprāpta-	adj. not (having) attained, reached 40c (fr. pra-√ āp)
apsarāḥ f. (°ras-)	n. apsaras, a heavenly nymph 78b
abhayam	n. absence or removal of fear; security, safety, protection from fear or danger 115a
abhi-√ vṛṣ	v. to rain down 38d (abhivarṣati)
abhivāñchita-	ppp. (strongly) desired 65b (fr. abhi-√ vāñch); as adv. abhivāñchitam, according to one's desire
abhi-√ i	v. approach, move toward: abhyeti 35b
abhimata-	ppp. wished for, ardently desired 2c (fr. abhi-√ man)
abhimānaḥ	n. pride; misconception, wrong notion 84b
abhyudita-	ppp. risen, appeared 7a (fr. abhy-ud-√ i)
abhram	n. cloud 37c
amara-	adj. immortal 23c, 115b
amaraḥ	n. 'the immortal one', god 83c, 105c
amala-	adj. immaculate 10a
amṛtam	n. nectar 7b, 9a, 107b, 116c
ameya-	adj. immeasurable 81c
ambaram	n. garment 83b
ambu nt.	n. water 41c

ambuvāhaḥ	n. 'water-carrier', cloud 7a
ambhojam	n. 'water-born', lotus 114c
ayam	*see* idam
ayaḥ nt. (ayas-)	n. iron 86c; iron instrument 49c
ayorasaḥ	n. molten iron 58b
aravindam	n. a lotus (Nymphea stellata) 90a
arciḥ nt. (arcis-)	n. a ray of light, flame 56b
arṇavaḥ	n. ocean 12a
arthaḥ	meaning 108c
arthaṁ	postp. (with gen.) for the sake of 101c
ardita-	ppp. tortured 39a, 39b (fr. √ ard)
arpita-	ppp. (having) bestowed, caused 46d (fr. √ ṛ caus. arpayati)
alakaḥ	n. a curl, lock of hair 78a
alpa-	adj. little, small 2b
alpapuṇya-	adj. having (only) few virtues or merits 2b
avakāśaḥ	n. opportunity, occasion 98a
ava-√ tṝ	v. to descend: avataranti 11d
ava-√ ruh	v. to descend: avarohati 48d, avaroḍhum 49b
avalīḍha-	ppp. licked 36c (fr. ava-√ lih)
avaśa-	adj. having no will of one's own, powerless 87a, 103b
avaśyam	adv. necessarily, certainly 18c
ava-√ āp	v. attain: avāpa 4b
avidyā	n. ignorance 103a
avīciḥ m.	n. the hell Avīci 104a

ava-√i	v. to descend; to enter (a certain state): avaiti 18b
avadānam	n. heroic deed (of the Buddha) 1a
aśaknuvant-	adj. unable (to do) 49b, 51c (fr. √śak)
aśaraṇa-	adj. having no shelter or protection, unprotected, helpless 42c, 98c, 99a, 106a
aśita-	ppp. eaten 95b (fr. √aś)
aśuci nt.	n. impurity, filth 19a, 21a
aśubha-	adj. unpleasant 89c
aśrānta-	adj. not exhausted or tired, tireless 102a
aśru nt.	n. tear 58c
aśvaḥ	n. horse 109d
√as	v. to be: asti 65d, 92c, 93c, 93d, 96d; āsīt 93b; san 77b
asakṛt	adv. 'not once', many times 91b, 93a
asahana-	adj. not enduring, impatient; intolerable 66d
asiḥ m.	n. sword 42d
asipattra-	adj. having leaves consisting of swords 42b, 79d, 105b
asipattravanam	n. the forest in which the leaves are as sharp as swords 105b
asuḥ m.	n. spirit, life 15c, 45c
asuraḥ	n. demigod 100b
asulabha-	adj. not easy to attain 107c
asau	*see* adas
asthi nt.	n. bone 52a, 54c, 55c
asmad-	pron. we: vayam 72d
√ah	v. to say, speak: āhuḥ 99b

aham	*see* mad
aho	interjection (showing surprise or wonder) 101d
ā	prep. (with abl.) from; until, up to 53c
ā-√ i	v. to come (together): etya 95a
ākaraḥ	n. mine, source of origin 54b (*see* śikhākaraḥ)
ākīrṇa-	ppp. scattered, spread (over) 109a (fr. ā-√ k)
ākula-	adj. confused, distracted; whirling around 33d, 61a, 79c, 82c; loose, weak 22a; full of; afflicted by 44b, 55a, 58b, 61c
ākulita-	ppp. scattered, whirled around; flickering; dishevelled 36a, 65c, 78a (fr. ākulay, denom. of ākula-)
ākrandaḥ	n. cry, crying 33d
ā-√ kṛṣ	v. to drag away, along: ākṛṣyate 34d; to pull out: ākṛṣyamāṇaḥ 49d
āgata-	ppp. come 67b (fr. ā-√ gam)
āgamaḥ	n. arrival 38a, 67a (*see* kusumāgamaḥ)
ācāryaḥ	n. teacher 116+
ājavaṁjavam	n. the torrent of birth and death 96a
ātapaḥ	n. heat, pain 43a
ātapatram	n. parasol 4c
ātmā m. (ātman-)	n. self; adj. own (in the beg. of a comp.) 3d, 23c
ātmīya-	adj. own 61a
ādagdha-	ppp. burnt, singed 59a (fr. ā-√ dah)
ādīpta-	ppp. blazing 49a (fr. ā-√ dīp)

ā-√ dṛ	v. to respect, honor; to care for: ādriyante 9d
ādhānam	n. placing; doing, creating 100d
ānanam	n. face 99c
ānīla-	adj. dark-blue 36b
√ āp	v. to attain: āpnuvanti 9b; anāpnuvantaḥ 50d
āpātaḥ	n. burst; first encounter 45c, 74a
āpūrṇa-	ppp. (completely) filled with 86c (fr. ā-√ pṝ)
ābha-	adj. having the splendor of, resembling, liking 45a
ābhogaḥ	n. curving, winding; circumference; vault 72b; enjoyment 113c
āmodaḥ	n. joy, pleasure, delight 116a
ā-√ yā	v. come, approach: āyāti 67a
āyāsaḥ	n. toil 115c
āyuḥ nt. (āyus-)	n. life 65d, 67d, 68d
ā-√ ruh	v. to mount, climb: āruhya 18b, ārohati 46b; caus. to plant: āropayanti 63b
ārgalaḥ	n. a bolt or bar 109c
ārta-	adj. afflicted, tormented; miserable 40b, 48b, 110d, 111d, 112d
*ārtivat-	adj. suffering from illness (Tib. nad kyis thebs pa) 9d (Ms. mutilated)
ārdra-	adj. wet, slimy 21b
ārya-	adj. noble 12c, 15a
ālayaḥ	n. dwelling-place 22d
ā-√ liṅg	v. to embrace: āliṅgyate 44d

ālokaḥ	n. (bright) light, splendor, radiance 102a, 114a, 116d
āvartaḥ	n. whirl, whirlpool 96b
āvaliḥ f.	n. line, row, series, chain 13c
āvalī f.	n. line, row, series, chain 54a, 81b
āvila-	adj. turbid, impure, dark-colored, stained; filled with 70a
ā-vi-√ bhā	v. to manifest: āvibhāti 60d
ā-√ viś	v. to enter: āviśya 19c
āśā	n. hope [28d (in jīvitāśā; text of the Ms. not correct)], 57b
āśīviṣaḥ	n. (poisonous) snake 47b
*āśayaḥ	n. receptacle; heart, mind; mental disposition, intention 8a, 112a (Ms. in both cases āśraya-, Tib. in both cases bsam pa)
āśrayaḥ	n. shelter; vessel, recipient *7d (Tib. brten nas, Ṭippaṇa rten)
āsanna-	ppp. near, nearby 68a, 72c (fr. ā-√ sad)
āsāraḥ	n. a sharp or hard-driving shower (of anything) 111b (Tib. has shugs drag for dhārāsāra-)
ā-√ sev	v. to devote oneself to: āsevate 62d
āstīrṇa-	ppp. spread (out) 79a (fr. ā-stṝ)
āsthita-	ppp. having obtained, reached, got 77c (fr. ā-√ sthā)
*āsyam	n. mouth 40d (Tib. kha)
āhata-	ppp. beaten (at) 58c (fr. ā-√ han)
āhita-	ppp. placed, done; created 3c (fr. ā-√ dhā; cf. ādhānam)

√**i**	v. to go (to): eti 37a; to attain (a certain state): eti 28c, 40d, 88b, 88d
iti	adv. so, thus 31a (twice; iti ceti ca), 66b, 67b, 67d, 72d, 107a, 113a, 116+
idam	pron. this (here): anena 113b; amī 57b, 90d; ayam 20c, 29c, 30c, 35b, 67a, 98a, 101c; asmin 84a, 94a, 99a, asya 28a, 33c, 36c, 37c, 39d, 99d, 101d [twice]); idam 30a, 39d, 66a, 90c, 101d; iyaṁ 102c
indīvaram	n. the blue lotus 90b
induḥ m.	n. moon 90a
indriyam	n. organ of the senses 29a
indhanam	n. fuel, firewood 59c
iyam	*see* idam
iva	1c, 2d, 4d, 5d, 6a, 7a, 7b, *9d (Tib. bzhin), 11a, 15a, 17a, 20b, 21c, 21d, 25d, 26b, 27a, 27b, 32b, 33d, 47a, 54d, 59d, 72d, 85d, 86d, 96b, 99d, 104d
iha	12b, 16a, 63d, 93b, 97d, 98d, 99b, 99d, 101c, 103d
ugra-	adj. horrible, terrible 21b, 54a, 90c
ugragandha-	adj. of bad smell, stinking horribly 21b, 54a
ujjvala-	adj. radiant 5b
ujjhita-	ppp. abandoned, bereft 26b, 109b (fr. √ ujjh)
ut-√ kram	v. to go out or away; to pass away, die: utkrāmati 28b
uttapta-	ppp. hot, heated 50c, 80c (fr.ut-√ tap)
uttama-	adj. highest, supreme 6a, 63b

uttara-	adj. higher; strong, surpassing 44c
uttitīrṣu-	adj. desiring to cross 12a (fr. ut-√ tṝ, desiderative)
uttrāsita-	ppp. terrified 46a (fr. ut-√ tras, caus.)
ut-√ (s)thā	v. to rise: utthātum 13b
utpanna-	ppp. born, arisen 52c (fr. ut-√ pad)
ut-√ paṭ	v. to tear up or out, to draw out: utpāṭayanti 47c
utpādaḥ	n. arising, appearance 115d
ut-√ sah	v. to bear, endure, stand: utsaheta 97d, 98d
ut-√ sṛj	v. to abandon, to leave behind: utsṛjanti 10c, utsṛjya 22b
udayaḥ	n. rising, appearance 5a
udaram	n. belly; womb 98a
udāra-	adj. noble, exalted, dignified 107b, 108b
udita-	ppp. risen, appeared 5d (fr. ud-√ i)
udgamaḥ	n. going up, rising; going out 58d
udgrīva-	adj. with the neck uplifted 86b (here used as noun)
uddhata-	ppp. raised up, elevated; high 37a (fr. ud √ han)
udyata-	ppp. persevering, diligent, active 13b (fr. ud √ yam)
unnata-	ppp. raised up, raising up 80a (fr. un-√ nam; *see* natonnata-)
*un-√ mīl	v. to open, gaze openly: ⟨unmīla⟩*yan 4b; Ms. defective, Tib. spyan 'byed gzigs mdzad cing)

unmukha-	adj. with the face raised; pointing up(ward) 48c
upakāraḥ	n. service (done to others) 5a
upa-√ i	v. to go to; to enter (a certain state): upaiti 43, upaiti 59c, upetya 65a
upa-√ gam	v. to go to, to approach; to attain (a certain state): upagacchati 29c
upacāraḥ	n. practice, performance, conduct, behavior 22a
upajāta-	ppp. born, risen, become 22b (fr. upa-√ jan)
upadruta-	ppp. attacked 31b (fr. upa-√ dru)
upabhogaḥ	n. enjoyment, tasting; experience 20d
*upabhogya-	adj. to be enjoyed: upabho⟨gyaṁ⟩ 8c
upamā	n. simile, comparison 52a
uparuddha-	ppp. obstructed 19a (fr. upa-√ rudh)
upārjita-	ppp. acquired 113a (fr. upa-√ arj)
upeta-	ppp. having gone to; having attained (a certain state) 53c (fr. upa-√ i)
upalaḥ	n. stone; rock; meteorite 38b, 41d
upoḍha-	ppp. collected, accumulated, brought near 19b (fr. upa-√ vah)
uragaḥ	n. 'breast-walker', serpent, snake 94d
uraḥ nt. (uras)	n. breast, bosom 55c
uru-	adj. broad, huge 6b, 55a
ulbam	n. the membrane that surrounds the embryo 21b
ulbaṇa-	adj. intense, dense; huge 21c, 27b, 37b
ulmukaḥ	n. firebrand, torch; here tree stump (?) 36d (thus Tib.: mgal dum)

uṣṇa-	adj. hot 86a
uṣṇam	n. heat 99c
uṣmā m. (uṣman-)	n. heat 40d (or ūṣmā; second part of a compound)
ūḍha-	v. carried, worn 6b (fr. √ vah)
ūruḥ m.	n. thigh 80d
ūṣmā m. (ūṣman-)	n. heat 40d (or uṣmā; second part of a compound)
ūhuḥ	*see* vah
eka-	adj. one; single, sole, only; unique 2d, 4c, *5b (Tib. gcig pu), 10a, 10b, 43d, 96d, 97c, 110d, 111d, 112d, (pl.) some 51a
ekākin-	adj. single, alone, on one's own 14a
ekatra	adv. in one place, together 75c (here for ekasmin), 95b
ekadīpaḥ	n. the sole lamp or light 10b
ekarasa-	adj. of (only) one flavor, of a unique flavor 7b
ekānta-	adj. 'having only one end', exclusive, exclusively devoted to 102d, *109d (Ms. defective, only (sā)kāntaṁ, Tib. gcig pu)
ekāntarasika-	adj. having only one feeling or emotion 102d
etad	pron. this (here): asya 38a; etad 66a, 66b, 67c; ete 102d; eṣa 16c, 48b, 67b, 104d; eṣā *102c
etya	*see* ā-√ i

enad-	defective pron. this, that: enam 98b (used in a dependent clause)
eva	ind. (limiting or intensifying the preceding word) just, only 18c, 23b, 23d, 28d, 29d, 40c, 46b, 61d, 65b, 77c, 91d, 92d, 100a, 101a, 108b; (after a pronoun or any form derived fr. a pronoun) same 3d, 14d, 19c, 20d, 35b, 43d, 45d, 49b, 60b (twice: tad eva; sa eva), 62c, 86d, 90d, *102c
evam	adv. thus, in this manner 30a, 30b, 30c, 76d
eṣa	*see* etat
oghaḥ	n. abundance, mass 15a, 27b, 35c, 46c, 63c, 99a
auṣṇyam	n. heat 60b
kaḥ	*see* kim
kakṣā	n. a girdle 105a; *see* baddhakakṣa-
kaṅkaḥ	n. heron 47d
kaṭatkaṭaditi	onomatopoeic: the sound of bones breaking in the fire 55c
kaṭāhaḥ	n. frying-pan, cauldron 50b
kaṭu-	adj. acrid 54a
kaṭuka-	adj. sharp, pungent; disagreeable, unpleasant 74b
kaṭhora-	adj. hard (also figuratively) 22b
kaḍevaraḥ, °ram	n. body 32c
kaṇṭakaḥ, °kam	n. thorn 34b, 46c
kaṇṭhaḥ, °ṇṭham	n. throat 40c, 53b

kati	pron. some, several (here in combination with ke 'pi) 95c
katham	interrogative adv. how, in what manner 12c, 30a, 30b, 30c, 93d
katham api	adv. somehow; desperately 57b
kathaṁ cit	adv. somehow; with great effort 20b, 61b, 87b, 95d, 100c
kathā	n. story; sermon 116c
kadā cit	adv. at some time; (with negation) never 76d
kanakam	n. gold 38c
kapālaḥ, °lam	n. the skull, skull-bone 59a
karaḥ	n. hand 54b (here ākaraḥ is also possible; *see* śikhākaraḥ), 114a
karaṇam	n. doing 105a
karatalaḥ, °lam	n. the palm of the hand 114a
karāntaḥ	n. 'end of the hand', finger 47a
karī m. (karin-)	n. 'having a hand or trunk', elephant 25d
karuṇam	adv. mournfully 31d, 83b
karuṇā	n. compassion 3c
karkaśa-	adj. harsh, rough 37d, 44d
karṇaḥ	n. ear 53b
karma nt. (°man-)	n. action, deed; the consequences of one's deeds 14b, 39c, 57c, 60c, 61a, 82c
karmamaya-	adj. consisting of deeds, made of deeds 51d
kalāpaḥ	n. a band, bundle; a group, multitude 59b
kalilam	n. a large heap, confused mass 86a
kalpa-	adj. similar, resembling 6a, 73a

kalpaḥ	n. aeon; end of the world, universal destruction 55d
kalpataruḥ	n. the wish-fulfilling tree 79a
kallolaḥ	n. a large wave 37b
kaviḥ m.	n. poet 90b
kaś cit	*see* kiṁ cit
kānanam	n. forest, grove 1d, 105d
*kāraṇaṁ	n. cause, reason, factor 7c (Ms. mutilated, Tib. rgyu)
kāntāraḥ, °ram	n. a large or dreary forest 12c
kāntā	n. beloved one 79b
kāmaḥ	n. desire; object of desire 73b, 93b
kāmam	adv. indeed, really; however 75a
kāyaḥ, °yam	n. body 51b, 53c
kārya-	adj. to be done 66a (fr. √ kṛ)
kāla-	adj. dark, black 34d, 47a, 66c, 85b
kālaḥ	n. time 20a, 55d, 95c
kālakramaḥ	n. lapse of time, course of time 20a, 95c
kāladaṇḍaḥ	n. the black club of the Lord of Death 66b, 85b
kiṅkaṇīkaḥ, °kam	n. a small bell or tinkling ornament 81a (usually f.: kiṅkaṇī, kiṅkaṇīkā, kiṅkiṇī or kiṅkiṇīkā; the Ms. has kiṅkanīka°)
kinnaraḥ	n. kinnara, a heavenly musician 1b, 82a
kim	interrogative pron. who, what: ka 12b, 63d, 99d; kā 91a; kās 91c; kim 16d, 57d, 69a, 70c, 91b; ke 49b, 50a, 50b; ko 82d, 97d, 98d
kiṁ cit	indefinite pron. whosoever, whatsoever: kaś cit 102c; ke cit 49b, 50a, 50b

kiyant-	interrogative pron. how much 113a
kiraṇaḥ	n. ray 1c
kiśorakaḥ	n. a colt, the young of any animal 109d
kukūlaḥ, °lam	n. chaff; the hell Kukūla 80c
kukṣiḥ m.	n. belly 40a; the interior of anything 50b
kugatiḥ f.	n. a lower form of existence (as animal, ghost, or hell-being) 82c
kupita-	ppp. angry 66d (fr. √ kup)
kumbhīpākaḥ	n. the hell Kumbhīpāka 86a
kuliśaḥ, °śam	n. thunderbolt, lightning bolt *31b (Ms. kukṛtaih, Tib. rdo rje), 38b, 41b, 48a
kuśalam	n. well-being 26b
kusumaḥ	n. flower 67a, 83a, 110b
kusumāgamaḥ	n. 'the arrival of flowers', spring 67a
kūṭaśālmaliḥ f., m.	n. a species of the kūṭaśāmali tree (which has sharp thorns) 46c
kūpaḥ	n. water-hole, well 42c, 77a
√ kṛ	v. to do: karoti 26c, 39b, 87d, 101a, 104d; kartum 51c, 101c; kuryāt 65b; kurvan 102a; kṛtvā 86b, 99d, 113b
kṛtaghna-	adj. 'killing what has been done for one', ungrateful; impudent 96d
kṛta-	ppp. done 30a, 30b, 33d, 48b, 62b, 92b, 95b, 98a, 115a (fr. √ kṛ)
kṛtāntaḥ	n. the Lord of Death 34c, 66d, 109b
kṛtārthatā	n. 'the state of being successful', success 116d
kṛtiḥ f.	n. work, composition 116+
kṛpaṇa-	adj. miserable 98c

kṛpāṇaḥ	n. a sword 4d
kṛpā	n. compassion 111b
kṛśānuḥ m.	n. fire 80c, 114a
keśaḥ	n. hair 35c, 53a
koṭiḥ f.	n. the sharp, pointed edge, tip 41d, 48a
kopaḥ	n. anger, wrath 59d
ko 'pi	whoever 95c (ke 'pi, preceded by kati)
krakacaḥ	n. saw 44d
kramaḥ	n. progression, course 20a, 95c
kramaśaḥ	adv. gradually 29a
krameṇa	adv. gradually, successively 18c
kriyā	n. act, deed 56d
krīḍā	n. play; playful sporting 78b, 115b
krodhaḥ	n. anger, wrath 86c
kleśaḥ	n. defilement 72d, 115c
kva cit	indefinite adv. somewhere 55a
√ kvaṇ	v. to sound 55c (kvaṇantam)
kvathita-	ppp. boiled 43a (fr. √ kvath)
kvathitam	n. boiling brew 86a
kṣaṇaḥ, °ṇam	n. instant, moment; (in the beg. of a comp. = kṣaṇam) 55b, 109a
kṣaṇam	adv. lasting for a single moment 99c
kṣaṇam api	adv. lasting (only) a single moment 65d, 86b, 87c, 105d
kṣaṇāt	adv. after a while 66b
kṣata-	ppp. wounded, smashed 41b (fr. √ kṣan)
kṣatam	n. wound 52d
kṣatajam	n. 'arisen from a wound', blood 35d

kṣama-	adj. enduring, capable to endure 112c
kṣamā	n. forbearance 110a
kṣayaḥ	n. decay 28c
kṣāra-	adj. acid 41c
kṣut f. (kṣudh-)	n. hunger 99c
kṣuraḥ	n. razor 42a
*kṣema-	adj. comfortable 100a (Ms. illegible, Tib. has bde, "pleasant, comfortable")
kṣobhaḥ	n. agitation 87b
khaḍgaḥ	n. rhinoceros 46a
khara-	adj. hard; sharp; acid 78c
kharaḥ	n. ass; mule 46a
khalu	ind. indeed (enforcing the meaning of a preceding pronoun or negation) 60c, 77d, 109d
khinna-	ppp. exhausted 43a (fr. √ khid)
gaganam	n. heaven 106c, 115b
gaganasarit f.	n. the heavenly river Ganges (which in Indian mythology descends from heaven to earth) 106c
gaganasalilam	n. the heavenly water (of the river Ganges) 115b
gajaḥ	n. elephant 24d, 54d
gajacarma nt.	n. elephant's hide 54d
gajavat	adv. like an elephant 24d
gaṇaḥ	n. host, multitude 69c
gata-	ppp. gone; gone to, dwelling in 12b, 96c (fr. √ gam)

gatiḥ f.	n. gait 28b, 103a; form of existence 16b, 18d, 20d, 61c, 82c, 91a, 100b; life 30b
gadita-	ppp. told, said, declared 73b (fr. √ gad)
gandhaḥ	n. smell, scent 19a, 21b, 54a
√ gam	v. to go: agamat 3b; gatvā 81a; gantum 98d; caus. to make go: gamitāḥ 95c
gamya-	adj. suited to be gone; accessible 72d
garbhaḥ	n. womb 6d, 19c, 90d
garbhanilayaḥ	n. 'the dwelling-place womb' 6d, 19c, 90d
√ gal	v. to trickle down, to stream down: galad- 58c
galaḥ	n. throat, neck 34d, 56b
galita-	ppp. trickled down; hanging down 47a, 49d (fr. √ gal)
gahana-	adj. deep, dense, thick 74c
gāḍha-	ppp. dived or plunged into, deeply entered; strong, intense, excessive 35b, 46d, 72b, 101b (fr. √ gāh)
gātram	n. body; limb 45b, 59d, 79d
√ gāh	v. to dive or plunge into, enter deeply: gāhante 104a
giriḥ m.	n. mountain 50a, 60a, 68c
girinadī	n. mountain stream 60a
girīndraḥ	n. 'lord of the mountains', a high mountain 22c
gīta-	ppp. sung, praised 1b (fr. √ gā)
guṇaḥ	n. quality; degree; virtue 3c, 5b, 13c, 15a, 63c
guṇita-	ppp. multiplied, increased 116b (fr. √ guṇ)

guru-	adj. heavy, strong 56d, 68b
guruḥ	n. weighty, venerable person; teacher 14d
gurutā	n. the state of a teacher 14d
guhā	n. cave 72b
gṛdhraḥ	n. vulture 47d
gṛhīta-	ppp. seized 33a (fr. √ grah)
goṣṭhī	n. meeting, assembly; discussion 95b, 116c
√ gras	v. to devour: grasituṁ 27c
grāmaḥ	n. village, hamlet; (in the beg. of a = grāmya-) relating to a village, rural, vulgar 87d
grāsaḥ	n. devouring, eating 101a
ghana-	adj. hard, solid; thick, dense 19b, 43b, 110b
gharghara-	adj. gurgling 56d
gharmaḥ	n. sweat, perspiration 83a
*ghāṭita-	ppp. closed, shut (Ms. ghaṭitaṁ; I follow Tib. bcad gyur pa; confirmed by the Ṭippaṇa bcad pa) 57c (fr. √ ghaṭ, caus.)
ghātaḥ	n. a blow, strike, hit 34c
ghāsaḥ	n. food 101a
ghṛṇā	n. compassion; disgust, aversion 21d (both meanings are suitable; Tib. skyon gyis is unclear)
ghora-	adj. dreadful, terrible 16b, 34c, 49c, 74b, 81c
ghoratara-	adj. (even) more dreadful or terrible 32b
ghoṣaṇam, °ṇā	n. proclamation 115a

ca	conj. and *7c, 16b (twice), 18d (twice), 29a, 31a (twice), 60b, 73b, 74abcd, 75a (twice), 76b, 77c, 90b, 94b, 95b, 95d (twice), 100a
cakram	n. wheel 18a
cakṣuḥ nt. (cakṣus-)	n. eye 10a
√ cañc	v. to move, waver, shake: cañcaj- 41a
cañcala-	adj. moving, shaking; unsteady 68d
caṭaccaṭaditi	onomatopoeic: the crackling sound of sparks 55a
caṇḍa-	adj. fierce 36c, 65c
candraḥ	n. moon 1c, 73a, 104b, 116d; the author Candragomin 1c, 116d
candragomī (°min-)	n. Candragomin, name of the author of the Śiṣyalekha 116+
candanaḥ, °nam	n. sandal 36b
candanataruḥ m.	n. the sandal tree
capala-	adj. moving, trembling 74d, 91c
cayaḥ	n. assembly, multitude 59d
caraṇaḥ, °ṇam	n. foot 80d
caritam	n. life and acts 1a, 113b
carma nt. (°man-)	n. hide 54d (*see* gajacarma)
cala-	adj. moving, fickle, unsteady 65c
cāmaraḥ, °ram	n. a bushy yak tail used as fly-whisk or fan and considered a sign of royalty 91c
cāru-	adj. lovely, sweet 69d, 91c
cit	particle (used after interrogative pronouns and adverbs); *see* kathaṁ cit, kadā cit, kiṁ cit, kva cit
cittam	n. mind 31a

cintāmaṇiḥ m.	n. the wish-fulfilling gem that grants every wish to its possessor 2d, 63c
ciram	adv. for a long time 12d, 43d, 80b
cūḍā	n. crest, plume, diadem, head ornament 6a
cūrṇita-	ppp. pulverized, pounded, ground (to pieces) 41b, 45b (fr. √ cūrṇ)
cetaḥ nt. (cetas-)	n. heart, mind 17d, 48d, 53c
ceṣṭitam	n. gait; course; conduct 26a, 61a
codita-	ppp. driven, instigated 111b (fr. √ cud)
chadaḥ	n. a covering, cover 110b
channa-	ppp. covered 114b (fr. √ chad)
chamacchamaditi	onomatopoeic: the hissing sound of burning fat 55b
chāyā	n. shadow 110c, 111c
chedaḥ	n. cutting off (also figuratively) 112c
jagat nt. (jagat-)	n. the world; the people of this world 5d, 10a, 88a, 88c, 91a, 92b, 93b, 94a, 94c, 99a, 116a
jagdha-	ppp. eaten up 52d (fr. √ jakṣ)
jaghanam	n. the buttocks 69b
*jaṭā	n. mane (of hair) 41a
jaṭharaḥ (°ram)	n. abdomen, belly 56c; womb 93c; cavity 13a
jaḍataratvam	n. the state of total numbness 53c
√ jan	v. to be born; jāyate 88a, 88c, 89b, 89d
janaḥ	n. being; people 2b, 8c, 16a, 33c, 66b, 67c, 84b, 94c, 111a, 113b; group (of) 31d, 72a, 106a, 116c

jananam	n. birth 87b, 115c
janana- (f. °nī)	adj. producing, bringing forth 15a
jananī	n. mother 15a
janita-	ppp. (having) produced 37b (fr. √ jan, caus.)
jantuḥ m.	n. creature, living being 51a, 52c, 60a, 61d
janma nt. (°man-)	n. birth; life (in which one is born) 9a, 12a, 63a, 75c, 75d, 84d, 94a
jarā	n. old age 9a, 25c, 27d
jarjara-	adj. worn out 56a
jarjarita-	adj. worn out, torn to pieces, splintered, eaten away 51b, 52b, 78d
jalam	n. water 7b, 60a, 70d, 78a, 83d
jaladaḥ	n. cloud 38a
jaladhiḥ m.	n. the ocean 63a, 85c
jalalavaḥ	n. a drop of water 40d
javaḥ	n. speed, swiftness 42a
javena	adv. with speed, quickly 42a
jahāti	*see* √ hā
jāta-	ppp. born, risen 24d, 52c (fr. √ jan)
jātiḥ f.	n. birth 62c
jālavyālaḥ	n. water-snake 112b (= jalavyālaḥ)
jinaḥ	n. the Victorious One, the Buddha 73b
√ jīv	v. to live: jīvanti 51d
jīvaḥ	n. life 20c, 51d, 60a, 83d
jīvalokaḥ	n. the living beings 77d
[jīvitam	n. life 28d; *see* the next entry]

*jīvitā	n. the state of being alive (?), desire for life (?) 28d (*see* commentary on pp. 191–92)
jīvitāśā	n. the wish or hope to live 28d (the unmetrical reading of the Ms., which is hardly correct)
jṛmbhita-	ppp. unfolding, flaring up 55b (fr. √ jṛmbh)
√ jval	v. to burn, blaze: jvalan 58a
jvalita-	ppp. burning, blazing 44b, 56a (fr. √ jval)
jvālā	n. flame 103c
tajja-	adj. resulting from that 9a
taṭaḥ	n. slope, declivity, precipice 22c, 41c, 50a, 77a
√ taḍ	v. to beat: tāḍyamānā 86c
tad	pron. he, she, it; that: tad 3d, 8c, 10c, 10d, 20d, 35b, 43c, 57c, 60b, 60c, 62c, 63d, 65b, 83d, 84c, 84d, 85a, 91b, 91d, 92b, 92c, 92d, 93a, 93d, 94d, 99b, 101d; tam 21a, 27a, 86d; *tasmai 8d; tasya 17d, 25a, 90c; tān 96a; tām 46c; tāsu 90d; tāḥ 91c, 92a, *97c, 98c; te 9c, 13d, 14c, 60a, 93b, 103d [twice]; teṣām 48a, 59d, 99d; taiḥ 14d; sa 19d, 20a, 23a, 24a, 26a, 29d, 33a, 60b, 102c; sā 29d, 69a, 70c, 100c; so 18c, 36c, 37c, 93c
tataḥ	adv. then 20a, 23a, 28a, 113d; (comparative) than that 16d, 96d
tatra	adv. there 21a, 38a, 43d, 47d, 49b, 62c, 82d
tathā	adv. thus, in that way 45d, 60c
tathāpi	conj. despite, nevertheless 20c, 26a
tadā	adv. then 39d, 57d

tadvat	adv. so, like that 77d, 87a
tanu-	adj. thin, tiny 53a (?), 87d
tanuḥ f.	n. body 21b
tanutara-	adj. thinner; very thin 89d
tantuḥ m.	n. cord 85a
tapta-	ppp. heated, hot 37c (fr. √ tap)
tamaḥ nt. (tamas-)	n. darkness 81d
taraṅgaḥ	n. wave 73a, 78c, 106c
taraṇam	n. crossing 106a
taralataratā	n. great shakiness; great hollowness 88d
taralita-	adj. shaking, tremulous, undulating 17d
taruḥ m.	n. tree 36b
talaḥ, °lam	n. surface, ground 111c; palm (of the hand) 114a
tāpaḥ	n. heat; pain 7c, 39a, 104d, 110d, 111d, 112d
tāluḥ m.	n. palate 56b
tāvat	adv. to that extent; that long 16a
tāvatkālam	adv. extending that much time 87b
tāvat tāvat	ind. to exactly that extent 88b, 88d, 89b, 89d
timiraḥ, °ram	n. darkness 6d, 32b, 109c
tiryañc-	adj. oblique, traverse, horizontal 66c
tiryak m., nt.	n. animal 62b (fr. tiryañc-)
tiryagnirīkṣaṇam	n. a sidelong glance 66c
tilakam	n. ornament, beauty-mark 67b
tīkṣṇa-	adj. sharp 48c
tīkṣṇatara-	adj. very sharp, piercing 34b
tīraḥ	n. bank (of a river) 70d, 72c

tīrṇa-	ppp. crossed (over) 106a (fr. √ tṝ)
tīvra-	adj. fierce, intense 43a
tu	ind. but, however 76d, *104c, 106c
tuṅga-	adj. high 11c, 22c
turagaḥ	n. 'moving swiftly', horse 102a
√ tul	v. to compare: tulayanti 90b
tuhina-	adj. cold 39a
tṛṇam	n. grass 56a
tṛptiḥ f.	n. satisfaction 93b
tṛṣita-	ppp. thirsty 35b, 101b (fr. √ tṛṣ)
tṛṣṇā	n. thirst; greed 87d, 99c, 112c
tṛṣṇāmaya-	adj. made of greed 85a
√ tṝ	v. to cross: taranti 106b
tejaḥ nt. (tejas-)	n. strength; dignity 101d
tejasvin-	adj. strong 15c
tailam	n. 'made of sesamum', sesame oil 20a, 50b
tailayantram	n. oil press 20a
tomaraḥ, °ram	n. an iron club; (the sharpened edge of an) arrow 58a
√ trā	v. to save, protect: trātuṁ 103d
tribhuvanam	n. the triple world 10b
tvad	pron. you: tvam 110d, 111d, 112d

dakam	n. water 73a
daṇḍaḥ	n. club; rod 34c, 58c, 66c, 85b (*see also* kāladaṇḍaḥ)
datta-	ppp. given 85d (fr. √ dā)
dantura-	adj. jagged, dentate; uneven 114b

danturatā	n. jaggedness 36d
danturita-	adj. notched, serrated, bristling 81b
damaḥ	n. discipline 110a
dayita-	adj. dear, beloved, cherished 32d
darī	n. cavity, crevasse, crevice 13a, 22c, 40c
darśanam	n. beholding, sight 2b
dalaḥ, °lam	n. a small shoot or blade, petal, leaf 43b
daśanaḥ, °nam	n. tooth 27b, 53a
daśā	n. condition, situation 29c, 95d
dasyuḥ m.	n. thief, robber 97d
dahana-	adj. hot, burning 39a
dahanaḥ	n. fire 39b, 58b
daṁṣṭrā	n. tusk, fang 41b
dāruṇa-	a. hard, cruel, harsh 37c, 60d, 78d, 87a
dārāḥ (m. pl.)	n. wife 100b
dik f. (diś-)	n. direction 54b, diśi diśi 115d
digmaṇḍalam	n. the whole world 54b
digdha-	ppp. smeared, anointed; covered 83a (fr. √ dih)
divaṁ	*see* dyauḥ
divyaḥ	adj. heavenly, divine 69b, 70a
diśi diśi	adv. in every direction, everywhere 115d
dīpaḥ	n. lamp 10b, 65c
dīpita-	ppp. kindled, blazing 59b (fr. √ dīp, caus.)
dīpta-	ppp. lighted, kindled 56b (fr. √ dīp)
dīrgha-	adj. long *9d, 85a
durgandhi-	adj. stenchy, stinking 90a
durgama-	adj. difficult to go or travel 34a

durlabha-	adj. difficult to obtain, attain, rare 2b, 61d, 65a
durlalitam	n. bad behavior, roguish trick, naughty prank 20d, 73c, 97c
durvāra-	adj. difficult to ward off 74d
duṣpūraṇa-	adj. difficult to fill, satiate, quench 92d
dustara-	adj. difficult to cross 12a
duḥkham	n. sorrow, suffering; pain, grief 3b (twice), 3d, 16d, 19d, 20d, 57b, 57d, 78d, 83c, 84a, 87a, 87c, 88c, 93a, 94b, 99a, 99b, 103b
duḥkhita-	adj. suffering 98c (= ppp. of the denom. duḥkhāyate)
duḥsaha-	adj. difficult to bear, unbearable 43a, 87c
dūtaḥ	n. messenger 33b
dūrataḥ	adv. from afar 57a
dūrāt	adv. from afar 35a
dūrvā	n. a kind of grass 77b
dṛḍha-	ppp. fixed, firm, strong 20a, 33b, 47b, 57c, 85a (fr. √ dṛṁh)
√ dṛś	v. to see: paśya (108d)
dṛṣṭa-	ppp. seen 96a (fr. √ dṛś)
dṛṣṭiviṣaḥ	n. 'whose gaze is poisoning', snake 22d
dehaḥ	n. body 43a, 49a
doṣaḥ	n. fault, moral fault 5c; disturbance of the three humors in the body 21c
doṣā	n. night, the darkness of night 5c
dyauḥ f. (dyaus-)	n. heaven: divaṁ 81a
dravīkṛta-	ppp. liquified, molten 58b (fr. dravī-√ kṛ)
druta-	ppp. running; quick, swift 46b (fr. √ dru)

drumaḥ	n. tree 108b, 110d
dveṣaḥ	n. hatred 94d
dhagiti	adv. in a moment, at once 56b
dhanya-	adj. blessed, fortunate 68d
dharmaḥ	n. the holy Dharma, the teaching of the Buddha 7a, 7b, 116a
dharmakāvyam	n. a poem dealing with the holy Dharma 116+
dharmamaya- (f. ī)	adj. consisting of, containing the holy Dharma 17a
√ dhā	v. place: dadhānāḥ 11b, dadhatu 114d, dhatte 102b
dhī	n. heart, mind 98b
dhārā	n. stream of water, shower 111b; the sharp edge of a sword 4d
√ dhāv	v. to run: dhāvañ 42a
dhīra-	adj. wise 106b
dhūmaḥ	n. smoke 38b, 54a, 56b, 58d
dhūmra-	adj. smoky, dark, murky 54a, 103a
√ dhṛ	v. to hold; to keep: dhārayanti 9b
dhṛta-	ppp. held, held up 47b (fr. √ dhṛ)
dhvanitam	n. sound 56d (= ppp. of √ dhvan)
na	part. (the negation) not 9b (thrice), 9d, 12d, 15d, 20c, 23b, 30b, 30d, 33c, 65d, 67c, 72d, 75b, 76d, *77c, 82d, 83d, 91a, 91b, 91d, 92a (twice), 92b (twice), 92c (twice), 93a (twice), 93b, 93c (twice), 93d, 94c (twice),

	96d, 100a (twice), 100b (four times), 102c, 105c, 106c, 109d
nata-	ppp. bowed down, bowing 80a (fr. √ nam)
natonnata-	adj. 'bowing down and rising (up)', elastic 80a
√ nad	v. to sound; to shout, scream: nadantaḥ 53d
nadī	n. river, stream 60a, 70d, 92a
nandana-	adj. delighting, pleasing, gladdening 107 (nominalized; twice)
nandanam	n. name of Indra's grove 69a, 105d
namaḥ	ind. bow, salutation, obeisance, homage (with dative) 0, 8d
nayanam	n. eye 4b, 47c
naraḥ	n. man 115b
narakaḥ, °kam	n. hell 29d, 53c, 55d, 60b, 86d, 114d
narakapālaḥ	n. guardian of the hell 58c, 62a
nartanam	n. dancing 17c
nalinam	n. the lotus flower 104c
nalinī	n. lotus-pond 104c
naṣṭa-	ppp. lost; disappeared 48d, 96a (fr. √ naś)
naṣṭacetas-	adj. having lost one's mind, stupefied 48d
nā m. (nṛ-)	n. a man; mankind: nṝṇāṁ 76b
nāgaḥ	n. a serpent-like mythological being 82a
nādaḥ	n. screaming 48b
nāma	ind. indeed (enforcing the preceding word); ko nāma who on earth 82d, 97d, 98d; (in a compound) entitled 116+

nārakaḥ	n. inhabitant of the hell 86d
nārācaḥ	n. arrow; iron arrow 38d
nāsikā	n. nose 58d
ni-√ gad	v. to proclaim, say, speak: nigadatā 113a
nikaraḥ	n. mass, multitude 41a, 81b, 104b
*nicita-	ppp. covered, overspread 42d (ni-√ ci)
nija-	adj. own, inborn, innate 11d, *13c, 32c, 87c
nitambaḥ	n. the buttocks 80b
*nitya-	adj. constant; constantly (in the beg. of a comp.) 109a
nidrāy	v., denom. to sleep: nidrāyante 109d
ni-√ pīḍ	v. to harrass, pain, trouble: nipīḍyamānā 21d
nibaddha-	ppp. bound, fettered 51d (fr. ni-√ bandh)
nibha-	adj. resembling 48a, 103c
nimīlita-	ppp. closed 29a (fr. ni-√ mīl)
nimna-	adj. deep 8a
niyatam	adv. certainly 28d, 89c
niyamaḥ	n. restraining; vow; certainty 14a, 17d
niyamena	adv. with certainty, certainly 17d
niraṅkuśa-	adj. unrestrained, unchecked 24d
nirata-	ppp. devoted to 5a, 100d (fr. ni-√ ram)
nirayaḥ	n. hell 16b, 19c, 61b, 73d
*nirāśraya-	adj. without shelter, protection 81c
nirīkṣaṇam	n. a look 66c
nir-√ īkṣ	v. to look at, behold: nirīkṣya (35a, 43b, 57a)
nirupāya-	adj. without means, having no means 27d

ni-√ rūp	v. to observe carefully, investigate, examine: nirūpyamāṇāḥ 75a
nirodhaḥ	n. confinement, enclosure, control 84a
nirgata-	ppp. gone out, going out 44a (fr. nir-√ gam)
nirjharaḥ, °ram	n. spring, waterfall 72c
nirdayatā	n. mercilessness 59c
nirdayam	adv. merciless 44c
*nir-√ dṝ	v., caus. to tear or rend asunder: *nirdāryamāṇaḥ 48b
nir-√ bhid	v. to tear open: nirbhidyamāna° 46d
nirbhinna-	ppp. torn open, ripped open 48d (fr. nir-√ bhid)
nilayaḥ	n. abode, dwelling 19c, 61b, 90d
ni-√ lī	v. to lie, rest upon, settle, dwell: nilayat 6d
niveśita-	ppp. fixed on, laid on 34d (fr. ni-√ viś, caus.)
niśita-	ppp. sharpened, whetted, sharp 4d, 25c, 42a, 49c, 58a, 79c (fr. ni-√ śā, √ śi)
niścayaḥ	n. certainty 65d
niśvāsaḥ	n. inhaling, breathing 86b
niṣevya-	adj. to be used; to be worshipped 108c (fr. ni-√ sev)
niṣ-√ kṛṣ	v. to draw or pull out; to tear asunder: niṣkṛṣyate 41d
niṣ-√ pīḍ	v. to press, squeeze: niṣpīḍyamāna 20b
[niṣphala-	adj. fruitless 97c, in tannisphalah; unclear and most probably corrupt; tentatively emended as *tā vatsala-]

niḥsaṅga-	adj. without company, lonely 69d
niḥsaṁgama-	adj. without company, lonely 68c
niḥsṛta-	ppp. coming out, protruding 56c (fr. niḥ-√ sṛ)
√ nī	v. to lead: nayanti 68d
nīta-	ppp. lead 95d (fr. √ nī)
nīla-	adj. dark green or blue 43b
nṛ-	*see* nā
nṛpati-	n. king 100a
netram	n. eye 59a
nauḥ f.	n. ship: nāvam 17a
nyasta-	ppp. placed on 25b, 30d (fr. ni-√ as)
pakṣaḥ	n. side, part; half (of the lunar month) 5b
paṅkaḥ	n. mud 35d
paṅkajam	n. 'mud-born', lotus 1d
paṅkajatā	n. the state of being a lotus 4b
paṭṭaḥ	n. strip 57c
√ pat-	v. to fall: patati 23a, 42c, 62d, 77c; patanti 13d, 50a, 55d, 73d, 81d
patita-	ppp. fallen down or into 12c, 23b, 96b, 103b (fr. √ pat)
pattram	n. leaf 43c, 114b
pathaḥ	n. way, road 109c
pathikaḥ	n. wanderer, wayfarer 72d
padam	n. foot 11b, 25b, 30d, 50d, 80a; step 46b; place 11b, 92c
padavī	n. place, position 11c, 17b; path 80b
paddhatiḥ f.	n. way, path; line, row 11b

payodharaḥ	n. female breast 97b
para-	adj. the other: 3a, 3b, 24c, 66a, 99d, 100d, 101c, 105a, 113d; (at the end of a comp.) the highest (form of) 32d , 67d, 83c, 86d; (at the end of a comp.) eagerly devoted to 13b
*paranirvṛtiḥ f.	n. the highest (form of) liberation; the highest (form of) refreshment 7c (Tib. has mya ngan 'das pa mchog, not yongs su mya ngan 'das pa) [nevertheless most likely a corruption of *parinirvrtiḥ]
parama-	adj. the highest or adv. (in the beg. of a comp.) exceedingly 2a, 3b, 10d, 12a, 13b, 60d, 61d
parasparam	adv. mutually, one another 62b
parārtham	adv. for others 2d, 4a, 99b
parārthe	adv. for others 99b, 104c
parikaraḥ	n. who or what helps or assists; equipment 100a (thus Tib. yo byad); a girth, waist-band 72b
parikvathita-	ppp. boiled, boiling 50b (fr. pari-√ kvath)
parigata-	ppp. surrounded; filled with 103a (fr. pari-√ gam)
parigrahaḥ	n. taking (of rebirth) 94a
pari-√ ṇam	v., caus. to make ripe, mature, develop, transform: pariṇāmayanti 60c
pariṇāmaḥ	n. transformation, ripening, consequence 39c
*parinirvṛtiḥ f.	n. complete liberation; complete refreshment 7c [alternative restoration of *paranirvṛtiḥ]

paripiṇḍita-	ppp. (completely) squashed together 19d (fr. pari-√ piṇḍ)
paripūrṇa-	ppp. completely filled, full 5b (fr. pari-√ pṝ)
paripluta-	ppp. swimming around 85c (fr. pari-√ plu)
parimardaḥ	n. hit, bump, collision; *burden (thus Tibetan: khur) 8b
parimalaḥ	n. perfume 70a
pari-√ vṛt	to turn around, revolve: parivartamāna- 18a, 21a, 94b
pariśoṣaḥ	n. complete drying up 40d
pariślatha-	adj. completely slackened, weakened 28c
paryanta-	adj. (in the beg. of a comp.) from all sides 44a
paryasta-	ppp. swung around, hurled around; perverted, perverse 85b (fr. pari-√ as)
parśukā	n. rib 56a
palitam	n. grey or white hair of an old person 25c, 27b
pallavaḥ	n. bud 79a, 110a
paśuḥ m.	n. animal, cattle 101a
√ pā	v. to drink: pibati 101b; pibataḥ 40b, pibanti 9b, 58c
pākaḥ	n. ripening; result 21c
pātaḥ	n. falling, fall (down) 13d, 43c, 79c, 80a
pātālam	n. the last of the seven netherworlds, inhabited by Nāgas 6d
pātram	n. vessel; recipient *7d, 8b

pādaḥ	n. foot; added to a name to express respect 116+
pādapaḥ	n. tree 84d
pādapīṭham	n. footstool 82b
pāpa-	adj. sinful; evil-doing 16b, 61b
pāpagatiḥ f.	n. a sinful state of existence 16b
pāraḥ, °ram	n. the further or opposite bank of a river or ocean 63a, 81c
pāśaḥ	n. chain, rope 33b, 34d, 47a, 51d
piñjara-	adj. reddish-yellow, tawny, gold-colored 82b
piṭakā	n. a small boil or pimple 52c
piṇḍita-	ppp. pressed or rolled into a ball or lump 52b (fr. √ piṇḍ)
pipāsu-	adj. thirsty (fr. √ pā, desiderative)
piśaṅga-	adj. reddish-brown, reddish, of a tawny color 38c, 59b
piśaṅgita-	adj. reddened; deep crimson 66c
pīṭham	n. a seat in general; a stool, chair, bench, sofa, etc. 82b
√ pīḍ	v. to torment: pīḍyamāṇas 87a
pīta-	ppp. drunk, having drunk 95b, 97b (fr. √ pā, to drink)
pīna-	ppp. fat, large; full, round 68a (fr. √ pyā)
pīvara-	adj. fat, large, massive 41a, 48c
puṇyam	n. virtue, merit 2b, 113a
punar	adv. again, once again 45d, 46b, 62d, 81d, 84d, 106b; however, but 4c, 15d, 51a, 67c, 105c
purā	adv. in former times 91b, 93a

purāṇa-	adj. old 56a
puruṣaḥ	n. man 82d, 101c, 103d; servant 34c
*puruṣarūpa-	adj. having the form of men, consisting of men 8d
pulinaḥ, °nam	n. bank of a river 92a
puṣpam	n. flower 108a, 108b, 108c
puṣpita-	adj. decorated with flowers; variegated, spotted 26d
pūrva-	adj. former, previous 1a, 21c
pūrvasmṛtiḥ f.	n. the memory of (deeds done in a) former life 21c
pūtiḥ f.	n. filth; secretions 35c, 90a
pūyaḥ, °yam	n. pus, discharge from an ulcer or wound 35c
pūrita-	ppp. filled 104a (fr. √ p, caus.)
pūrṇatara-	adj. very full, overflowing 41c
pṛthu-	adj. broad, wide 40c
pṛthutara-	adj. very broad, wide; copious, abundant 111b
pṛthvī	n. the earth 4d
pṛṣṭham	n. the back, hinder part, rear 69b
pauruṣam	n. (true) humanity 101d
prakaṭa-	adj. clear, brilliant 5a, 8a, 112a
prakaraḥ	n. heap, multitude 19a, 36d, 54b, 58a, 59c, 82b, 84a
prakarṣaḥ	n. excellence, eminence; high degree 108d
prakāśa-	adj. illuminating 5d
prakṛtiḥ f.	n. nature, natural form; by nature 16c, 102c, 112c

pra-√ kḷp	v., caus. to invent, devise, plan: prakalpya 14a
prakḷpta-	ppp. devised, established 17b (fr. pra-√ kḷp)
pragīta-	ppp. sung 95a (fr. pra-√ gā)
pracura-	adj. much, plenty, abundant 48c, 97c
prajñā	n. wisdom 110b
praṇayaḥ	n. affectionate love 44c, 97b
praṇidhiḥ f.	n. vow 110c
praṇihita-	ppp. placed down (a bait); (as noun) serious intention, vow (= praṇidhiḥ) 85b (fr. pra-ṇi-√dhā)
pratata-	ppp. extended, prolonged 57b (fr. pra-√ tan)
pratijñā	n. promise, vow 15d
pratisama-	adj. equal to, a match for 99d
prada-	adj. granting 110c
pradānam	n. granting, charity 110b, 111a
pradīpta-	ppp. blazing 103b (fr. pra-√ dīp)
prapātaḥ	n. fall, falling down 62d; precipice 13a, 40c
prabandhaḥ	n. continuance, continuity, succession 115c, 116a
prabhā	n. splendor, radiance 82b
pramathita-	ppp. destroyed 103c (fr. pra-√ math)
pramādaḥ	n. negligence 112b
pra-√ mṛj	v. to wipe out, remove: pramārṣṭi 6d
pra√ mlā	v. to fade, wither: pramlāyamāna 83a
pra-√ yat	v. to endeavor, strive; to care for: prayatate 101c

pra-√ yā	v. to go to, march to: prayāti 18d, 35d, 36b, 36d, 37d, 75c, 82c, 96d; prayātu 113d, 116d; prayānti 11c, 57b, 75d
pra-√ lī	v. to become dissolved, melt away; to be absorbed in: pralayatā 52a
pravālaḥ, °lam	n. sprout, shoot, new leaf 77b
pra-√ vṛt	v. to set out: pravartate 27c
pravṛtta-	ppp. begun, set in motion 54d (fr. pra-√ vṛt)
praśamaḥ	n. appeasement 27d
praśamita-	ppp. appeased, put to rest 111c (fr. pra-√ śam, caus.)
praśānta-	ppp. subdued, quelled, extinguished 114a (fr. pra-√ śam)
praśāntiḥ f.	n. calmness 110c
prasannatara-	adj. very clear, crystal clear 112a
prasahya	adv. forcibly, violently 47c, 48a
pra-√ sṛ	v. to come forth, bulge out: prasarad 56c
pra-√ sṛp	v. to go forth, to spread: prasarpad 104b
prastāraḥ	n. thicket, wood 34a
pra-√ has	v. to laugh loud: prahasan 27a
prahīṇa-	ppp. cast off, worn out (as a garment) 67d (fr. √ pra-hā)
pra-√ hṛṣ	v. to rejoice: prahṛṣyati 67c
*prahva-	adj. sloping, slanting, inclined; devoted to, attached to; friendly, gently bowing down 112a [Tib. byin (gyis) gzhol (ba)]
pra-√ āp	v. to get, obtain; attain: prāpya (17a, 63a)
prāpta-	ppp. got, obtained, attained 91d (fr. pra-√ āp)

prāpya-	adj. to be obtained, obtainable 100c (fr. pra-√ āp)
prāsaḥ	n. a dart, a barbed missile 42d
prītiḥ f.	n. happiness, joy 100d
prema nt. (°man-)	n. love 44c
plavaḥ	n. ship 12b
phaṇaḥ	n. hood (of a snake) 47b
phaṇī m. (phaṇin-)	n. snake 6b
√ phal	v. to bear fruit: phalati 108b
phalam	n. fruit 90c, 108c, 110c
phulla-	adj. flowering, blossomed, in full blossom 67a, 114c
phenaḥ	n. foam, frost 37b
bakaḥ	n. heron 47d
baḍiśam	n. a fish-hook 85d
baddha-	ppp. bound, fixed 85a, 105a (fr. √ bandh)
baddhakakṣa-	adj. 'having the girdle girded one,' ready, prepared 105a
bandhaḥ	n. manifestation, display, exhibition 116c
bandhanam	n. sinew 32a
bandhuḥ m.	n. companion, friend; relative 31d, 43d, 83b, 94c, 96c
balāt	adv. forcibly 25a
bahala-	adj. abundant, plentiful, great, strong 9c, 21b, 54a
bahalataratā	n. abundance, plenty 88b

bahu-	adj. much, plentiful, abundant, great 40a, 111a
bahutara-	adj. more, greater 89b
bahuśaḥ	adv. frequently, repeatedly 94b
bāla-	adj. young, foolish; as noun: fool 73d
bāliśa-	adj. childish, puerile; foolish, ignorant 23d
bālyam	n. childhood 22b
bāṣpaḥ, °ṣpam	n. tear 31c
bisam	n. the lotus plant 114b
bījam	n. seed 63b, 84d
buddhaḥ	n. Buddha, the Enlightened One 115d
budbudaḥ	n. bubble 83d
bodhiḥ f.	n. enlightenment 11a, 63b
bodhisattvaḥ	n. a being seriously striving for enlightenment, a Bodhisattva 0

bhakṣaṇam	n. eating, devouring 62b
bhaṅgaḥ	n. breaking 106c
√bhaj	v. to honor, revere: bhaja 107d, 109b; bhajeta 82d; adhere to; bhajante 106d
bhayam	n. fear, threat, danger 26b, 61c, 82d, 109b
bharaḥ	n. a great number, large quantity, multitude 112c
bhavaḥ	n. existence 85c, 110d, 111d, 112d
bhavanam	n. house, palace 100b
bhāj-	adj. (at the end of a comp.) sharing or participating in 78d, 97c
bhāraḥ	n. burden, load, weight 102b, 112c

bhāvaḥ	n. nature, character, heart *22b (partly restored, bh⟨āvaḥ⟩); state 65a
bhāvanā	n. contemplation, visualization 89a, 89c
bhāvyamāna-	*see* √ bhū
bhāṣitam	n. speech, utterance 33c
bhāsura-	adj. sparkling, radiant 81a, 107b (nominalized; twice)
bhidura-	adj. splitting; clearing away 5c
bhinna-	ppp. split, split open, fully opened 21d, 52c, 70a (fr. √ bhid)
bhīma-	adj. formidable, dreadful, terrifying 29d, 37a, 40a, 85b, 94d
bhīṣaṇa-	adj. dreadful 45a, 54c
bhujaḥ	n. arm 80d
bhuvanam	n. the world 14c, 103b
bhuvanamaṇḍalam	n. the whole globe 14c
√ bhū	v. to become: babhūva 3a, 4d, *7d, 94c; bhava *110d [restored], 111d, 112d; bhavati 8c, 57c, 69a, 76c; bhavatu 116a; bhavantu 115d, 116b; caus. to visualize, contemplate: bhāvyamānā 89a
bhūḥ f.	n. the earth; ground 16d, 20b, 50c
bhūta-	ppp. become 14c (fr. √ bhū)
bhūtalam	n. the ground of the earth
bhūdharaḥ	n. 'supporter of the earth', mountain 13a
bhūmiḥ f.	n. the earth; place, position 11d, 114c
bhūmikā	n. place, region 69a
bhūyaḥ	adv. again 17b, 78c, 79c
bhūṣaṇam	n. ornament, decoration 54c, 107a (twice)

bhṛśam	adv. much, very much, intensely 53d
bhedaḥ	n. splitting, breaking; section, category 37b, 61c
bhairava-	adj. frightful, terrifying 84a
bhairavaḥ	n. the god Bhairava 54d
bhogaḥ	n. hood (of a snake) 94d
√bhram	v. to wander about, roam, err: bhramati 102a; bhramanti 78c, 79c, 80d
bhramaḥ	n. erring 103a
bhraṣṭa-	ppp. fallen, deviated, strayed from 12d (fr. √bhraṁś)
maṅgala-	adj. auspicious, lucky, propitious 107d (nominalized; twice)
majjā m. (majjan)	n. the marrow of the bones and flesh 52d
maṇḍanam	n. ornament 44b, 68a
maṇḍalam	n. a circular globe, disc 14c, 54b, 68a (*see* digmaṇḍalam, bhūmaṇḍalam)
maṇḍita-	ppp. adorned, decorated 44b (fr. √maṇḍ)
matiḥ f.	n. mind, mental capacity 28b, 77d
matsyaḥ	n. fish 85d
mad-	stem of the pronoun of the first person, I: mama 67c, mayā 30a, 30c, 113a
madaḥ	n. intoxication, drunkenness; rut 9c, 24d
madhu nt.	n. honey 108d
madhukaraḥ	n. bee 108d
madhura-	adj. agreeable, sweet 72c, 74a
madhyaḥ, °dhyam	n. the middle, center, interior 12c, 96b
manaḥ nt. (manas-)	n. mind, heart 14a

manuṣyaḥ	n. man, human being 65a
manorathaḥ	n. wish 2c, 113c, 116b
manorama-	adj. pleasing 5c
mandākinī	n. the heavenly river Mandākinī or Ganges 78a
mandībhūta-	ppp. having become weak; having died down 87c (fr. mandī-√ bhū)
√ man	v. to think, believe; to consider, regard: manyata 23d; manyante 86d
maraṇam	n. dying; death 9a, 83c, 87b, 115c
marīciḥ m., f.	n. mirage 73a
maruḥ m.	n. desert 110d, 111d, 112d
marut nt. (marut-)	n. wind 37d
marutā	n. the state of being a desert 37d
marma n. (°man-)	n. a vital, vulnerable part of the body; any joint (of a limb) 32a
malayaḥ	n. name of a mountain range at the western coast of India 36b
mastiṣkam	n. the brain 59b
mahant-	adj. great 3c, *8d, 9c, 9d, 19d, 40b, 76d, 102c, 110d, 111ad
mahāghanaḥ	n. a great cloud 111d
mahādrumaḥ	n. a great tree 110d
mahāviṣam	n. a strong poison 76d
mahāsamudraḥ	n. the great ocean 40b
mahāsvara-	adj. having a loud voice
mahāhradaḥ	n. a great lake *8d, 112d
mahotsavaḥ	n. a great festival 116a
*mahauṣadham	n. an effective medicine 9d

mātra-	adj. (at the end of a comp.) 'measuring as much as', only 51c, 56d, 74a
māthin-	adj. crushing 31a
mānavaḥ	n. a man, human being 83d
mānasam	n. mind, heart 77b
mānuṣyakam	n. existence as human being 61d, 63d
mābhairvādaḥ	n. the utterance "have no fear" 111a
māyā	n. illusion 73a
māraḥ	n. Māra ('killer'), the tempter of the Buddha, often identified with Kāma, the God of Love 1d, 115a
mārgaḥ	n. way, road 34b
mālā	n. garland 44b, 58b
mukta-	ppp. released, escaped 61b, 87b (fr. √ muc)
mukhara-	adj. talkative; noisy, jingling 81a
mukham	n. mouth; beak; the foremost part, tip 40a, 48a, 49c, 58d
mugdhamugdha-	adj. very innocent 69c
√ muc	v. to abandon, give up, let go: muñcanti 13c
mudgaraḥ	n. hammer, mallet, mace 86c
muniḥ m.	n. seer, sage 17b, 116c
munijanaḥ	n. the seers, sages 116c
munīndraḥ	n. the best among the seers 24a
murajaḥ	n. a kind of drum or tabor 72c
muhuḥ	adv. again, repeatedly 57a
muhūrtaḥ, °tam	n. a moment, an instant 66a
muhūrtāt	adj. after a moment, after a while 66a
mūrtiḥ f.	n. shape, body 42b, 43c, 48d

mūrdhajaḥ	n. 'grown on the head', hair 33a
mṛtyuḥ m.	n. death 47a, 84c, 116b
mekhalā	n. a belt, girdle 68b
medaḥ nt. (medas-)	n. fat 55b
meruḥ m.	n. Mount Meru 80b
meṣaḥ	n. ram 45a
mokṣaḥ	n. release, esape 57b, 86b
mohaḥ	n. delusion 9c, 10d, 74c, 88b, 88d, 109c
mohāy	v., denom. to roam about bewildered: mohāyate 22d
mohita-	ppp. deluded, blinded 9c, 24b, 26 (fr. √ muh, caus.)
mauliḥ m.	n. the head, the crown of the head 14c, 82b
mlāna-	ppp. withered 83b (fr. √ mlā)
mlecchaḥ	n. barbarian 62a
yakṣaḥ	n. a class of demigods, attendants of Kubera, the God of Wealth 82a
√ yat	v. to attempt, endeavor, strive: yatante 103d
yatnaḥ	n. effort, exertion, attempt 32d
yatra	relative adv. where 82a, 92b, 92c
yathā	relative adv. how, in what manner 19c, 60d
yad-	pron. who; which: yad/yad- 6c, 7d, 10a, 10b, 10c, 16c, 35b, 63a, 65b, 83c, 91b, 93a, 99b, 99d, 113a; yasya 1b, 2b, 3d, 4a, 93c; yaḥ 3a, 7a, 17a, 18b, 94c; yā 69c, 70d, 91a; yām 29c, 100d; yāsām 92a, 97a, 98a; yāḥ

	91d, 98b; ye 9b, 13c, 14b, 103d; yena 5d, 62d; yeṣu 8b, 73d; yaiḥ 93b, 95a
yad	conj. that 20c, 84b, 90b, 90d, 101c, 102a, 102b, 102d
yadā	relative conj. when 49c, 57c
yadi	conj. when; if 29d, 37a, 62c, 96d
yadṛcchā	n. chance, accident 101b
yadvad	relative adv. in what manner 77a, 86d
yantram	n. any instrument or machine 20a
√ yam	v. to offer, give, bestow: yacchati 25d
yamaḥ	n. Yama, the Lord of Death 33b
yaśaḥ nt. (yaśas-)	n. fame 111b
√ yā	v. to go: yāti 20b, 24b, 67d, 89c; yānti 14d, 57d, 63a
yāta-	ppp. gone 91a, 92c (fr. √ yā)
yānam	n. vehicle 100a
yāvad yāvat	relative adv. to exactly which extent 88a, 88c, 89a, 89c
yukta-	ppp. united (with); (properly) used 76c (fr. √ yuj)
yugmam	n. a pair, couple 45a
yojanam	n. a measure of distance (equal to 8 or 9 miles) 40a
yauvanam	n. youth 22c
rakṣita-	ppp. protected, cared for 32d (fr. √ rakṣ)
racita-	ppp. made of 54c (fr. √ rac)
rajaḥ nt. (rajas-)	n. dust; passion 111c
rata-	ppp. devoted to 113d (fr. √ ram)

ratiḥ f.	n. pleasure, joy 69a, 70c
ratnam	n. gem, jewel 6a, 107a
randhram	n. hole, aperture, cavity, chasm 42d, 55c
rabhasaḥ	n. violence, force, impetuosity; rashness 24c
rabhasena	adv. recklessly, in a rash manner 24c
√ ram	v. to enjoy: ramante 105d
ramya-	adj. pleasant, lovely 70c, 95c, 99c, 113c, 115b
rayaḥ	n. the stream of a river, current 78a
ravaḥ	n. crying, noise; sound, voice 33d, 72c
raviḥ m.	n. sun 102a
raśmiḥ m.	n. a beam, ray of light 58b
rasaḥ	n. juice 58b, 97b; love, affection (for) 2d, 102d
rasika-	adj. having a feeling, emotion (for) 102d
rahita-	ppp. quit, left, separated; without 52a (fr. √ rah)
rāgaḥ	n. desire, passion 89b, 89d, 91d, 92d
rājiḥ f.	n. streak, line, row 38c
rāśiḥ m.	n. a heap, mass, collection 80c, 108c
ruk f. (ruc-)	n. light, luster, splendor; beauty, loveliness 99c
ruddha-	ppp. encircled, obstructed 54b (fr. √ rudh)
rūḍha-	ppp. mounted, climbed 77a (fr. √ ruh)
romāñcaḥ	n. a thrill, bristling of the hair 104b
raudra-	adj. fierce, savage, terrible, wild 46b
lakṣita-	ppp. noticed 30d (fr. √ lakṣ)

lakṣmīḥ	n. welfare 100a
lagna-	ppp. locked together 53a (fr. √ lag)
lajjā	n. shame, modesty 15a
latā	n. creeper; branch; string 38c, 42b
√ labh	v. to obtain, to attain: labhante 62c, 100d
labdha-	ppp. obtained 58d, 86b, 101b (fr. √ labh)
lalita-	adj. handsome 23d; ppp. played, frolicked 95a (fr. √ lal)
lavaḥ	n. a piece, fragment, bit, drop 40d, 45c, 77b, 87d
lasīkā	n. pus, matter, lymph 52d
lābhaḥ	n. attaining, attainment 77c
lālasa-	adj. ardently longing for, craving 29b, 77b
lokaḥ	n. the world; human beings, men 2c, 5a, 61c, 77d, 84b, 87d, 102b, 102d
locanam	n. eye 53b
loma nt. (loman-)	n. hair 53a
lola-	adj. tremulous, moving; fickle, inconstant 37a, 60a, 83d
lohaḥ, °ham	n. iron 48c
vaktram	n. mouth 42d
vacanam	n. word 108a, 108c
*vatsala-	adj. child-loving, affectionately loving, tenderly loving 97c (Ms. nisphalāḥ, Tib. byams pa bsten pa)
√ vad	v. to speak, to call: vadanti 72d
vadanam	n. mouth; face 1d, 84c
vadhaḥ	n. killing 26d

vanam	n. forest 42b, 70d, 79b, 105b
vanadāvaḥ	n. a forest-conflagration 36c
vanalekhā	n. a long tract of forest 72b
vanasthalī	n. a wood, forest ground 68c, 69d, 79d
vandhya-	adj. barren, fruitless, useless 116b
vapuḥ nt. (vapus-)	n. body 2a, 28c, 46d, 48b
vayam	*see* asmad
*va⟨ra-⟩	adj. the best 6b (Tib. mchog)
vargaḥ	n. group, troop, flock, multitude 83b
varṣaḥ, °am	n. rain 38d
varṣaṇam	n. raining, showering, rain 58a
varṣin-	adj. raining down, showering down 116c
√ vas	v. to dwell, to live: vasanti 105b
vasā	n. fat, marrow 52d
vasumatī	n. 'bearer of wealth', the earth 102b
√ vah	v. to bear, carry: vahati 84b, ūhuḥ 98b
vahniḥ m.	n. fire 87c, 89b, 89d, 103c
vā	conj. or 62a, 62b, 76c, 101b
vāñchā	n. wish, desire 108d
vāñchita-	ppp. wished, desired, longed for 65b (fr. √ vāñch)
vāñchitam	n. wish, desire 57d
vātaḥ	n. wind 45c
vānta-	ppp. vomited, spitted out 56b (fr. √ vam)
vāyasaḥ	n. crow 47d
vāyuḥ m.	n. wind 114d
vāri n.	n. water 31c, 40b, 68b
vārinidhiḥ m.	n. the ocean 37a

vārivāhaḥ	n. cloud 38d
vāridaḥ	n. cloud 68b
vāluka-	adj. made of sand 50c
vāsaḥ	n. dwelling, dwelling-place 92b
vikīrṇa-	ppp. scattered, dispersed 54a, 99a (fr. √ vi-kṝ)
vikṛta-	ppp. mutilated, deformed, loathsome 90a (fr. vi-√ kṛ)
vi-√ kṝ	v. to scatter, dispel: vikira 109c
vikriyā	n. agitation, perturbation, excitement of passion 23b
viklava-	adj. affected by, overcome with 98b
vigamaḥ	n. disappearance, cessation, end 99c
vigrahaḥ	n. body 23c, 44d
vighātin-	adj. destroying, cutting 115c
vi-√ cint	v., caus. to think, consider; ponder over: vicintyamāne 66b
vi-√ cūrṇ	v. to grind to pieces, crush, pulverize: vicūrṇayan 24c
vi-√ chid	v. to cut off or asunder: vicchidyamānam 4a
vicchinna-	ppp. cut off or asunder 42b, 79d (fr. vi-√ chid)
vijita-	ppp. to conquer, defeat; to surpass, excel 55d, *115a (fr. vi-√ ji),
vijihma-	adj. crooked, bent 26a
vijṛmbhita-	ppp. open, expanded 54b (fr. vi-√ jṛmbh)
vijjalatā	n. sliminess 35d
viḍambanam, °nā	n. imitation, appearance 70b

vi-√ dal	v. to burst, crack: vidalanti 28a
vidita-	ppp. known, understood, grasped 11a (fr. √ vid)
vidyut f. (vidyut-)	n. lightning 38c
vinayaḥ	n. modesty, discipline 110a
vinipīḍita-	ppp. squeezed, tormented 32a (fr. vi-ni-√ pīḍ)
viparīta-	ppp. reversed, perverted 39d (fr. vi-pari-√ i)
vipākaḥ	n. ripening; digestion 74b
vipula-	adj. extended, spacious 112a
vipūtiḥ f.	n. filth; secretions 51b [an intensification of pūtiḥ; here used as an adjective?]
vipralabdha-	ppp. deceived (fr. vi-pra-√ labh)
viphala-	adj. fruitless, in vain 57d
viphalī-√ kṛ	v. to render fruitless, spoil: viphalīkaroti 63d
vibhavaḥ	n. wealth 73b
vi-√ bhā	v. to appear: vibhāti 39d
vibhinna-	ppp. divided, cut, pierced 43c, 49a (fr. vi-√ bhid)
vibhūṣaṇam	n. ornament 6a
vibhūṣita-	ppp. adorned 111c, 114c (fr. vi-√ bhūṣ)
vibhramaḥ	n. error; roguish trick 73c
vibhrānta-	ppp. erring about, whirling 37d (fr. vi-√ bhram)
vimardaḥ	n. pounding (as of waves) 112c
vimala-	adj. immaculate, pure 8a, 35a
vimānaḥ, °nam	n. a celestial chariot 81b

vimiśrita-	ppp. mixed 35c (fr. vi-√ miśray)
vimukta-	ppp. released 56d (fr. vi-√ muc)
vimokṣaḥ	n. liberation, salvation 109c
vimohita-	ppp. deluded, confused 39c (fr. vi-√ muh, caus.)
virata-	ppp. abstained from, indifferent 72a (fr. vi-√ ram)
virāgaḥ	n. passionlessness 93d
vi-√ ru	v. to scream: virauti 33a
viruta-	ppp. screaming 115a (fr. vi-√ ru)
virutam	n. screaming 43d
vilasitam	n. appearance, manifestation 10d
vivaram	n. hole, cavity, hollow; intervening space, opening 57a, 58d
vivarjita-	ppp. deprived of, destitute of, without 112b (fr. vi-√ vṛj)
vivartanam	n. tossing, whirling around 17c, 96a
vivaśa-	adj. without any will of one's own, helpless 18c, 22a, 61a, 97a, 99a
vivikta-	ppp. separated, lonely 70c (fr. vi-√ vic)
vi-√ vṛt	v. to turn back, revert: vivartamānāḥ 11d; to roll about, be tossed about: vivarta-mānāḥ 18b
√ viś	v. to enter: viśann 32b, viśanti 50d, 90d
viśāla-	adj. broad, vast 17a, 72a, 84c
viśīrṇa-	ppp. shattered, broken to pieces 45b (fr. vi-√ śṝ)
viśuddha-	ppp. completely purified, pure 6c (fr. vi-√ śudh)
viśrānta-	ppp. resting 68b (fr. vi-√ śram)

viśva-	adj. all, everything 39d
viṣatā	n. the nature of poison 75c, 75d
viṣam	n. poison 37c, 74a, 74b, 74c, 74d, 75a, 75b, 75c, 76a, 76c
viṣama-	adj. uneven, rugged; unpleasant, bad; dangerous, terrible 13d, 18d, 41d, 50a, 75b, 77a, 95d
viṣayaḥ	n. object of the senses 22d, 29b, 74a, 74b, 74c, 74d, 75a, 75b, 75d, 76d, 100c, 109a
viṣādaḥ	n. dejection, sadness, depression of spirits 67d
visaṁkaṭa-	adj. frightful, dreadful; dangerous 45a (Tib. has no equivalent)
visaraḥ	n. extension; multitude; large quantity 110a
vi-√ sṛ	v. to spread, be extended or diffused: visarad 49d, visarati 89a
vi-√ sṛj	v. to abandon: visṛja 109a
visṛta-	ppp. spread, extended, diffused 50c (fr. vi-√ sṛ)
vistīrṇa-	ppp. expanded, wide, broad 8a (fr. vi-√ stṝ)
visphuṭita-	ppp. burst open 59a (fr. vi-√ sphuṭ)
visphuliṅgaḥ	n. a spark of fire 38b, 44a
vi-√ has	v. to smile: vihasad 4c
vi-√ hā	v. to abandon: vijahāti 32c, vihāya 24a, 98c
vi-√ hṛ	v. to play, sport, enjoy oneself: vihṛtya 79b, 80b
vihṛta-	ppp. sported, played; enjoyed 92a (fr. vi-√ hṛ)

vihāraḥ	n. sporting 78b
vi-√ īkṣ	v. to see, observe: vīkṣamāṇaḥ 96b, vīkṣya 103b
vīkṣita-	ppp. seen, looked at 31d, 83b (fr. vi-√ īkṣ)
vīryam	n. energy, striving 110a
vṛkṣaḥ	n. tree 43b
vṛtta-	ppp. turned; round 6c (fr. √ vṛt)
vṛttam	n. nature 6c
vṛttiḥ f.	n. behavior 2d
√ vṛdh	v. to grow, increase: vardhata 28d, 91d, 92d
vṛddhiḥ	n. growth, increase 89c
√ vṛṣ	v. to rain: vavarṣa 7b
vṛṣaḥ	n. a bull 77a
vegaḥ	n. vehemence, speed 13d, 74d, 86a
veṇiḥ f.	n. a braid of hair 70a
vepita-	ppp. made to tremble 52b (fr. √ vip, caus.)
velā	n. the seacoast, seashore 36a
veṣṭanam	n. band, bandage 103c
veṣṭita-	ppp. surrounded, enveloped 21b (fr. √ veṣṭ)
vaitaraṇī	n. the river of hell Vaitaraṇī 41c, 78c, 106b
vyatikaraḥ	n. contact, union 106d
vyathita-	ppp. shaken, tormented; painful 31c, 53b (fr. √ vyath)
vyayaḥ	n. disappearance, destruction; decay, downfall 109a
vyasanin-	adj. endeavoring for 15d
vyākula-	adj. completely bewildered 103a

vyājaḥ	n. pretext; semblance 109c
vyālaḥ	n. snake 112b
vyoma n. (°man-)	n. heaven 92c
√ vraj	v. to go; to enter a state: vrajati 76a, vrajanti 83c
vraṇaḥ, °am	n. wound 21c
vrataḥ, °am	n. practice, custom 62a
śaṁsin-	adj. praising, giving thanks for v 38a (Tib. translates 'dod na (yang) ≈ *āśaṁsino (*'pi) 'longing for')
śakalaḥ, °lam	n. piece, fragment, bit 54c
śaktiḥ f.	n. ability, faculty 29b; a kind of missile, a sharp instrument, razor 42c
śakraḥ	n. Indra, the lord of the gods 82a
√ śaṅk	v. to think probable, to suspect, fear: śaṅke 66d
śaṅkuḥ m.	n. a peg, nail, spike 48c
śatam	num., n. a hundred 43c, 44a, 52c
śataśaḥ	adv. a hundred times 18c, 45d, 91a
śatruḥ m.	n. enemy 98d
śanaiḥ	adv. slowly, gradually 113d
śamaḥ	n. tranquility 107d, 109b, 116c
śamathaḥ	n. tranquility 110b
śayita-	ppp. lying down, sleeping 93c (fr. √ śī)
śarat f. (śarad-)	n. autumn 67b
śaravat	adv. like an arrow 26d
śalyam	n. an arrow; any cause of poignant or heart-rending grief; pain 46d, 49a

śaśāṅkaḥ	n. moon 67b
śaśī m. (śaśin-)	n. moon 5d, 68a
śastram	n. any sharp weapon, knife 43c, 49c, 79c
śākhā	n. branch 110b
śāntiḥ f.	n. tranquility *109b (Ms. defective; it has only sā, the second syllable being omitted); cessation, stop 76a
śāsanam	n. teaching 6c, 10c
śikharaḥ, °ram	n. top, summit 110c
śikṣā⟨padam⟩	n. moral commandment, precept 11a
śikhā	n. tongue (of a flame), flame 36c, 44a, 54b, 59b, 65c, 89b, 89d, 104a, 104d
śikhākaraḥ	n. either 'hands of the flames', tongues of flame (śikhā + karaḥ, thus Tib.), or 'mine of flames', i.e. fire (śikhā + ākaraḥ) 54b
śita-	ppp. sharpened, whetted, sharp 41d, 42c, 49a (fr. √ śā, śi)
śithila-	adj. weak, feeble 22a
śiraḥ nt. (śiras-)	n. head 4a, 6b, 25b, 27c, 30d, 59a, 103c
śiraḥkapālaḥ, °lam	n. the skull 59a
śilātalam	n. a slab of rock, the surface of a rock 69b
śiva-	adj. auspicious 63b, 107b
śivā	n. a jackal 46a
śiśira-	adj. cool 104b, 112b, 116d
śiśuḥ m.	n. a child, an infant 97a
śiṣyalekhaḥ	n. 'letter to a disciple', title of the work 116+
śīkaraḥ	n. spray, thin rain, drizzle, mist 36a, 114d
śīta-	adj. cool 36a, 53d

śītam	n. cold, coldness 39b, 52b
śīrṇa-	ppp. torn asunder, rotten 36d (fr. √ śṝ)
śīlam	n. disposition, nature, character, custom; morality 12b, 62c, 68d, 110c, 111c
śukla-	adj. white, pure, bright 5b
√ śuc	v. to grieve: śocati 12d
śuci-	adj. pure 70d, 114c
śuddha-	ppp. purified, pure 15b (fr. √ śudh)
śubha-	adj. white; blissful; pleasant 6c, 89a
śuṣka-	adj. dried 59c (fr. √ śuṣ)
śūna-	ppp. swollen 51b (fr. √ śvi)
śūlaḥ, °lam	n. spear, lance 42c, 49a
śṛṅgam	n. top, peak (of a mountain) 68c
śeṣaḥ, °ṣam	n. rest, remainder 56d
śaityam	n. cold, coolness 45c
śailaḥ	n. a mountain; a rock, bog stone 34a, 45a, 72a
śaivalaḥ	n. a kind of aquatic plant, moss 35c
śokaḥ	n. grief 59d
śokamaya-	adj. consisting of grief 31b
śobhā	n. beauty 114d
śraddhā	n. faith 113b
śramaḥ	n. exhaustion 99c
śravaṇaḥ, °ṇam	n. ear 58d
śrīḥ	n. wealth, riches, prosperity 91c
√ śru	v. to hear: śṛṇoti 33c
śreyaḥ	adv., n. better, the better 75b
ślatha-	adj. weak 98b

śvabhram	n. a hole, chasm, den 77c
śvaḥ	adv. tomorrow 66a
śvā (śvan-)	n. dog 46a
sa-	ind. together with, possessing 31c, 38b, 52d, 54d, 56b, 114d
saṁyata-	ppp. restrained, fettered 33b, 47b (fr. saṁ-√ yam)
saṁrambhaḥ	n. turbulence, agitation 86a
saṁ-√ śṝ	v. to wither away 80d (saṁśīryamāṇa-)
saṁsāraḥ	n. the cycle of existence, samsara 13a, 17c, 18a, 96c
saṁsārin-	adj. samsaric being 93d
saṁsṛṣṭa-	ppp. mixed 76a (fr. saṁ-√ sṛj)
saṁstaraḥ	n. a bed, couch, layer; a bed of leaves 42a, 79a
saṁsthita-	ppp. stored 8c (fr. saṁ-√ sthā)
saṁhatiḥ f.	n. accumulation 104d
sakala-	adj. all, whole, entire, complete 88a, 88c
sakta-	ppp. clinging 73d (fr. √ sañj)
sakhā m. (sakhi-)	n. friend 79b
saṁkaṭa-	adj. narrow; hemmed, obstructed 19b, 34b
saṁ-√ kuc	v. to shrink: saṁkucanti 1c
saṅgaḥ	n. contact 50d, 106d
saṅgin-	adj. having contact with
saṁghaṭṭaḥ	n. crashing together 45b
saṁghaṭṭita-	ppp. united, locked together 53b (fr. saṁ-√ ghaṭṭ)
saṁghātaḥ	n. multitude, assemblage 51b

sajjanaḥ	n. a good man, a virtuous man 16d
saṁcayaḥ	n. accumulation, heap; large quantity 56a
saṁcālaḥ	n. movement 51c
saṁ-√ cūrṇ	v. to pulverize, crush, grind: saṁcūrṇyate 45d
saṁjñā	n. notion 88a, 88c
satata-	adj. constant, perpetual 112b, 113c
sattvaḥ	n. being 85c, 93c
satyam	n. truth 15d
sadā	adv. always 102b, 115d
sadyaḥ	adv. all of a sudden, immediately, at once 16c, 20c
sant-	adj. good, noble 105b, 109d (*see also* √ as)
saṁtānakaḥ	n. one of the five trees in Indra's paradise or its flowers 70b
saṁ-√ tyaj	v. to abandon, give away completely: saṁtyajanti 15c
saṁtrāsita-	ppp. frightened, terrified 56c (fr. saṁ-√ tras, caus.)
saṁdaṣṭa-	ppp. clenched together 53a (fr. saṁ-√ daṁś)
saṁdhi- m.	n. joint 28a
samabhyadhika-	adj. superior 63c
sama-	adj. even, regular; pleasant, good 18d, 34c, 95d, 114a; same 62a
sam-adhi-√ gam	v. to approach; to adopt (a teaching): samadhigamya 10c
samarpita-	ppp. restored, given back 45c (fr. sam-√ ṛ, caus.)
samasta-	ppp., adj. whole 45b (fr. sam-√ as)

samāpta-	ppp. completed 116+ (fr. sam-√ āp)
samīhita-	ppp. desired 115d (fr. sam-√ īh)
samudita-	ppp. assembled, collected, united 14b (fr. sam-ud-√ i)
sam-un-nī	v. to raise completely up, elevate; to bring together, unite: samunnayanti 14b
samṛddha-	ppp. prosperous; rich in, abounding in 113c (fr. sam-√ ṛdh)
sameta-	ppp. assembled; united; accompanied by 115b (fr. sam-ā-√ i)
saṁparkaḥ	n. union, contact, touch 78d
saṁpātaḥ	n. meeting together, encountering 72a
saṁpādita-	ppp. accomplished, fulfilled 2c (fr. saṁ-√ pad, caus.)
*⟨sa⟩ṁbhogaḥ	n. enjoyment 100c
sanmantram	n. a good or effective spell 76b
sarit f. (sarit-)	n. river 34a, 70c, 72c, 106c
sarva-	adj. all 0, 8b, 8c, 16a, 16b, 18d, 22a, 60d, 67c, 87d
sarvajñattvam	n. omniscience 113d
sarvadā	adv. always 3a, 108a
salilam	n. water 35a, 101b
√ sah	v. to endure: sahate 19d
saha	prep. together with 78b
saha-	adj. standing, enduring 8b (fr. √ sah)
sahaja-	adj. inborn, natural, innate 16c
sahasram	num., n. one thousand 46a
sahāyaḥ	n. companion, consort 105c
sāgaraḥ	n. ocean, sea 17c, 96c

sādhāraṇa-	adj. common, general, universal 10b
sādhu-	adj. good, excellent, perfect 14c
sānuḥ m., sānu nt.	n. mountain ridge 36a
sārameyaḥ	n. dog 41a
sārthaḥ	n. a company of merchants, caravan; company 12c
sārdham	prep. together with 95a
sita-	adj. white 4c, 54c
√ sidh	v., caus. to accomplish; to prepare, cook: sādhyamānam 76b
simisimāyita-	ppp. slightly moving, crawling, swarming (as of tiny insects) 51a (fr. simisimāy, onomatopoeic) [Tib. correctly has lcig lcig 'dug pa]
sukṛtin-	adj. acting well or kindly; virtuous, wise; benevolent 103d
sukha-	adj. pleasant 80a
sukham	n. happiness, bliss 3a, 3d, 18b, 77d, 84b, 86d, 87d, 91b, 94b, 99b, 100c, 100d, 101d, 102d, 106d, 107d, 109b
sukham	adv. happily, pleasantly; easily 15c, 79b, 86b, 105b
sukhita-	adj. (made) happy 113c
sukhin-	adj. experiencing happiness, happy 3a
sugataḥ	n. epithet of the Buddha 108a, 108c, 113b
sucaritam	n. good conduct 107a
sucira-	adj. very long 109d, 116b
suduṣkara-	adj. very difficult to accomplish 1a
sunirdayam	adv. without the least bit of compassion 25b

sundarī	n. a beautiful woman 1b, 105c
supathaḥ	n. the right way, the right path 12d, 24b
supuruṣaḥ	n. a good man 99b
subahu-	adj. very many 86c
subhaga-	adj. lovely, blessed, fortunate 69d, 72a, 112c, 116d
suraḥ	n. god 1b, 70c, 79b, 82a, 100b
surabhiḥ m.	n. fragrance 114c
sulabha-	adj. easy to obtain 101a
suśiṣyaḥ	n. a good disciple 14d
sūkṣma-	adj. tiny 51a
sūcī	n. needle 40a
sūtram	n. thread 49d
sevanīya-	adj. to be worshipped (108a)
sevita-	ppp. followed, practiced 24a; inhabited, dwelt in 69c (fr. √sev)
saikatam	n. sand 37c, 80c
sopānaḥ	n. steps, stairs, a staircase, ladder 11b
saukhyam	n. happiness 88a
saudham	n. any great mansion or palace 11a
saubhāgyam	n. auspiciousness; beauty 2a
skandhaḥ	n. the trunk or stem of a tree 110a
strīḥ	n. woman 73b
stabaka-	n. a bunch, cluster 70b
sthagita-	ppp. covered, hidden; interrupted 55b (fr. √sthag)
sthalakamalinī	n. a land-growing lotus 114b

√ sthā	v. to stand: tiṣṭhati 43d, 94d; tiṣṭhanti 53d; tiṣṭhantu 16a
sthānam	n. place 92b
sthita-	ppp. standing; resting, residing 21a, 38a, 47d, 97a, 98a (fr. √ sthā)
sthitiḥ f.	n. constancy, lasting 15d, 65d
snehaḥ	n. love 98b
sparśaḥ	n. contact, touch 80a
spaṣṭa-	adj. clear, manifest; bright 114a
spṛhā	n. longing, desire 17d
sphīta-	ppp. abundant 114d (fr. √ sphā)
sphuṭa-	adj. opened, expanded, full-blown 104c
√ sphur	v. to shake, tremble, quiver; to struggle, become agitated; to dart: sphurant- 47c, 55a, 56c, 103c
sphuliṅgam, °gaḥ	n. a spark of fire 50c, 55a
smṛtiḥ f.	n. remembrance, memories 21c
sruta-	ppp. flowing 52d, 83a (fr. √ sru)
svapnam	n. sleep; dream 73c
svabhāvaḥ	n. character, nature 75b
svayam	adv. oneself; of one's own accord 101a, 106d
sva-	pron. own 33d, 101d
svātmā m. (°man-)	n. one's own self; oneself 26d
svaraḥ	n. sound, voice 111a
svārthaḥ	n. one's own interest 4c, 102c, *104c
hata-	ppp. destroyed, wasted; perished 29b, 30b (fr. √ han)

hariṇī	n. a female deer, doe 69c
harita-	adj. green, verdant 72b
√ has	v. to laugh: hasaty 66d
hasita-	ppp. laughed 95a (fr. √ has)
hastaḥ	n. hand; hold 12b
hastipakī (°kin- ?)	n. elephant-driver 25d
√ hā	v. to give up, abandon: jahāti 12b, 16c, 17b, 20c, 21d, 23b; hātum 97d, hīyate 28b
hāraḥ	n. a garland or necklace of pearls 81b
hāsaḥ	n. laughter, laughing, smile 37b, 42d, 70b, 91c, 104c
hāhāravam	n. roaring laughter 54d
hita-	adj. beneficial 111a
hitam	n. welfare, benefit 7a, 76c, 100d, 102d, 105a, 113d
himaḥ	n. snow 104b
hi	adv. for, because 65d
hutavahaḥ	n. 'carrier of offerings', fire 104a, 104d
hṛdayam	n. heart 15b
hṛdya-	adj. pleasant 2a
hetuḥ f.	n. cause, reason; source 107d
hradaḥ	n. pond, lake *8d, 112d (in

Facsimile of a Palmleaf Manuscript of the Śiṣyalekha

Bibliography of Works Cited

Editions of the Mahārājakaniṣkalekha

For canonical editions of the Tibetan text, see "About the Texts and Translations," *supra*, p. 185, and "Variant Readings in the Tibetan Text of the Mahārājakaniṣkalekha, *supra*, pp. 213–14.

Hahn, Michael. "Mātṛcetas Brief an den König Kaniṣka." In *Études bouddhiques offertes à Jacques May, Asiatische Studien/ Études asiatiques* XLVI (1992): 147–79.

Thomas, Frederick William. "Mātṛceṭa and the Mahārājakaniṣkalekha." *Indian Antiquary* 32 (1903): 345–60.

Editions of the Śiṣyalekha

For Sanskrit manuscripts, see "About the Texts and Translations," *supra*, pp. 186–88.

For the Tibetan translation, see "About the Texts and Translations," *supra*, pp. 189, 191–93.

"Poslanie k učeniku" [Letter to a Disciple]. In *Zapiski vostočnago otdelenija imperatorskago russkago archelogičeskago obščestva* [Memoirs of the Oriental Section of the Imperial Russian Archeological Society] 4 (1889): 29–52. [edition and incomplete Russian translation by I. Minaev]

Tibetskij perevod "Poslanija k učeniku" [The Tibetan translation of the "Letter to a Disciple"]. In *Zapiski vostočnago otdelenija imperatorskago russkago archelogičeskago obščestva* [Memoirs of the Oriental Section of the Imperial Russian Archeological Society] 4 (1889): 53–82.

COMMENTARIES ON THE ŚIṢYALEKHA

Prajñākaramati. Śiṣyalekhavṛtti. D 4183, Q 5683. See "About the Texts and Translations," *supra*, p. 190.

Vairocanarakṣita. Śiṣyalekhaṭippaṇa. D 4191, Q 5691. See "About the Texts and Translations," *supra*, p. 189.

WORKS BY INDIAN AUTHORS

Śākyamuni Buddha. Lalitavistara. *The Voice of the Buddha: The Beauty of Compassion*, translated by Gwendolyn Bays. Berkeley: Dharma Publishing, 1983.

Āraṇyaka. Gurulekha ["Letter to the Spiritual Teacher"]. In *Die buddhistische Briefliteratur Indiens. Nach dem tibetischen Tanjur herausgegeben, übersetzt und erläutert* by Siglinde Dietz, 214–71. Asiatische Forschungen 84. Wiesbaden: Otto Harrassowitz, 1984.

Āryaśura. *The Marvelous Companion: Life Stories of the Buddha.* Berkeley: Dharma Publishing, 1983.

———. *Once the Buddha Was a Monkey*, Ārya Śūra's *Jātakamālā*, translated from the Sanskrit by Peter Khoroche. Chicago, London: University of Chicago Press, 1989.

Aśvaghoṣa. *The Buddhacarita; or, Acts of the Buddha.* Part 1, Sanskrit text, Part 2, Cantos i to xiv. Translated by E. H. Johnston from the original Sanskrit supplemented by the Tibetan version. Calcutta: Baptist Mission Press, 1935–36.

Aśvaghoṣa and Mātṛceta. *Neue Aśvaghoṣa- und Mātṛceṭa-Fragmente aus Ostturkistan* [New Aśvaghoṣa and Mātṛceṭa Fragments from Eastern Turkestan]. Translated by Jens-Uwe Hartmann. Nachrichten der Akademie der Wissenschaften in

Göttingen. I. Philologisch-historische Klasse. Jg. 1988. Nr. 2. Göttingen, 1988.

Atiśa. Vimalaratnalekha ["Letter Consisting of Flawless Jewels"]. In *Die buddhistische Briefliteratur Indiens. Nach dem tibetischen Tanjur herausgegeben, übersetzt und erläutert* by Siglinde Dietz, 302–19. Asiatische Forschungen 84. Wiesbaden: Otto Harrassowitz, 1984.

Avalokiteśvara. Briefwechsel zwischen Avalokiteśvara und Rab gsal gzhon nu ["Letter Sent to the Monk Rab-gsal gZhon-nu by the Noble Avalokiteśvara"]. In *Die buddhistische Briefliteratur Indiens. Nach dem tibetischen Tanjur herausgegeben, übersetzt und erläutert* by Siglinde Dietz, 132–41. Asiatische Forschungen 84. Wiesbaden: Otto Harrassowitz, 1984.

Bharata-Muni. *The Nāṭyaśāstra. A Treatise on Hindu Dramaturgy and Histrionics. Ascribed to Bharata-Muni.* Completely translated for the first time from the original Sanskrit with an Introduction, Various Notes and Index by Manomohan Ghosh. 2 vols. Calcutta: Manisha Granthalaya, 1950–1961.

Buddhaguhya. Bhoṭasvāmidāsalekha ["Letter to the Ruler, Nobility, and Subjects of Tibet"]. In *Die buddhistische Briefliteratur Indiens. Nach dem tibetischen Tanjur herausgegeben, übersetzt und erläutert* by Siglinde Dietz, 358–99. Asiatische Forschungen 84. Wiesbaden: Otto Harrassowitz, 1984.

Candragomin. *Candragomins Lokānandanāṭaka. Nach dem tibetischen Tanjur herausgegeben und übersetzt. Ein Beitrag zur klassischen indischen Schauspieldichtung*, by Michael Hahn. Asiatische Forschungen 39. Wiesbaden: Otto Harrassowitz, 1974.

———. *Difficult Beginnings. Three Works on the Bodhisattva Path.* [By] Candragomin. Translated, with commentary by Mark Tatz. Boston, London: Shambhala, 1985.

———. *Joy for the World, A Buddhist Play by Candragomin.* Translated with an introduction and notes by Michael Hahn. Berkeley: Dharma Publishing, 1987.

Carpaṭi. Avalokiteśvarastotra. In "Buddijskija molitvij. I" ["Buddhist Prayers. I"], edited by I. Minaev. *Zapiski vostočnago otdelenija imperatorskago archeoločeskago obščestva* [Memoirs of the Oriental Section of the Imperial Archeological Society] 2 (1887): 125–36.

Daṇḍin. *Mirror of Composition.* Edited with commentary by Pandit Rangacharya Raddi Shastri. 2nd ed. Poona: Bhandarkar Oriental Research Institute, 1970.

Jitāri. Cittaratnaviśodhanakramalekha ["Graded Course of the Purification of the 'Mind-Jewel'"]. In *Die buddhistische Briefliteratur Indiens. Nach dem tibetischen Tanjur herausgegeben, übersetzt und erläutert* by Siglinde Dietz, 142–213. Asiatische Forschungen 84. Wiesbaden: Otto Harrassowitz, 1984.

Kamalaśīla. Duḥkhaviśeṣanirdeśa ["Description of the [Eight] Kinds of Suffering"]. In *Die buddhistische Briefliteratur Indiens. Nach dem tibetischen Tanjur herausgegeben, übersetzt und erläutert* by Siglinde Dietz, 340–57. Asiatische Forschungen 84. Wiesbaden: Otto Harrassowitz, 1984.

The Mahāvastu. Vol. I, translated from the Buddhist Sanskrit by J. J. Jones. London: Pali Text Society, 1949, 1973.

Mātṛceṭa. *The Śatapañcāśatka of Mātṛceṭa,* translated by D. R. Shackleton Bailey. Sanskrit Text, Tibetan Text, Commentary and Chinese Translation. Cambridge: Cambridge University Press, 1951.

———. *Das Varṇārhavarṇastrotra des Mātṛceṭa* [The Varṇārhavarṇastotra of Mātṛceṭa]. Translated by Jens-Uwe Hartmann. Abhandlungen der Akademie der Wissenschaften in Göttingen. Sanskrittexte aus den Turfanfunden. XII. Göttingen: Vandenhoeck & Ruprecht, 1987.

Mitrayogin. Candrarājalekhaka ["The Letter to King Candra"]. In *Die buddhistische Briefliteratur Indiens. Nach dem tibetischen Tanjur herausgegeben, übersetzt und erläutert* by Siglinde Dietz, 320–39. Asiatische Forschungen 84. Wiesbaden: Otto Harrassowitz, 1984.

Nāgārjuna. "A Letter to a Friend." In *Golden Zephyr,* translated by Leslie Kawamura. Emeryville, CA: Dharma Publishing, 1975.

———. *Master of Wisdom, Writings of the Buddhist Master Nāgārjuna.* Translated by Chr. Lindtner. Berkeley: Dharma Publishing, 1986.

Sajjana. Putralekha ["Letter to the Son"]. In *Die buddhistische Briefliteratur Indiens. Nach dem tibetischen Tanjur herausgegeben, übersetzt und erläutert* by Siglinde Dietz, 272–301. Asiatische Forschungen 84. Wiesbaden: Otto Harrassowitz, 1984.

Shantideva. *A Guide to the Bodhisattva's Way of Life.* Translated by Stephan Batchelor. Dharamsala: Library of Tibetan Works and Archives, 1992.

Works by Tibetan Authors

Bu-ston. *History of Buddhism (Chos-ḥbyung) Part 2. The History of Buddhism in India and Tibet.* Translated by E. Obermiller. Heidelberg: Otto Harrassowitz, 1932.

dPal-byangs. Sārasaṁgralekha ["Letter that Summarizes the Essence (of the Doctrine)"]. In *Die buddhistische Briefliteratur Indiens. Nach dem tibetischen Tanjur herausgegeben, übersetzt und erläutert* by Siglinde Dietz, 400–529. Asiatische Forschungen 84. Wiesbaden: Otto Harrassowitz, 1984.

Tāranātha. *Tāranātha's History of Buddhism in India.* Trans. from Tibetan by Lama Chimpa [and] Alaka Chattopadhyaya. Ed. by Debiprasad Chattopadhyaya. Simla: Indian Institute of Advanced Study, 1970.

Zhechen Gyaltsab. *Path of Heroes: Birth of Enlightenment*. Berkeley: Dharma Publishing, 1995.

WORKS BY CHINESE AUTHORS

I-Tsing. *A Record of the Buddhist Religion as Practised in India and the Malay Archipelago (A.D. 671–695)*. Translated by J. Takakusu. Delhi: M. Manoharlal, 1966 (first published Oxford, 1896).

WORKS BY CONTEMPORARY SCHOLARS

Bendall, Cecil. *Catalogue of the Buddhist Sanskrit Manuscripts in the University Library, Cambridge*. Cambridge: Cambridge University Press, 1883.

Chari, V. K. *Sanskrit Criticism*. Honolulu: University of Hawaii Press, 1990.

Chattopadhya, Alaka. *Atīśa and Tibet*. Calcutta: Motilal Banarsidass, 1967.

Dietz, Siglinde. *Die buddhistische Briefliteratur Indiens. Nach dem tibetischen Tanjur herausgegeben, übersetzt und erläutert* [The Buddhist Epistolary Literature of India. Edited, translated and explicated on the basis of the Tibetan Tanjur]. Asiatische Forschungen [Asiatic Researches] 84. Wiesbaden: Otto Harrassowitz, 1984.

Eimer, Helmut. *Berichte über das Leben des Atiśa (Dīpaṁkaraśrījñāna)* [Records of the life of Atiśa]. Asiatische Forschungen 51. Wiesbaden: Otto Harrassowitz, 1977.

———. *Rnam thar rgyas pa. Materialien zu einer Biographie des Atiśa (Dīpaṁkaraśrījñāna)* [rNam thar rgyas pa. Materials for a life of Atiśa]. Parts 1 and 2. Asiatische Forschungen 67. Wiesbaden: Otto Harrassowitz, 1979.

Gerow, Edwin. *A Glossary of Indian Figures of Speech*. The Hague, Mouton: Columbia University, 1971.

Hahn, Michael. "Ajātaśatravadāna—A Gopadatta Story from Tibet." In *K. P. Jayaswal Commemoration Volume*, 242–76. Patna: K. P. Jayaswal Research Institute, 1981.

———. "A Difficult Beginning. Comments upon an English translation of Candragomin's Deśanāstava." In *Researches in Indian and Buddhist Philosophy: Essays in Honour of Professor Alex Wayman*, 31–60. Delhi: Motilal Banarsidass, 1993.

———. "Prakrit Stanzas in an Early Anthology of Sanskrit Verses." *Bulletin d'Études Indiennes* 11–12 (1993–94): 355–68.

———. "Über den indirekten Beweis bei literaturhistorischen Fragestellungen" ["On Indirect Evidence in Literary-Historical Issues"]. *Wiener Zeitschrift für die Kunde Südasiens* 36 (1992): 91–103.

Hartmann, Jens-Uwe. "Notes on the Gilgit Manuscript of the Candraprabhāvadāna." *Journal of the Nepal Research Centre* 4 (Humanities) 1980: 251–66.

Kölver, Bernhard. "Zur Frügeschichte der Rasa-Lehre ["On the Early History of the Rasa Doctrine"]. *Berliner Indologische Studien* 6 (1991): 21–48.

Masson, J. L. and M. V. Patwardhan. *Aesthetic Rapture*. Vol. I: Text, Vol. II: Notes. Poona: Deccan College, 1970.

Matsumura, Hisashi. *Four Avadānas From the Gilgit Manuscript*. Unpublished dissertation. Canberra, 1980.

Matsunaga, Daigan and Alicia. *The Buddhist Concept of Hell*. New York: Philosophical Library, 1972.

Matsunami, Seiren. *Catalogue of the Sanskrit Manuscripts in the Tokyo University Library*. Tokyo: Suzuki Research Foundation, 1965.

Minaev, I. "Buddijskija molitvij. I" ["Buddhist Prayers. I"]. In *Zapiski vostočnago otdelenija imperatorskago archeoločeskago obščestva* [Memoirs of the Oriental Section of the Imperial Archeological Society] 2 (1887): 125–36.

Rao, T. A. Gopinatha. *Elements of Hindu Iconography*. Madras: Law Printing House, 1914; New York: Paragon Book Reprint Corp., 1968.

Sāṁkṛtyāyana, Rāhula. "Second Search of Sanskrit Palm-Leaf Mss. in Tibet." *Journal of the Bihar and Orissa Research Society* XXIII (1937):1–57.

Srinivasan, Srinivasa Ayya. *On the Composition of the Nāṭya-śāstra*. Studien zur Indologie und Iranistik. Monographie 1. Reinbek, 1980.

Steiner, Ronald. *Untersuchungen zu Harṣadevas* Nāgānanda *und zum indischen Schauspiel* [Examination of Harṣadeva's Nāgānanda and Indian Drama]. Indica et Tibetica 32. Swisttal-Odendorf, 1997.

Steinkellner, Ernst. "Miszellen zur erkenntnistheoretisch-logischen Schule des Buddhismus" ["Miscellany regarding the epistemological-logical School of Buddhism"]. *Wiener Zeitschrift für die Kunde Südasiens* 28 (1984): 177–78.

Tatz, Mark. "The Life of Candragomin in Tibetan Historical Tradition." *The Tibet Journal* 7.3 (1982): 1–22.

Thomas, Edward Joseph. "State of the Dead (Buddhist)." *Encyclopedia of Religion and Ethics* 11 (1971): 829–33.

Willson, Martin. *In Praise of Tārā*. London: Wisdom Publications, 1986.

Index

Tibetan Translation Series

Calm and Clear

The Legend of the Great Stupa

Mind in Buddhist Psychology

Golden Zephyr (Nāgārjuna)

Kindly Bent to Ease Us, Parts 1–3

Elegant Sayings (Nāgārjuna, Sakya Pandita)

The Life and Liberation of Padmasambhava

Buddha's Lions: Lives of the 84 Siddhas

The Voice of the Buddha (Lalitavistara Sūtra)

The Marvelous Companion (Jātakamāla)

Mother of Knowledge: Enlightenment of Yeshe Tsogyal

The Dhammapada (Teachings on 26 Topics)

The Fortunate Aeon (Bhadrakalpika Sūtra)

Master of Wisdom (Nāgārjuna)

Joy for the World (Candragomin)

Wisdom of Buddha (Saṁdhinirmocana Sūtra)

Path of Heroes: Birth of Enlightenment

Leaves of the Heaven Tree (Jātaka)

Invitation to Enlightenment (Mātṛceṭa, Candragomin)